CONTENTS

SERIES EDITORS' INTRODUCTION

Although still relatively uncommon, interracial marriages in the United States are increasing in number. Furthermore, such relationships can constitute "laboratories" for the detailed investigation of race relations. In this book, Rosenblatt, Karis, and Powell explore the interpersonal dynamics and social contexts of 21 interracial couples in committed relationships. A unique contribution is the qualitative research design, enabling all participants to tell their own stories with a minimum of analytic baggage.

The reader may be struck by the number of fruitful contradictions in the lives of these couples. They are ordinary, but they are also exceptional. The couples are different from each other, but they also share many things in common. They report much support and sympathy from their families and from their communities, but they also experience considerable opposition and resentment. They are wounded and often oppressed by peers and members of both sides of their families, but they are also enriched and even blessed by their struggles. These couples are relatively successful in navigating the racial divide and in creating a reconciliation, yet this is never entirely possible.

Considerable depth of focus is given in this research to the identities of the couples, to their wider social networks, and to the effects on their children. This book should stand alone as testimony to an important contemporary phenomenon, and it will be useful to students of family life and ethnic studies alike. The research reported here also will inspire others to investigate similar issues with different samples, different temporal boundaries, and different data collection methods, enriched by the hypotheses that emerge from a close scrutiny of the data themselves and the authors' interpretations.

David M. Klein
University of Notre Dame

Bert N. Adams
University of Wisconsin

ACKNOWLEDGMENTS

We are grateful to many people for help and support with this project. To William D. Allen and Dr. Sheron L. Randolph for reading and commenting on a preliminary draft of the manuscript. To Paul R. Spickard, David Klein, Bert Adams, and an anonymous reviewer for their close and helpful reading of an almost-final draft. To Sara Wright for comments on Chapter 7 and for support in all phases of the project. To Vivian Jenkins Nelsen, Charles Willie, and their students for a summer course that sustained our interest and focus and affirmed many of our assumptions and beliefs. To Marie Welborn for conversations and reality affirmation. To Harold Grotevant for administrative support and for his valuing of diversity, research, and collaboration.

Books like this arise in part from teachings of all sorts. We have had more "teachers" than we can remember. But we want to be sure to give credit to William D. Allen, Rose Brewer, V. Lorraine Haley, Julie Palacio, Robert Staples, and Oliver J. Williams. They helped us think, see, and hear about matters dealt with in this book. A summer workshop on promoting diversity in teaching, funded by the Bush Foundation, taught by Rose Brewer and Susan Geiger, and involving a group of stimulating colleagues provided Paul with a strong impetus to engage in this project.

Acknowledgments go to Chrissie Mahaffy and her family, Claire Keister, Shelly Maloney Reichardt, and Jaya Duffin and her family for providing the loving child care that made it possible for Terri and Richard to participate in this project.

We are grateful, more than we can ever say, to our immediate families—Sara and Emily, Kahdeen and Jordan—who have sustained our work with love, laughter, caring, and much else.

Our thanks most of all to the 42 people whose voices give life and substance to this book.

Paul C. Rosenblatt
Terri A. Karis
Richard D. Powell

RACIAL BIAS AND
INTERRACIAL RELATIONSHIPS

In America, whites and blacks infrequently marry each other or enter into some other kind of committed sexual partnership together. For example, in 1990, only .10% of married white men had a black wife (U.S. Bureau of the Census, 1990, Table 13). In the past, black-white marriage was illegal in many states. Even at present, there is considerable opposition from both whites and blacks.

The most corrosive form of white opposition to interracial couples is *racism*. As a first step toward conceptualizing racism, one could define it this way:

> Racism is the assumption of inherent superiority of one race coupled with discrimination, prejudice, and stereotyping directed at people of at least one other race. To be racist, one must believe there are distinct physical differences between groups labeled as of different races and that many social, psychological, and other attributes are associated with the physical differences one uses as racial markers.

This definition, although reasonable conceptually, fails to convey what it is like to live as a member of a targeted category in a racist society. A person who has felt the sharp edge of racism might offer a more experiential definition of racism, such as the following:

> Racism is hostile actions with the intent to harm, based on the skin color of the intended victim. Such acts are on a continuum, with intent to kill at one end of the continuum. Those who have been the targets of racism but have not been killed are survivors.

Many people say that racism can be expressed only by those with relatively great power. In America, white people have had the power to enact their racist intent into law and to play out their racism in ways that limit the comfort, safety, opportunities, actions, and life chances of African Americans. By some standards, it is legitimate to write of black racism, but there is no comparison when one looks at the power and privilege that has supported and still supports white racism in America. In fact, a case can be made that what might be labeled black racism is only a reaction to and learning from white racism. That would make what appears to be black racism something else—perhaps reaction to oppression.

This book focuses on the experiences of black-white interracial couples, not on the differences between racism, prejudice, discrimination, and stereotyping. The people who are quoted in this book, however, use the terms *racism, prejudice, discrimination,* and *stereotyping* often enough that it is useful to point out distinctions between the terms.

Prejudice is an attitude, judgment, opinion, or belief held prior to getting to know a person that is applied, in ignorance, to that person and is adverse to that person. Discrimination is action that treats a person differently based on the social category into which one classifies that person. The term usually refers to treatment that is adverse to a person in a certain category, as when an African American is not granted a mortgage loan because of being an African American. Stereotyping is a process of ascribing simplistic, uniform, often negative, characteristics to all people whom one classifies in a particular category. For example, a white person might stereotype African Americans as being poor and on welfare. Typically, racism may involve prejudice, discrimination, and stereotyping; however, prejudice, discrimination, and stereotyping may be based on ignorance or fear, may not have an intent to harm, and may be responsive to education.

Often, the terms racism and discrimination are used to refer to the thoughts and actions of individuals, but there is also racism and discrimination at the level of social institutions. Institutionalized racism and discrimination involve actions supported overtly or covertly by a substantial societal institution—such as a state government, a university, a school board, the real estate dealers of a community, or a business.

Prejudice directed at interracial couples involves beliefs that exist prior to knowing a couple, that are adverse to the couple, and that might lead to action directed at the couple. The prejudicial beliefs might be that mixed-race relationships are immoral or vulgar.

Prejudice, discrimination, and stereotyping take many forms and occur in many different situations. Often, those who think and enact what could be labeled prejudice, discrimination, or stereotyping are unaware of their attitudes and actions; some are people who have every intention of helping rather than hurting or who in other situations behave in ways that are supportive of the people who are the target of their prejudice, discrimination, or stereotyping. The dynamics of power and privilege are important factors in understanding where prejudice, discrimination, and stereotyping might be most corrosive and where they might be least in the awareness of those who think or act in those ways. Those with the greatest power to have their prejudice, discrimination, and stereotyping make a difference in the lives of others have the greatest freedom to be unaware of the ways in which they affect the lives of others. One expression of the freedom to lack awareness is that, in America, white people have the power to live a life of unexamined privilege in innumerable ways that African Americans are denied (McIntosh, 1988). Because of this, some whites choose to be unaware of their comparative privilege. Others are aware of their privilege and are willing to defend it through racist acts. So when we write in this book about prejudice, discrimination, stereotyping, or racism directed at people in interracial couples, we are writing about situations in which white power and privilege are expressed or defended, whether or not that is how the people expressing prejudice, discrimination, stereo-typing, or racism think about them.

Often it is difficult for a person experiencing something unpleas-ant to know precisely what is going on, and often it is hard for us, hearing of people's experiences, to distinguish one demeaning pro-cess from another. Therefore, except when somebody who was interviewed specifically labels something as prejudice, discrimina-tion, or stereotyping, we will use the term racism as a generic term to encompass the varying forms of dehumanization. The choice of terms also represents a belief that racism directed at black Americans and at interracial couples sustains the prejudice, discrimination, and stereotyping directed at them.

This book would be unnecessary if there were no racism. If entering a committed interracial relationship made as little difference in a person's life as marrying someone of the same race, the people who were interviewed would not have had stories to tell like those that make up the bulk of this book. But in a country in which racism is part of the experience of all African Americans, black-white inter-racial couples experience difficulties that couples in which both partners are white do not. This book is written to give a voice to the members of 21 interracial couples and to understand their experi-ences. It is written with knowledge that racism is a central problem in America. It is written with a hope of improving the situation of all who are victims of racism. One way that we hope this book helps to improve the situation is that we hope that it offers to white Americans who are unaware of their racism an opportunity to understand what it is and how it victimizes people.

Interracial partnerships challenge racism. They may, for example, challenge a presumption that the races are culturally unequal (Kitchen, 1993, p. 65). If an interracial partnership produces a child, it challenges a way of thinking that requires discrete, nonoverlapping categories of people. Interracial couples also challenge a presumption that people of different races cannot get along. To the extent that an interracial partnership denies the validity of cultural inequality, it denies the validity of the economic and legal discrimination and the discrimination in housing, education, health care, hiring, and so on that presume the inequality (Kitchen, 1993, p. 65). Thus, interracial partnerships may be opposed by white people who hold racist beliefs because such partnerships threaten white privilege. Put another way, white acceptance of interracial couples may be an important sign that racism is being left behind. Some people have even gone so far as to say that such acceptance is the key to freeing all people from the binds of racism (Washington, 1970, chap. 1).

This book focuses on black-white interracial couples, but it is as important to understand the experiences of other interracial couples and to address hostility and opposition directed toward them because they are interracial. We focus on black-white interracial couples because such couples are at the heart of discussions in the mass media about interracial couples (Kitchen, 1993, pp. v-vi), because they are the most common interracial couple in the area in which we live, and because Terri Karis and Richard Powell would do the interviewing and themselves are a black-white interracial couple, we thought they would have the best rapport with similar interracial couples.

BLACK-WHITE INTERRACIAL
COUPLES IN AMERICA'S PAST AND PRESENT

Data on the number and location of interracial relationships are not necessarily reliable (Porterfield, 1982). There are, however, some educated estimates. According to the U.S. Bureau of the Census, in 1992 there were about 246,000 married couples in the United States in which one partner was an African American and one was white (U.S. Bureau of the Census, 1993, Table 63). The 246,000 black-white married interracial couples in a country with more than 50,000,000 married couples is a much smaller number than one would expect if blacks and whites were mating without regard to race of partner (Kalmijn, 1993; Staples, 1992).

Presumably, there are still powerful forces in society that make black-white interracial marriage difficult, unappealing to people who might be looking for a partner, or otherwise unlikely. Some of what is in society is no doubt a holdover from the past. Until a U.S. Supreme Court decision (*Loving v. Commonwealth of Virginia*) in 1967, such unions were illegal in many states. The fact that interracial unions were illegal does not mean that they were not occurring. In fact, in 1910, 73% of interracial married couples lived in states where such marriages were illegal (Kitchen, 1993, p. 75). On the other hand, the absence of a law prohibiting interracial marriage does not mean that interracial couples are free from terrorist threat or attack (Staples, 1992). At any rate, the 1967 Supreme Court decision that struck down laws against interracial marriage marked the beginning of a steady increase in black-white interracial marriages (Aldridge, 1973; Kalmijn, 1993; Monahan, 1976; Schoen & Wooldredge, 1989).

The history of black-white interracial relationships in America has been intensively studied (for reviews, see Adams, 1995; Roberts, 1994; Spickard, 1989, chap. 9; Staples, 1992). Many interracial couples are aware of that history (see discussion in Chapter 3). The history includes rape of slave women by white slave owners and men of their families; it includes intercourse or marriage between indentured black men and indentured white women, relationships between white women and African American slaves, prostitution, recreational sex, and much more (see Johnston, 1970, for a rich discussion of the troubled, painful, and complex history from the times of slavery). The history of interracial relationships also goes back to times following the Civil War when racism, economic exploitation, and sociopolitical oppression allowed white men to impose themselves sexually on black women and to bully black men into suppressing even the hint of interest in white women (Staples, 1992). The history of black-white interracial relationships is important for many reasons, but this book focuses on the present.

THE FOCUS OF THIS BOOK

This book is based on what the partners in 21 committed, heterosexual relationships in the Minneapolis-St. Paul metropolitan area had to say about their experiences. It does not speak to the experiences of all black-white interracial couples in America or even to the experiences of all such couples in the Minneapolis-St. Paul area. The Twin Cities area is not representative of America. It is urban, not rural; there are fewer blacks than can be found in most metropolitan areas, and many of the blacks in the area were born elsewhere. A relatively large percentage of blacks in the area have middle-class occupations. The metropolitan area has a relatively large number of interracial couples and has the reputation of being a good place for an interracial couple to live.

This book focuses more on what people had to say about their experiences than on theoretical ideas about racism, couple relationships, and related matters. We want the voices of the people who were interviewed to be the heart of this book. That means that we provide relatively little interpretation of what people said, relatively little of the sorts of social science insights that go well beyond people's words. The choice to give so much of this book to the people interviewed is in part an ethical choice—a matter of whose reality counts. It also represents a choice about what matters most at present about black-white interracial relationships. We think that Americans need to know what people in black-white interracial couples have to say about their experience, because what they say signifies much about society and contradicts societal stereotypes. An understanding that frames their experiences with someone else's terms would obscure their message. Their message needs to be read, partly because it is interesting and important in itself and partly because it is a counter to the stereotypes and presuppositions that make a great deal of the extra trouble that interracial couples and their children experience.

We hope that what we have to say will be less true with the passage of time, that the experiences of black-white interracial couples will become much more benign than those of the couples we have interviewed. We hope that this book will make a difference in the lives of interracial couples by giving them perspective on their experiences, giving their families a mirror for looking at themselves, and giving those who hope to be helpful to them (clergy, teachers, counselors, etc.) wisdom about them.

AVOIDING BIASED WRITING
IN A BIAS-FILLED SOCIETY

When we look at what has been written about interracial relationships, even things written recently by people who clearly want to support interracial relationships, we often see words that we consider to be prejudiced or stereotyping. That makes us wonder if, in a few years, people reading this book may consider it to be biased. Will the use in this book of the terms *black* and *African American* seem biased? Will our unwillingness to call black separatism *racist* seem racist? Will our thin discussion of the varieties of racism, prejudice, discrimination, and stereotyping seem a support of those biases, or simpleminded? We acknowledge our own prejudice and stereotyping. We recognize that we are surrounded by racism (and rude insensitivities about racial matters) in the media, in ordinary conversations, in the institutions that are central to our lives, and even in discussions directed at attacking racism and other forms of bias; all of that may make it hard for us to give up or even recognize some of our own bias. We hope that society is changing so that people are becoming more aware of racism and more accepting and supportive of difference and of interracial relationships. We hope that this book can help with that evolution. So even if we worry that this book might seem biased by the standards of some people, we hope it will eventually seem antiquated because racism will no longer be a force in society.

One reason to think of this book as well on its way to being outdated is that it uses racial categories. *Race* is a type of categorization applied to individuals and groups, constructed (and maintained as a construction) through sociocultural processes (Spickard, 1992). The social construction of race involves physical distinctions assumed to have a biological reality and to be unambiguously distinguishable in all people. The social construction of race also involves distinctions based on the geographical origins of one's ancestors (Spickard, 1992). Elaborate and indefensible structures of ideas about how racial groups differ rest on these distinctions. For all their vagueness and indefensibility, racial concepts and distinctions have been accepted as real and true by millions of people and are the basis of immense damage committed against millions of other people. Given that history, one can be wary of any writings that address matters of race. But we cannot study or write about interracial relationships without knowing where people fall in those sociocultural categories. We cannot write about problems arising from sociocultural race categories that classify individuals and couples without using those categories. We hope we make it clear in this book that we oppose racist use of those categories and that we see those categories as having none of the meaning attributed by those who act in racist ways.

The terms used to designate racial categories are highly politicized. People who strongly oppose racism may disagree with one another, and preferred terms change from time to time. At the moment this is being written, people we respect and whose opinions we value disagree about whether to call themselves *African American, black, Black, African, Afro-American,* or something else. There is disagreement about the designators *white, White, Caucasian,* or *Euro-American.* There is also disagreement about labels for black-white couples, a disagreement reflected in the discrepancy between the text and title of this book. In the text we use the term *interracial,* the most common designator in scholarly writings and the term we used while interviewing. However, the book title is *Multiracial Couples,* because *multiracial* is now the preferred term for many black-white couples we know. The term does not presume that a couple bridges or is located between races, and it reflects more accurately the identity of people in quite a few couples.

When we asked the people we interviewed how they identified themselves in terms of racial and ethnic background, we received quite a range of answers. A list of those answers follows and will help the reader to keep track of people as they are quoted in this book. (When quoting people, we identify some with a racial label when we think it might be especially important to understand what might be called the "racial standpoint" of the person quoted.) To keep the focus on black-white interracial couples, rather than on the issues involved in choice of racially descriptive terms, when we quote people we may identify them with the terms black, African American, or white. A glance at the list that follows, however, will make clear that there was a great deal of individuality in how people identified themselves.

HOW PEOPLE DEFINED THEMSELVES

All interviewees were asked how they identified themselves in terms of race and ethnicity. The diversity of their responses to the question provides a useful commentary on racial categories. Among the things that can be seen in the list is that whites claim national origin roots, whereas blacks whose roots go back to slavery have lost track of tribal/national/cultural roots. In the following list, responses are grouped by couple. All names have been changed, and anything quoted that would make it too easy to identify a specific person has been changed to similar information, with the changed material enclosed in brackets: For example, the person we call Isaac did not actually come from Akanland in Ghana but from another part of Africa. The partners are listed by couple.

HENRY African American.
DONNA Norwegian.

ISAAC I'm African . . . maybe a Pan-Africanist. . . . I'm an [Akan]. I was born in [Akanland], but I was raised in another tribal land . . . that is in the western part of [Ghana].
OLIVIA I guess [I am] Bohemian, Slovak. My great grandmother . . . came from Czechoslovakia. . . . She was actually born in Yugoslavia, but the boundaries had changed, and it was *Czech*oslovakia.

CHARLES Black . . . Afro-American.
JANET White. Byelorussian.

MANNING I identify myself as African and then American.
CHRISTINE I used to think of myself as a white. . . . I suppose I'm primarily, well, I'm European American. I'm primarily German, French, French Canadian, and a smidgen of Indian. God knows what else.

ROBERT I would identify myself as an individual . . . [and] as an American.
KATE European American I guess, by race.

GLORIA African American. From Jamaica.
KENT European. There's a number of them. I can list them off. . . . I have English, Irish, German, and Swiss. I tend to identify with English because of my name, which is English.

JOHN I'm from the West Indies. I'm from [Jamaica]. I consider myself black . . . , but I don't carry it around. I don't wear my race in my character.
LIZ I guess I call myself white, but I think of my background, my ethnic background is Norwegian.

GREGORY I'm African American . . . first-generation civil rights.
JOYCE I'm Polish and Swedish.

ED I'm African American.
ROSEMARY I'm white European (she laughs). I'm all Norwegian.

BAYARD I'm black.
ANN I guess I'm white. Ethnically I know I'm a real mix. I tend to identify
     more with the Irish part of me probably, because I look more Irish.

SHANE Afro-American.
SHIRLEY I'm German-Norwegian background.

HOUSTON I'm a black, African American.
EVE I never really, uh, we say Euro-American for me, because I don't like
    the term Caucasian. But I don't know, to me it's, I never really have
    to say what I am, you know. It doesn't really affect me, I guess, so.
    But I would say Euro-American, European American.

WILSON *I* am an Afro-American.
DOT I'm mostly German.

BARB I'm black.
ROGER I'm white.

WILLIAM Let's see, now I'm African American (he laughs).
LAURA I'm white. Apparently my blood background is mixed European,
      Scotch, Irish, English, German.

PATRICIA I'm . . . black. Afro-American is the term I prefer.
GARY White, Caucasian.

EMMETT Black American.
NORA I'm of German with a little bit of Russian descent, I guess.

JAMES African American and uh, French descent.
JILL I just basically am white.

FLORA I now use the term African American.
TIM White American.

WANDA African American.
ADAM White.

LORENZO African American, although our family has Indian heritage as
        well and that is something we also talk about.
VIRGINIA I would identify myself as white but my mother is Jewish; my
         father is Finnish with a piece of Lapp blood in there somewhere.

2

HOW THE RESEARCH WAS DONE

A ll interviews were carried out by Terri Karis and Richard Powell, both of whom have considerable professional experience talking to people about personal matters. Terri is experienced in research interviewing and in the provision of services to individuals, couples, and families. Richard, a licensed marriage and family therapist, has many years of direct service experience with individuals, couples, and families. Terri and Richard are themselves an interracial couple— Terri is white; Richard is African American. It was preferable for an interracial couple to carry out the interviews because they might better understand the issues that interracial couples deal with and might help the couples being interviewed to be more comfortable. In fact, some people said they were more willing to participate because the interviewers were an interracial couple.

WHAT WAS ASKED

The interview schedule was relatively simple, but Terri and Richard often asked additional questions for clarification, to fill in more information on issues people brought up, to get a better picture of why two partners might have different perspectives on something, or to check whether issues brought up by other respondents were relevant to the couple being interviewed. The interview began with basic background questions. There followed this set of questions, designed to pick up a range of issues and experiences in coming together and living together as an interracial couple.

1. You're in an interracial relationship. Does it matter to you that you are? If so, what is it that matters? If not, why does it not matter?

2. When you look back at your relationship since it started, has your view of yourselves as an interracial couple changed over time? (Has your view about whether or not it matters changed over time?)

3. Assuming that it matters to the larger community that you are an interracial couple, what do you think the community thinks of your relationship as an interracial couple?

4. If you wanted the larger society to know something about interracial relationships, what would it be?

5. What kind of concerns, if any, have been raised by your family (parents, siblings, etc.) or friends about your interracial relationship?

6. What kind of support, if any, have you received from your family (parents, siblings, etc.) or friends for your interracial relationship?

7. Have you experienced prejudice, discrimination, or racism as an interracial couple? If so, what have you experienced? How have you responded to these situations?

8. Have any of your relatives experienced prejudice, discrimination, or racism because of your relationship as an interracial couple? If so, what have they experienced? How have you or they responded?

9. What was significant in your family history that brought you to this relationship?

10. What was significant in your dating history that brought you to this relationship? Did you date outside of your race before this relationship?

11. Has race ever been an issue as a part of your conflicts with each other?

12. Have you experienced either internal or external pressures as an interracial couple that have made you consider splitting up? If so, what have the pressures been?

13. Have you had conversations with each other about this upcoming interview? What have you talked about with each other since we contacted you? Did you discover things that you didn't want to reveal to us? [Couples were told they did not have to reveal anything they wanted to keep confidential but that we would like to know whether there was anything they had not wanted to reveal.]

14. What have been the special blessings of your interracial relationship?

WHO WAS INTERVIEWED

We recruited couples through announcements made at workshops for interracial families, notices placed in a YMCA newsletter for multiracial families and in a newspaper that serves the African American community, and announcements posted at a YMCA that offers programs for interracial families. Friends suggested couples they knew, and some of the couples who were interviewed suggested other interracial couples who might be interested. Some couples who were interviewed learned about the research from acquaintances and then contacted us, and one couple contacted us after seeing an announcement about the research that was put up without our knowing about it at a community health clinic. We attempted to interview same-sex couples but had no success.

Racial categorization invariably simplifies. Underlining the simplifications of racial distinctions in the United States, two of the black partners who were interviewed did not trace their African ancestry to the time of slavery in the American South. A number of people who identified themselves as black said that they had ancestors who were not black. Two people who self-identified as black said that they were actually biracial, both black and white, and had been raised with "mixed" identity. In a number of other instances, a person who self-identified as black talked about a white grandparent or great-grandparent but did not claim a biracial upbringing or identity. In four cases, a black partner claimed to have Indian heritage (Cherokee in three cases, Choctaw in one). None of these four people spoke of active contact with Indian culture or kin, and each of the four called himself or herself black or African American. All four had been raised as black and had experienced racial discrimination directed against blacks. One white partner also claimed Indian heritage but also had no active contact with Indian culture or kin.

Twenty-one interracial couples were interviewed, all of them during 1991. In 16 couples, the African American partner was a man (76%); in 5, the African American partner was a woman. The frequency difference between couples in which the man was African American and those in which the woman was African American resembles that found in the Twin Cities metropolitan area and nationally. Welborn (1994, p. 66), for example, reported that in 1991, 273 (or 75%) of the 362 marriages in Minnesota that were between an African American and a European American involved an African American man and a European American woman. Similarly, Spigner (1990) reported that in 1987 U.S. Census data, there were more than twice as many black-white interracial couples in which the husband was black than in which the wife was black. Even though the U.S. Bureau of the Census reported that for 1960 there were as many interracial marriages in America that were white male with black female as black male with white female (Heer, 1974), data going back to the 1870s generally show that more black-white interracial couples have involved a black man with a white woman than a white man with a black woman (Bruce & Rodman, 1973).

The question of why there are more black-white interracial couples consisting of a white woman and a black man is a topic for another book. There is reason to believe that the factors influencing black men and women to enter interracial relationships are similar, even though the rates of entry into such relationships are different (Tucker & Mitchell-Kernan, 1990). Some of the people who were interviewed offered their perspectives on the issue. The following provides useful hunches about why it is that the majority of the couples in this study consist of a black man with a white woman.

> I think it's related to the status of male in society. Period. I think black males have fewer options, and certainly fewer freedoms, but if you look historically, males have always been able to make decisions about what they do; but I also think that if movement is to come in terms of change and ways of thinking, . . . it will come through women. . . . I know there's theories out there about the conquering and about being angry with your family and all that sort of stuff, and I really reject that

as a generalized notion. . . . I remember being very afraid. Gary seemed much more assured and confident than I did, and I called my brother. . . . "God, I'm involved with this person!" And he started laughing, and my brother who had dated interracially and did, it wasn't a big issue with him. . . . My brother, that was OK for him, because certainly I was raised by very traditional parents that, you know, men can do anything. But women can't do that. And so you had to walk a certain way and do a certain way. So I certainly wasn't going to ever be caught even thinking that I could be serious about Gary. You know, it was just kind of crushes, passing fancies kind of thing. But my brother, you know, my mother'd say, "[He] can go out there and stand in the street naked, and tomorrow morning he can get the best woman in town. You sit on that porch with your legs up and people will call you a whore." And that was kind of ingrained in me. And it limited what I thought I could do. (Patricia is black) [Note: All names and some other pieces of identifying information have been changed to disguise people's identities.]

One can read what Patricia said to suggest that more interracial couples involve a black man with a white woman partly because black families give men more latitude. Many other factors may be involved, however—some of which are mentioned in the next chapter, where people discuss ideas that the general public has about interracial attraction.

To be eligible to be interviewed, a couple had to be together at least a year. At the time of interview, the couples had been together from 1 year to 20 years. Nineteen of the 21 were married to each other. (Because two of the couples were not legally married to each other, we use terms such as *partnership, relationship,* or *committed relationship* to refer to couples in this study.) The age of the people interviewed ranged from 23 to 51, with only 5 of the 42 people interviewed in their 20s and only 1 in the 50s. As far as we know, all people interviewed were American citizens.

The sample was well educated. One person had never finished high school. All the rest had at least some education beyond high school. Of the 42 people interviewed, 29 had at least a bachelor's degree—15 African Americans and 14 whites; 20 had some education beyond the bachelor's degree—9 African Americans and 11 whites. There were quite a few professionals, managers, and entrepreneurs in the sample, and only 2 whose primary work could be called blue-collar.

Of the 21 African American partners, 14 had spent a great deal of their childhood in cities in the Midwest, East, or Northeast, and 2 had spent part or all of their childhood in the South. Of the 21 white partners, 12 had spent a great deal of their childhood in the Midwest, East, or Northeast, and none had grown up in the South. Three of the African American partners and 6 of the white partners had spent part of their growing-up years in the Twin Cities. The biggest difference between African American and white respondents in where they had grown up was that 9 of the white partners had grown up on farms or in towns of under 50,000 population in the Midwest; none of the African American partners had.

The sample is not representative of interracial couples in America, even of interracial couples in the Twin Cities metropolitan area. There were no elderly couples and no rural couples. There were no couples in public housing or on public assistance. There were no couples living in the neighborhoods of the metropolitan area that have the highest rates of violence, prostitution, and the drug trade. Nobody seemed intensely alienated from society. We think what we report in this book has importance and general relevance, but it is not definitive. Research still must be done with the full range of interracial couples—in terms of social class, age, region of the country, integration into society, and local culture.

ETHICAL ISSUES

Whose Reality Is This?

A question that is particularly important in a study of people who may be the object of racism is, Whose reality is this? Is this a book about the experiences and thoughts of the people being interviewed? Or is it about researchers' realities? Whose voice is speaking? Even if the people who were interviewed are quoted extensively, were the things they said shaped by questions that came from researchers' realities? Are the quotations a fair expression of what was said, or have the selection and editing of quotations distorted the realities of the people interviewed? We tried to interview in a way that would honestly and fairly represent the realities of people we interviewed. We try to capture those realities for the reader through extensive quotation from the interviews. In editing quotations, we eliminated most repetitions of words or phrases as people fumbled for words; most "continuing sounds" or "starter sounds," such as "uh" or "er"; many instances of "you know"; and the majority of partial clauses that were corrected by a restart. Any editing omissions more substantive than those are indicated by ellipsis dots.

It is challenging to represent fairly the diversity of experience and thought of a group of people. The reader should read with a critical eye for statements that seem to downplay variation among the people interviewed, for omissions of what the reader might expect to be part of the realities of the couples interviewed, and for places where our interpretations or summaries of what we quote seem to distort the meanings that can be seen in the interview quotations.

Does This Book Legitimate
Skin Color Categories?

"Race" is a category system that arises from and feeds racism. Racial concepts are tools of oppression. Can a book that deals with race avoid supporting racism? Edwards (1990) challenges those of us who are white (Paul, Terri), who have grown up in and live in a racist society, and who carry out research like this to question what we are doing. How can the white collaborators on this project do research that is not racist when there has been so much racism in our past, in our surroundings, and, presumably, in us? How can we escape our own racist views? One can presume that living in a racist society will affect an interracial relationship, but is it racist to ask about that and to suppose that what is learned from what people say could be useful both to the oppressed and the oppressor? Is it part of racist oppression to ask questions that could cause people to focus on past and current pain? The white coauthors of this book have every intention of writing a book that is antiracist and hope that the book also succeeds at being free of racism. We acknowledge, however, that it is not a simple matter to free our work from our own racism.

Part of the Problem Is the Labels

Racism operates with a category system and a set of labels. To carry out the research reported here and to write this book requires the use of labels. As has been reported in other studies of people in interracial relationships (e.g., Kerwin, Ponterotto, Jackson, & Harris, 1993), many people who were interviewed expressed concern about racial labels, the term *interracial,* and similar category terms. We agree with them and fear that using such terms can feed bias. In the following quotations from three different interviews, people challenge the concepts of race and of interracial relationship.

> The fact that I'm in an interracial relationship is, it's not a label that I apply to my relationship. . . . That's an external label that people outside have a need to categorize, and say, OK, [Mr. X] is married to [Ms. Y]. Gregory is black; Joyce is white, so . . . there's an interracial relationship, so that carries all that extra baggage with it. (Gregory)

> [Race] doesn't matter to us. . . . We don't even talk about it or think about it. It's not even like an issue. (Shirley)

EVE   We are just a married couple, and the outside world sees us as interracial. . . . I every day deal with that we're interracial, but it's mainly because other people are always telling us that we are . . .

HOUSTON   . . . I used to always say "interracial." I'm really against that now. People are just people. I think you need to stop saying things like, "Well, am I interracial?" I don't want my kids to grow up saying, "OK, we're interracial." I just want them to know that Mom's . . . white, and Dad's black. Simple as that. I don't want them to be labeled, 'cause I don't want to create a whole other uh, uh . . .

INTERVIEWER   Another minority?

HOUSTON   Yeah, you know. Everyone wants us to be separate. . . . It's kinda sickening. . . . I don't want my kids to have to grow up with people telling them that, "Oh, you're biracial," what not. No, they're just human beings. . . .

EVE   We're really careful I think in the last few years about the terms that we use, too; like, *biracial* bugs me, *mulatto* bugs me, *race* bugs me. I quit checking race on forms that I fill out. The only time I do it is like for the census, 'cause I wanted them to know that there are married couples like us that are happy and living together. . . . You know, like there's just the human race, and that might be like really idealistic, but we try to practice what we preach. . . . Both of us have really tried to change, even some of the words that we use.

HOUSTON . . . It's scary in this world that we live in. . . . If we keep buying this . . . "either-or" thinking, you know, either you're black or white. Everyone is more than just black or white. And we know that. So . . . either-or thinking is dangerous. I try not to even think like that.

We agree with what they say, but we are also trapped by the constructed social realities of race and of interracial relationships. Because race and interracial relationships have a reality for many people and because we want to illuminate how those realities affect certain couples, we use the terms coming from those realities. This book challenges those realities, but to write about them and their influence, the terms must be used. The partners in interracial couples may be similarly trapped (Frankenberg, 1993, p. 140) into using those terms. In that regard, Frankenberg talked about the " 'givenness' of a universe of discourse" that may limit discussion centered on racial matters at the same time that the discussion is intended to go beyond those limits. Even when people say "no" to racism, they are still captured by it in that they are taking it seriously enough to be talking about it. Discourse devoted to something oppressive is shaped by the oppression. One symptom of the problem is that people who are trying to escape the trap of having language and thought captured by racist terms find that the terms they use to designate interracial couples, their children, or the partners in interracial couples recurrently change (cf. Frankenberg, 1993, p. 141). Although the terms interracial and multiracial are used by people opposed to racist views, our expectation is that when these designators have been used too often in racist ways or can be interpreted as having racist meanings, they will be replaced by new terms.

In challenging the concepts of race and of interracial relationship, some of the people we quote in this chapter may seem to be "color-blind" about the reality of racial categories in society. Each showed in other places in the interview that they are not naive about their social world. They understand that even though they do not think of themselves or their marital or family relationships as meaningfully described by terms such as *white, interracial,* or *biracial,* they and their children must navigate wisely in a world where those terms have meaning to many people.

First Principles in Our Research Ethics

It can be oppressive to make people objects of research. The oppression may include putting words in someone's mouth, forcing people to respond to questions that they would rather not answer, making trouble between spouses, putting respondents in a subordinate position in relationship to the interviewer, and not respecting or acknowledging respondent realities. We tried to avoid such oppression. The respondents were interviewed as coequals, with every right to decline to answer a question, to stop the interview, and to raise issues that were important to them. The interviewers had a great deal of professional training and experience in listening and questioning. They take others seriously, listen well, are good at acknowledging other people's realities, and are good at functioning within those realities.

It also could be oppressive to objectify and idealize interracial couples as though they were a fascinating social experiment or heroic soldiers in a war on oppression. People's humanity, complexity, and diversity can be taken away from them by well-wishers as well as by those who resent them. As one white partner said,

CHRISTINE I think there [are] people who are kind of liberal or politically correct who find it, for me this is another kind of, it's not racism, but kind of peculiar stereotyping to think it's kind of "in" or interesting to know couples like us, and they grill you all the time about, you know . . .

INTERVIEWER What is this like?

CHRISTINE Yeah, what's the difference? What's it like? And so it's like this avid attention you get because again you're different, maybe not deviant, but different.

VALIDITY ISSUES

How can it be established that the interviews were competently done and that our presentation of the contents of the interviews accurately and fairly represents what people thought and experienced? We tried to interview in a way that left plenty of room for what people said to be clarified, explored, spelled out in detail, and heard accurately. We try, with the presentation of findings, to give the reader the words of respondents so that the reader can judge whether our interpretations are supported by our interview material. People do not automatically tell all to an interviewer. They may constrain what they say for all sorts of reasons. We hope that an interview that gives people room to say something such as the following would allow them room to relate significant experiences, impressions, and thoughts accurately.

> In an interview situation . . . you think to yourself, just how far should I go? How deep should the feelings be? What possible repercussions would they have? (James)

We hope that comments such as the one that follows suggest that the interview allowed people enough comfort to be honest and comprehensive in telling us about entering and living in an interracial relationship.

> I had no idea what the questions would be like, but I don't think you've asked anything to put me on the defensive or where I felt I couldn't say anything. (Jill)

All interview tapes were transcribed verbatim. All transcriptions were checked, usually by a person different from the original transcriber, and corrected as appropriate. The corrected transcriptions were read and reread closely for the topics that are at the focus of this book. Those topics emerged from our prior ideas about what might be important and also from what people said in the interviews. Excerpts were made from each transcript for each topic of interest. The excerpting results were supplemented by a computer key-word search of all transcripts. The categorization of the excerpts was checked and rechecked during the preparation of the book. The presentation of interview quotations throughout this book provides the reader with an independent opportunity to check if the documentation (the quotations from the interviews) fits our assertions about what people said.

Diversity Versus Stereotyped Unity

In characterizing the couples in this study, it is challenging to capture the trends and similarities in what they had to say but also to respect and represent honestly their diversity. It would be sad indeed to replace the stereotypes that some people have of interracial couples with new, social-scientist-generated stereotypes.

> The group that is multicultural families is not a monolithic entity. . . . There's variety and all this. (Barb)

> There's *too* much variety in interracial couples to stereotype. Actually, my sense is that in a very basic way, it's not that big a deal, not as big a deal as the rest of the community from outside is trying to think. (Virginia)

This last comment speaks not only of the diversity of interracial couples but also of the importance of affirming that life in an interracial couple is "not that big a deal." The next chapter expands on that point by exploring the claims of many of the people interviewed that their relationship is quite ordinary.

What Kind of Knowledge Is Provided by 21 Couples?

Interviews of 21 unrepresentative, volunteer couples from a single metropolitan area tell us nothing about the prevalence of things nationally or even in the metropolitan area. Statistical inference with so few couples and such an unrepresentative sample is meaningless. But the couples can provide us with ideas and ways of looking at the experiences of other interracial couples. A study such as this offers the knowledge of possibility and perspective, and it suggests hypotheses to inform and inspire future research.

3

FEELING ORDINARY
IN A RELATIONSHIP
OTHERS SEE AS UNUSUAL

MOST COUPLES SAW THEIR
RELATIONSHIP AS ORDINARY

Many of the people who were interviewed characterized theirs as a normal couple relationship. Most volunteered that the race of their partner made no difference to them. Most also said that they saw themselves as like other couples in dealing with the ordinary challenges and opportunities of a couple relationship, in working toward conventional goals, and in struggling with the everyday issues of making a living and maintaining a household.

We're no different than anybody else. We have the same concerns for a family, the kids—if you have any—my house, my dog, my job, my daily life concerns. (Manning)

I just look at this relationship as she is my wife and I am her husband.
. . . Everyone else is looking at it as a black and white couple, which I
think is really stupid because we are just a married couple. We are no
different than a Chinese couple that were married or a white couple
that were married or a black couple that were married. We're just a
couple of people who decided we wanted to be with one another.
(Houston)

I'm not in this relationship because of its interracial qualities. . . . [In-
terracial relationships] are just like any other relationship. (Charles)

DONNA You look for a person to be with, not a race or color. . . . I
would say that there's nothing different about this relationship than there is with, I mean, a relationship is based on a
few basic things, has nothing to do with color at all. . . .

HENRY I don't think we ever viewed ourselves as an interracial
couple.

When I met Tim, I didn't look at him as a white man. I looked at him
as somebody there for me when I needed to go out. . . . We live and
breathe and pay taxes and do . . . and everything else, just like anybody
else. Have a home and work. (Flora)

Many emphasized that they were in their relationship because of
the love, companionship, compatibility, and other positive aspects of
relationship that anyone might want, not because the relationship
was interracial (see Tizard & Phoenix, 1993, chap. 9, for similar
accounts from Britain).

There's nothing wrong with it. [We] are people. I don't think it's a matter of color . . . or race or whatever, to decide if [two people] are going to be happy or not. And they shouldn't let other people choose
their destiny for them, you know, like my family. They tried their darn-
dest. And I just had to stand up and say, "This is a person. He's not
black; he's a person. He's a man, and I love this man." (Olivia)

SHIRLEY We face the same stresses and problems that everyone else
does. Maybe we're an exception, but I don't think our
problems are magnified because we are interracial; I don't

think that affects them at all. We have our bills, our money problems, everything else. We go on vacations, we shop in places where everyone else shops, and we just don't encounter that much of a problem. I guess I would just want the larger society to see that we are normal. I'm not in this because I'm a white woman that thinks it's really "cool" to be with a "black man." . . .

SHANE   We're all in this world for a little time, not a long time, you know, and if you love somebody, be with them.

The relationship is not the difference of . . . skin. . . . People get attracted to each other and get married for probably similar reasons no matter what. . . . My sense is that if they're willing to risk the possible or likely disapproval of other people, then there must be something strong in that relationship that you should pay attention to and learn from, rather than see it as something irresponsible to do, that these are people who are choosing to risk more hurdles than other people have to do, so rather than see it as negative, see it as something you learn from, particularly if it lasts. (Gary)

Color has never been an issue in my life. . . . I [didn't] fall in love with my husband [based on color]. Color isn't there. I didn't see categories of color. I'm looking for someone who loves us. . . . I don't feel it's any different from any other couple out there. (Jill)

A relationship is a relationship is a relationship. You find common ground with another person and you make compromises and you develop a trust, an understanding, hopefully love, and you live like everybody else. (James)

Some people said that at first they were more self-conscious about being in an interracial relationship, reflecting expectations established by family members and others that interracial partners would have trouble getting along with each other and trouble getting along in society.

I guess I was looking for something that was going to mean something, or that people were going to react some way. . . . My mother said, "Oh, you're going to have so much trouble; you're going to have so much trouble." That might have been the influence. . . . When we first got together, I expected that there was going to be something about . . . the fact that he was black, and . . . you keep looking. . . . So there's this small whatever it is that happens in your mind. (Janet)

Some people said that at first they were more self-conscious about being in an interracial relationship because of their own sense of the differences in an interracial couple.

We marry for the same reason that anybody else does. . . . You get what you bring, just like anything else in this lifetime. Basically I don't think there's any essential difference. . . . Race just really hasn't made a lot of difference; it hasn't intruded very much. Early on, it's still early on, I would kind of look over and realize there was this white woman (he laughs) with my name (still laughing). How did that happen? Or sometimes I'd forget; . . . and when I see her relatives, "Oh, that's right, these are my in-laws (laughing). How odd." But most of the time, I don't think about it. She's Laura. (William)

Also, in the beginning, matters of physical attractiveness and the meaning of entering an interracial relationship might have been more important. A white man who was like other people in the study in claiming that race did not matter to him might seem to have contradicted himself by saying that he was and still is attracted to black women. His statement, which follows, however, might be something that many people who were interviewed could say, "Race does not make any difference, but I am certainly attracted to my partner and people like my partner, and there is much more to race than skin color."

In the beginning I was very attracted, both physically and mentally, and I think it had to do with her race. I have a different outlook and different philosophy about interracial marriages; I believe that at some point in time if we don't blow this place that we call earth up, that there won't be any races. And so to me it doesn't matter at all. . . . Other than . . . cultural differences, people are people. And so I don't think that race should be a barrier of any kind in a man-woman relationship. I like black women; I think they're very attractive. I think their eyes are beautiful, and their eyelashes are beautiful, and their skin color is beautiful, and their bodies are beautiful. (Tim)

On the other hand, Tim might be different from many people who were interviewed in being more aware of race on an ongoing basis. Similar to findings in other studies (Kouri & Lasswell, 1993; Porterfield, 1978), some people in the present study said that normally they were not aware of their partner's race, that they only think about their relationship as interracial when an outsider brings the matter of race up or when something happens that reminds them that others see them as an interracial couple.

JOHN I would think that emotions really don't follow any color scheme. . . . It's only now that we're discussin' it that it's an interracial relationship. Not that it has been classified or defined as such. I just basically see it as a relationship, and . . . the race issue only come into fore since we're discussin' it as such, her being Norwegian or whatever, and me being whatever I am. . . . I don't think our relationship is interracial. I think that our behavior, or interaction with each other might be racial, but when we're not into those aspects of being with each other, I don't see her as a different race.

LIZ Yeah, . . . I don't think of John as being black and me as being white. There's difference, but I just see him as John.

There is no white and black to me. We're all, I mean, I know there is white and black, but when I'm with Rosemary, it wasn't for her whiteness or her nonblackness, or when I had my first wife it wasn't for her blackness. It was for the companionship and the company and the chemicals of the intertwining of the two people. Color, the color is secondary. I talk about it, and it is significant when you are dealing with the world, but in this house it doesn't mean anything. . . . It's not different than the same-culture or same-race relationships. I mean, you mustn't fight and you have fun and you experience life and you make love, and there's no difference. (Ed)

Most people in most couples said that their relationship was ordinary and that there was nothing strange about loving their partner and living an everyday life with that partner. But when someone in an interracial couple characterizes her or his relationship as ordinary, it may be viewed as a challenge by those who oppose or stereotype interracial couples. From the perspective of the people who were interviewed, claiming ordinariness may be a counter to those who see them as unnatural, strange, doomed to fail, trouble-makers, or otherwise inappropriate or defective. By saying, "We are ordinary," a person in an interracial couple is telling those who single them out as different that they are wrong and is also trying to defend against any words, stares, and so on that could have the potential to intrude on ordinary couple life. One clue to how the claim of ordinariness can be a counter to opposition and stereotyping and a defense is that, while talking about being in an ordinary couple, some people also talked about those in their family or the larger society who singled them out as odd.

What makes a biracial couple happy? Probably the same, they love like a single-race couple love. . . . I just want society as a whole to leave me be. Don't look at me any differently than you look at any other couple, because we are all married by the laws of God. . . . We all said the same vows. . . . We may come from different racial backgrounds, but there's no difference. Why do you find me so unique, society? . . . Gee whiz . . . , can't you see that we no different than anybody else? Can't you see that we no different than yourself? You and your wife? We sit up to the table, just like you eat. Wear the same type of clothes. We've got jobs. Blue-collar, some are white-collar, some are no collar at all, but the point is that we're no different. So just sit back and shut up. Just take it easy! Leave us alone. We live our life in luxury just like we supposed to live our life, just like you. That's all that we ask for. And I think that once you do that, society, you'll find that couple hopefully becoming less tense themselves. Because surely we are tense from time to time, because there are some factors that are pushing against us hard all the time. There are those who don't want that to happen. There are some blacks who don't want blacks to marry whites. Whites don't want [whites] to marry blacks, OK. But if everybody just sit back and leave us alone, live our lives like we want to, you can marry who you want to marry, date who you want to date, then we can truly live out the powerful words [of] the Constitution. (Robert)

I didn't marry Ann because she's white. I married her because I loved her, thought she was the right person for me. . . . It's obvious . . . she's

white and I'm black, and I'd knew that there'd be some issues to deal
with, but I think that our relationship has progressed to the point
where we're so comfortable with each other that it doesn't make any
difference anymore. I see ourselves as a successful marriage, couple
relationship regardless of . . . what our races are. . . . With interracial
families . . . there obviously is some differences, because they've got
to deal with race and race issues, sometimes on a daily basis for some
families, depending on where they live and their situations, but if there
wasn't that to deal with, interracial families are the same as other families. They have the same problems, problems with kids, problems with
schools, problems with whatever. . . . And if race wasn't such an over-
riding factor . . . interracial families would fit in anywhere. (Bayard)

ANN Interracial couples are like all other couples, and . . . the fact
that we are interracial is not the most outstanding or significant day-to-day thing in our lives. . . . We didn't marry each
other from hidden agendas, you know. That's another big
stereotype.

INTERVIEWER What do you think people think those agendas are?

ANN Oh, that you're rebelling from your family or you have low
self-esteem. . . . That's, I guess, what they think about me, or
that Bayard . . . needs a white woman to elevate his status or
to reject his own culture. All that kind of stuff just really
bothers me, that [society can't] just allow people to choose
their mates simply because they love them. And then you got
Spike Lee making his *Jungle Fever* movie, and everybody's
talking about it again, and I just hate that. . . . It's like here's
another interracial couple on the big screen, and this is the
one couple that everybody's going to go see, and there's all
kinds of other issues tied up with that relationship, and like
when you see this on *Oprah Winfrey* they starting talking
about not just this movie, but then it all becomes interracial
couples, and it's just one little couple in one little story, and
it becomes this forum for the whole world, and it's not even
accurate. It just bothers me.

I guess when you fall in love you sort of become color-blind. I guess I
don't believe in loving somebody just for their culture, . . . but I don't
believe in not liking them because of that either, so I guess once you
kind of clear a lot of that out, . . . falling in love is the thing that really

makes the difference. And then you have to face yourself and say, "Is
this love strong enough to withstand what our families might think,
what the world might think, our friends might think?" (Nora)

Quite a few people said that at times they were blocked from their
identity as an ordinary couple. Sometimes, the blocking came in part
from knowing that they were out of the ordinary.

> I think that in the beginning we were very aware that we were [an] in-
> terracial couple, especially from where we were from. When we first
> met, we basically spent time in [a] community . . . where there was
> Flora and her family who were black, and then one other black family
> in the entire community, OK? So in that situation I think that we both
> were aware. (Tim)

For most couples, the blocks to being ordinary came mostly from
others. Many people said that they wanted to go for walks, go
shopping, take vacations, and in other ways live as an ordinary
couple, but the reactions of others recurrently defined them as not
ordinary. The reactions, discussed in detail in Chapter 7, might most
often involve privacy-invading stares. Many people also talked about
occasional words and actions directed at them as an interracial couple
that conveyed racist sentiments. These words and actions might hurt
a couple; threaten them; and deprive them of comfort, safety, and
the rights and opportunities that a same-race couple might have. In
short, those words and actions, at least at the time they occur, can
deprive a couple of the freedom to be ordinary. Some people talked
about struggling to achieve ordinariness. Some talked about being
very self-conscious—especially at first, when people stared or reacted
to them in some other way—but learning how to deflect, avoid, or
minimize those stares and other reactions.

> When we first got together and then married, there were I guess cer-
> tain feelings of being . . . an interracial couple when what I perceived
> from the general public as well as from my family is there was some-
> thing unusual (he laughs) about the situation. So I guess at that point it
> mattered [that we were in an interracial couple]. However, over a pe-
> riod of, say, 4 or 5 years, [as we] supposedly grew together, I really
> didn't care that we were of different color. All that concerned me then

was how we were going to live together and be able to coexist as individuals. . . . [I] kind of phased out of that concern for what other people thought and my family, et cetera, even though at some point . . . , even today, . . . you get certain feelings or vibes once we've gone outside. . . . But it . . . really does not matter. (Manning)

Some people talked about not being able to ignore reactions in public, about not being able to escape, at least in public, the sense that they were in a relationship that was anything but ordinary.

I saw Dot as a very kind and intelligent individual. And this is what attracted me to her. . . . But then, the thought of her being, uh, constantly thinking of being as a white woman, that kind of vanished, but whenever you're in society you become aware because the people, well, you become an oddity. And sometimes it's uncomfortable. Over the years, I've learned to deal with it psychologically myself. There's always a (pause) (snort) I guess it's always an awareness when you're out in the public, that makes you self-conscious. . . . But . . . I think of Dot as a wonderful human being. (Wilson)

Even if a couple could resist being affected by reactions of the larger society, they still had to deal with people who thought of their interracial relationship as a political act, as a statement beyond simply, "This is the person I love and want to be with." If not transparently negative or curious, there were the reactions that seemed to say to them, "We know what your politics are because of the relationship you are in."

Because of our relationship, [I] sometimes feel called upon by people to make a speech. . . . They are making presumptions about . . . my political beliefs, and that our relationship is somehow a philosophical decision that had been made . . . and that I should be able to make an eloquent speech. . . . I've always felt . . . I'm not up to the task. I didn't choose to marry her to make speeches. (Gary)

The awareness of societal reactions seemed to give the couples a dual reality. In that dual reality, they could think both that "we are an ordinary couple" and "we are in the spotlight, are special in some ways, and must be careful because people are watching and judging."

JOYCE It's sort of like a duality. I mean, we're just like everybody else, but there's this duality that, no, we also have to have this consciousness and an awareness of how we're seen. . . .

GREGORY On the one hand, like Patricia said, we're pretty much the same; money's short, money's short, it doesn't matter inter-racially or not. Kids get sick, they get sick. They go to birthday parties, you have a good time; you get together with your family and have a wonderful time. So in a lot larger sense it's very much the same. But . . . in the United States today see how the social-political climate forces you into this box, or this category, and so definitely we're different. How much do we see ourselves as different, and how much we want to wear the mask about what society projects about who we are and where we're going and what we're doing. . . . Like Patricia alluded to earlier, there's certain stereotypes that people have about interracial couples. One of the most common ones was the pimp and the hooker, and so in a lot of ways, we've tended to be sort of victims of pretty biased, pretty negative stereotypes. And maybe that's partly . . . the kind of bogeyman the culture has about relationships that are different. . . . The relationship cannot be built on anything other than sex. And that's the only reason that you . . . got together is because this great mystique around black male sexuality, and white women just lust after black males. That all came out of slavery days in America. . . . Patricia and I got married, but . . . unwantingly and unwillingly, this other baggage came with the relationship (laughs). You go to open your suitcase, you say, "Oh, this is nice; my God, what the hell is this? I didn't ask for this!" And it's like, "Well, you married one another, and here we are, we're not leaving!" . . . There's sort of this . . . ostracism by society. I don't think anybody gets into a relationship or marries someone to be ostracized, but I know that's certainly in there. It's really not . . . our problem; it's not our problem.

A lot of the problems in the relationships . . . aren't generated within the relationship . . . but from outside. I [am] sure that you will get in interviews people having been told by their parents, "Well what about the kids?" You know, "It's fine for you. I understand that. But what are you doing to the kids?" Well, the kids don't have a problem other than the attitude that you have just demonstrated. Those kind of tensions come from the outside. I think that . . . relationships and marriages . . . are under great strain in our modern society. . . . It's hard enough to be in a relationship anyway. Why would you make it more difficult? And I think what people have to realize is that the couple goes into it not being fooled. The mere fact that they're in the relationship shows that it isn't a source of tension for them. When we get angry at each other, our anger isn't expressed across racial lines. That tension isn't in the relationship. That all comes from the outside. . . . Yes, there is a statement in being an interracial couple. It is a statement about the ability to blend various cultures. . . . There is a communication there that in other elements of society [doesn't] exist. There are positive things in the fact that there can be interracial couples. I wouldn't want that set up as an ideal in relationships, because that's not what it's about. But at the same time it says good things about the society without being a norm that we need to strive towards. (Emmett)

For some couples, there also was a duality of history. Some people who were interviewed could feel ordinary and think of much of their everyday life as ordinary, but quite a few also referred to the history of black-white relationships in America. One man, for instance, talked about the carryover from slavery of a mystique about black male sexuality and of beliefs that white woman lust for a sexual relationship with a black man because of his sexuality. Similarly, one man referred to the forbidden fruit motif and the need to get past such burdensome historical memories to a place of mutual respect.

This [is] the type of picture I had painted of white people, for sure. . . . White women? Nothin' doin', because we've always learned and read, and heard through oral history, that the white man use her for the bait to trap the black man. The black man look at the white woman the wrong way; "Oh, he raped me!" . . . So therefore he have to pay lashes and whips and thrown in jail for something he never did. So those are the viewpoints that I carry with me. . . . Part of the way the system was for 350 years. . . . It's so important . . . for each couple to deeply respect the cultural makeup of a particular race. Because unless you gonna be aware of that, and especially it is so profound I think in black-white relationships, because it took on a negative tone back in the slave days. (Robert)

A black woman, referring to the forbidden fruit motif, talked about the absurdity of it.

> There's all these assumptions being made about those . . . relationships
> and that those relationships existed because it was somehow forbidden,
> as opposed to there being some real attraction to one another. . . .
> That history thing is false . . . because . . . it's a myth that the *only*
> reason that these people got together was because it was somehow
> forbidden and we . . . do what we are told not to do. (Wanda)

The history of relationships between African Americans and whites may be a special part of the awareness of a couple in which the woman is African American and the man is white. Even if the couple feels not directly affected by that history, they can be aware that others, particularly other African Americans, may look at their relationship with a memory of an oppressive history.

> I think we would probably get a stronger reaction from black males
> and . . . females because of the whole thing about slavery . . . and
> associating with the oppressor. (Gloria)

In Chapter 14, support groups for interracial couples and families are discussed. If a couple is not already thinking about the historical background of their interracial relationship, they may be pushed to think that way in a support group.

> Anita Brooks . . . did this; we were involved with one workshop and
> she had this whole diagram . . . going back to the slavery times, and
> kind of the different possibilities of black-white relationships. And
> they were pretty negative. (Joyce)

In fact, the history of black-white relationships in America can be said to affect everybody, not only people in black-white interracial couples but also people who have any reaction at all to a black-white couple. One woman talked about how much that history makes a black-white interracial relationship uncomfortable for everyone.

> I [assume] that of all the various couplings, that the world at large likes
> this kind the least. I do believe that. . . . I think I've read . . . things

that will take it back to the psychological reality of slave times, reactions to [an interracial couple] . . . and enmity between black and white, that it's just so fierce; it's still so fierce. . . . It's the least comfortable alliance for the world. (Laura)

Many of the people interviewed could claim that their relationship was ordinary, but many could also frame their relationship in a centuries-long history of oppression, myth, legal control, exploitation, and enmity.

What Might "Being Ordinary" Mean?

Most people who were interviewed talked about how they were an ordinary couple. They talked about following a daily routine, keeping a job, seeking love and happiness, arguing, and other things that are common to couples in America.

Why did people say "we are ordinary" rather than "we are unique"? Partly, it is that many of them were answering the question, "If you wanted the larger society to know something about interracial relationships, what would it be?" That question may invite people to focus on ways in which interracial and same-race couples are not different. Had people been asked, "What is unique about interracial couples?" fewer might have spoken about ordinariness. There are, however, more significant and interesting reasons why people may have claimed (and perceived) ordinariness in their relationship.

There may be things to be gained by an interracial couple's ignoring or minimizing the ways in which they are not ordinary. An obvious thing is that it means they have to focus less on the painful and difficult things they also discussed in the interviews—family racism and opposition, societal racism and curiosity, the challenges of raising biracial children, their own identity concerns, the history of oppression by whites of African Americans, and so on.

Another thing that may be gained by thinking that one's relationship is ordinary is that one does not add the extra burden of making one's relationship a political statement. Making one's couple life a political statement may burden the relationship. It requires political vigilance, a playing to audiences, and a willingness to speak about the politics that the relationship represents. As a number of people quoted in this chapter indicate, coping with the complexities of relationship life is difficult as it is. Adding to that difficulty by having to cope with the privacy invasion and division of attention that might occur if one claimed one's relationship as a political statement could be very burdensome. So even if people at times were aware that their relationship was a political statement, they could protect themselves from the burdens of being political by denying that there was anything political about their relationship.

> If you're going to put yourself in the position [where] you're always justifying or explaining why you're in these relationships, then you need to get out of them. . . . Those are very personal decisions, and that's your intimate business, who you're involved with in a relationship. (Patricia)

Claiming ordinariness may also be a way of claiming an achievement over racism. If racism denies an interracial couple the right or even the possibility of relating to each other as intimates and equals (Frankenberg, 1993, p. 113), claiming ordinariness may be a way of saying, "We have achieved what racism would deny us." Included in that achievement might be a transcendence of the dispositions that go along with racism (e.g., seeing each other in color terms or assuming oppressor and oppressed roles).

From another perspective, perhaps it is part of life for most people to take whatever their life is like as normal and every day. For example, people who live with a chronically ill child (Kirschbaum, 1994) reach the point where, if there is a routine to that living, that routine becomes normal. They may, for example, have to monitor the child's life signs around the clock, constantly administer medications, aspirate the child's breathing passage every few minutes, feed the child through a stomach tube, and recurrently rush the child to a hospital emergency room. As extraordinary as such a life routine may be by the standards of others, it can become ordinary for the parents living like that. Of course, they can step back and say what is extraordinary about that life in comparison to other families or in comparison to the expectations they had for parenting. But perhaps most of the time they experience what they do as their ordinary life. Similarly, people in the Twin Cities metropolitan area experience a winter with many subzero days, snow drifts that may be taller than they, and recurrent challenges with weather-related transportation problems. Yet that, too, becomes ordinary. The lives of interracial couples may be similarly ordinary.

Costs in Seeing One's
Interracial Relationship as Ordinary

If African Americans and whites were culturally identical, it would be easy to say that the only challenge to an interracial relationship is the racism of people around them. Although there is quite a range of European American and African American cultures (and maybe *because* there is such a range), it is easy to say that interracial relationships involve cultural differences. The partners bring different values, standards, practices, expectations, and experiences to family rituals, the expression of emotion, the management of money, purchasing, dealing with illness, matters of etiquette, and dealing with police, teachers, physicians, and other authorities. Cultural differences are likely to challenge any couple relationship (McGoldrick & Garcia-Preto, 1984). Perhaps the challenges are greater in couples who deny the differences by thinking of themselves as an ordinary couple. They might be less prepared to deal with differences and more likely to blame their differences and difficulties on matters of personality—"It's your fault,"—rather than saying, "Because we come from different cultures we have different ways and must find a way to deal with our differences." In fact, all couples, however similar their backgrounds may seem to them to be, may in some sense come from different cultures and may benefit from acknowledging that difference.

SUMMARY AND CONCLUSIONS

Nobody who was interviewed said that she or he had intended to have an interracial relationship. There was nobody who said that she or he fit the *Jungle Fever* stereotype of a person whose sexual energy and curiosity requires a partner of another race. Almost everybody said that theirs was a relationship that clicked because they were two people who were drawn to each other and got along well. They connected as people, not categories.

> It wasn't because of that racial issue that draw us together. It was because this is the woman who I really love, and care very deeply for. (Robert)

In addition to the claims of ordinariness, there are other layers of reality to being in an interracial couple. The people in these couples could often feel onstage when in public, and all were aware of the long and difficult history between whites and African Americans. As subsequent chapters show, many of these couples had to deal at times with family opposition, societal hostility, and invasive curiosity. Those with children also had to deal at times with the challenges of raising a biracial child in a racist society. Many in the 21 couples also had to struggle with their own doubts, their own feelings and assumptions about race, and their identity issues connected to being in an interracial relationship. Although people spoke eloquently and sincerely about the ways in which their lives were ordinary and how much they wanted that ordinariness, as subsequent chapters show, ordinariness was reached, by most or all of these couples, by traveling paths that couples in which the partners are of the same race do not travel.

We do not want to diminish the claims of ordinariness. The couples had good reason to claim that they were like most couples in their everyday life. But we also do not want to diminish the duality of their ordinariness. Even if one argues that many same-race couples experience difficulties like those the couples who were interviewed experienced with family opposition, cultural differences, antagonistic neighbors, and so on, there is a set of experiences shared by many of the couples interviewed that are unlikely to be part of the experience of same-race couples. The chapters that follow deal with those experiences.

4

IN THE BEGINNING

It cannot be assumed that partners entering interracial relationships are free of racism. People can be unaware of their racism, can put it aside when dealing with a specific person, or can put it aside at the beginning of a relationship only to have it burst out later. In part, these possibilities can arise because the choice of someone with whom to have an intimate relationship may be based on processes that are insulated from the attitudes and predispositions that make up racism.

> I think it's accident [that we came together]. I think it's happenstance, and tolerance probably has something to do with it, but I suspect that it doesn't have to. I suspect that you can find as many interracial couplings in the South and . . . not necessarily between people who are tolerant. (Roger)

He may be right that people come together by chance. The interviews, however, explored whether people thought there were nonchance factors leading to their choice of a partner. Those factors might include family values, family precedents, a personal disposition to be a pioneer in escaping from familial and cultural constraints, being an independent thinker, having a hunger for diversity, a white partner growing up with antiracist influences (e.g., family involvement in the civil rights movement), dating history, feeling secure, and the perception that they and their partner were very similar.

FAMILY AND COMMUNITY VALUES OF RACIAL TOLERANCE

White Partners Who Learned Tolerance From Family or Church

Some white people said that they grew up in an environment in which racial tolerance was advocated, if not practiced. For them, parental teaching and example, or religious teaching, communicated the importance of tolerance and racial equality.

> My parents were involved in the civil rights movement, and they would never, if they felt anything inside they would never publicly state they felt any racial prejudice. . . . My parents' general view that all people were created equal . . . I think that opened my mind to look at things, to experiencing things that I wouldn't have. (Janet)

> For me, part of it was . . . (small laugh) even though they didn't really mean it, when I went to Catholic school for 12 years, they kept telling us that all God's children are equal. . . . They really didn't mean it, but I believed it. (Christine)

> The thing that my natural parents did very well, my values, the things that they taught me were very significant, and one of those was that you don't limit yourself or close yourself to knowing another person that may be from somewhere else or looks different than you, and to always keep an open mind, and to be kind and treat people as . . . you would like to be treated yourself. (Kate)

> [My siblings and I] knew that the word *nigger* was bad. We said it once because we . . . heard it, and my grandma said, "Don't ever say that

word again!" So we knew that the attitude was, "Don't act like that; don't say stupid things; don't hate people because they're different than you." And of course my [siblings] grew up the same way. We liked to think that we were Christian and loving and, so [my siblings] grew up thinking that we are all God's children and so they accepted Shane. (Shirley)

I think there was some permission in my family just because of what people did, that there was permission to be different. . . . I think the other piece is, being brought up Catholic there was a real sort of . . . theoretically accepting people, and the church was very involved in civil rights, and making those kind of connections that wouldn't happen in my neighborhood otherwise. . . . I really think I got this sense of how people are connected. . . . And then I was pretty involved in the civil rights movement, and even kind of coming out of a Polish-Catholic church, the priest that was sort of my mentor became really radical and burned draft files and left the church. . . . It's kind of like he . . . weaned me along to come from praying the rosary once a week . . . to marching with Father Groppi, to getting an awareness of the war. . . . That conservative community center that was our life, I mean, I went to church every day, was sort of the catalyst, and I kind of grew with his awareness. So it's kind of like there was that permission even though I think my mom wouldn't kind of like what he did, but on one level it was OK too. (Joyce)

There were no [racial] taboos [in my family]. And not that my parents ever spoke to me about [race], but that they were very progressive. My father was a high school teacher and always aware of current reality and in touch with kids, and they were very compassionate, humanitarian people, and kind of politically oriented. So we were real aware of what was going on in the 60s and early 70s, encouraged to (laughs) go with it. Almost unspoken, we would participate in moratoriums and things like that, got their encouragement. . . . We never really dealt with race, specifically. It's just that it was an open door. (Laura)

In some cases, the experience was more mixed, with both tolerance and intolerance fostered. One white woman, for example, talked about being taught Christian values of loving one's neighbor but also being taught to stay away from black children.

> I think with my family it was just the *real* Christian values that they
> gave me, . . . 'cause I just was really at some point curious to know
> about other people. It took me all the way to Africa twice. I think the
> *real* Christian values about loving your neighbor as yourself and all
> that is what really comes through for me where I want to see people
> as people. . . . My parents were somewhat racist. . . . When we went
> . . . once to visit some of their friends, there was some black kids and
> I wanted to go play with them, and they wouldn't let me. And it was
> kind of like they were really protective. . . . Or then these black kids
> used to come up from Chicago to play. It was like a church interchange
> program. And they wouldn't let me play with those kids. (Liz)

Similarly, some white people grew up in families in which racist
things were said but doing good for people who were not well-off
was valued. This led to support for helping people (including African
Americans) who were not well-off but not to support for an intimate
relationship with an African American.

> I started working in the inner city, in low-income, white-black-
> Hispanic areas. Worked for the YMCA. And I think my family's
> reaction at first was . . . that it was a good thing to do. . . . But as
> my mother said, "We never expected you to marry one." . . . I was
> working [in] the inner city . . . when I was 19. If somebody could
> have said to my father at that time, "Ten years from now he's going
> to marry a black woman," he would have had a heart attack. (Gary)

Black Partners Who Learned
Tolerance From Family or Church

Some African American partners, like some white partners, talked
about learning tolerance, but the learning situation in the two groups
differed. For white partners, the learning could be rather abstract.
Many lived where African Americans were rarely seen, and they
typically grew up with privileges that were generally unavailable to
African Americans. So for white partners, tolerance was a value of
the privileged. For African American partners, the learning was much
more challenging in that all lived in contact with white racism. The
tolerance an African American learned was directed toward people

from a group that was more privileged and that included people who committed oppressive acts. Because of the differences in experience, in some ways it would be better to have different words for white tolerance and African American tolerance. It is quite a different thing to learn tolerance of people who are in a weaker power situation than to learn tolerance for people who come from a group with many oppressors. Learning tolerance of a privileged group with members who oppress one, one's family, and other people like one, is challenging. Nonetheless, quite a few African Americans talked about learning tolerance.

INTERVIEWER Was there anything significant in your own individual family history that possibly brought you to this relationship?

MANNING For me, not specifically, other than the fact that I was reared to respect and hopefully accept people as they are, [regardless of what] color they were.

My growing and my being raised, there was all kind problems out in the open for black people. And it would be very easy to hate a white person. And at home I didn't sense that hate. I sensed an understanding of what was going on, a dislike for what was going on, but not a hate for the individual. And I think I've always had an open mind. . . . [My dad] had several white friends that would come by and sit around and eat and laugh and talk. (Wilson)

My folks always taught me . . . treat everybody else how you want them to treat you. I think that more than anything it opened my eyes to let everything fall, based on what happened. Get involved with a person, not because of any color, size, whatever like that. But simply because about what that person is. (Robert)

I think [my mother] probably had some intrinsic value that said people are people. Yeah, there are whites, and yes, there are black people, and yes, there are Indian people and Chinese people, and Hispanic people, but people are people, and you should try to accept the person for who they are first before you dare to judge them based on, ya know, not, I mean, like Martin Luther King said, not the color of the skin, but the content of the character. (Gregory)

My mother, she taught . . . the golden rule you live by, "Do unto others as you would like them do unto you." And that applied to all people. So I don't think in my family we have that kind of racism thing. . . . Black people can be racists just like whites can. (Shane)

Me and my father, we talked a lot about black-white relationships. Dad always told me, "Never be afraid to talk to white people." Because a lot of his friends that he worked with in construction were white, but you know my father like, what is he, 57 years old, he grew up down South. Yeah, and he tells me, "Look, when I was growing up, I had to call young white kids [my] same age . . . 'Sir' and 'Mister.' " . . . But he always told me, "Never be afraid to talk with white people." That was his thing; never be afraid to talk with them. Talk with them so that you know that all of them aren't bad people. That's one thing he told me. All of them aren't bad people. And never be afraid. . . . The neighborhood I grew up in, there was like what they call "gray areas," . . . because . . . this area was predominantly a white neighborhood, and those elderly people still live here. . . . I had a chance to meet a lot of those . . . elderly white women, and they were really nice. (Houston)

One African American grew up in an atmosphere of both racial tolerance and urbane openness to diversity.

LORENZO We had the world at our house. We really did. And so I grew up with lots of different cultural influences. . . .

VIRGINIA Also you grew up in a really integrated environment at a time when that was not common and [your] family integrated the neighborhood.

WHITES WHO GREW UP
KNOWING NO AFRICAN AMERICANS

Some whites who grew up in all-white communities had no, or almost no, experience with African Americans. If they learned tolerance, it was an abstract process, unrelated to concrete experiences. There were also whites who grew up without contact with African Americans and who never heard race or racial tolerance discussed.

So in a sense, some whites did not learn tolerance but learned nothing at all about black people.

> Growing up where I did, nobody ever even talked about black people, to make even negative remarks, usually. Because they just weren't part of our lives, and so it may have been that if I grew up in a city, where we had to deal with interracial things, I may have heard a lot more negative things. . . . I knew a lot of racial things, hurtful things, about Native American people and about Jews . . . , but . . . there was that benefit of not having all the negatives things in your face. (Christine)

> [I] lived in [name of small city]. There was a nun at the high school who was, I believe, from the Bahamas. And Lou Brock played for a couple of years for the [city's minor league baseball team] in the early 1960s. Other than that, I suspect that black people who came [there] filled up the gas tank and kept on going. There wasn't much reason to think very much about [race]. (Roger)

That African Americans (and the enormously important African American challenge to racism that was occurring throughout the country as the interviewees grew up) could be ignored speaks of white privilege. There is a covert message of racism in a white family and community that can be completely indifferent to what goes on in the lives of African Americans. In contrast, however, to the bitter and outspoken racism that might often be part of the socialization of whites growing up in other families and communities, indifference like that in the statements just quoted can seem rather benign.

MIXED-RELATIONSHIP PRECEDENTS
IN FAMILY AND COMMUNITY

Quite a few people spoke of others in their family or community who had a mixed-race relationship. In some cases, we could not tell whether those other relationships occurred before the mixed relationship of the person being interviewed. But at the very least, it seems that some people who were interviewed could argue that they were not an isolated extreme.

In my father's family there's . . . a cousin who had adopted a black child. . . . And then [a] cousin . . . married [a] Hawaiian man, and . . . her sister married [a] Mexican, and this was before me. So it's just like there was some history of that happening in our family, and the other thing [that] . . . would kind of dispose me this way, I think in my family, it started opening up more. Like my oldest sister married a Presbyterian, which was . . . like, "Ohh!, you don't marry out of the Catholic faith," so that was kind of . . . a breaking of the traditions. My next oldest sister is a lesbian . . . , and I kind of think we're all a little bit unconventional. . . . I feel like it was probably harder for . . . my older sister to do what she did, 25 years ago. Or maybe comparable. But that was really a big thing. And she had at first been dating a Communist when she was at the university. And when my father found out they threw him out of the house! (Joyce)

Both of my sisters married white men. Their children are biracial. And they're black, and their husbands are white. My grandmother on my father's side was German, so I've been white and black all my life. My grandmother was white. She's a coal miner's daughter from Pennsylvania. . . . When . . . I was a kid, across the alley there was a mixed couple, a black man and a white woman, a German woman. And her name was [Fritzi]. And the experience that I had being over [at] their house was so warm and wholesome. And she would be teaching me German. And I was this little kid learning this German, and [Fritzi] and this strong black man. . . . The experience that I had from that . . . first opened my eyes to [see that] black and white live, or, could be married. And that they were friends of my mother and father's solidified it. (Ed)

When we first met, we met through a friend who was in an interracial marriage. And I guess almost everyone in that area was in interracial relationships. . . . It was like . . . the norm. . . . It was like a subculture, and it was very rare even to see black women there. It was mostly black men and white women. (Dot)

My family's pretty thoroughly mixed anyway. One of the first things I told Laura was that she reminded me a lot of my grandmother, who looked a lot like Laura and had blue eyes. (William)

I remember the time when I was speaking with my family, and my mother in particular, about marrying Patricia. And mother, I've always

been very close to her, and a good little boy, never did anything wrong.
And her saying, "How could you choose to be married with someone
who's so different from you?" And I remember thinking at the time,
"Well, let me look at this family history." . . . My older brother had
married a white woman, but she's Catholic and . . . a divorcee, quite
different from him. And my older sister's first husband was Arab.
Her second husband was Jewish. . . . Quite different from her. (Gary)

Most of the men that come from our family have married Caucasian
women. . . . All of my uncles have married someone not black. (James)

My brothers were married interracial prior to me, so . . . that wasn't
a real shock [to my family]. . . . I had cousins that were closest to me
who dated interracially prior to my doing that. . . . My dad's father
was of an interracial relationship. (Wanda)

[In] my family . . . there's a tradition of mixed marriages, really not
so much interracial, although I have a cousin who is married interracially. . . . But there's a history in my family of religiously mixed.
. . . My grandmother who was Catholic married a Jew. . . . And my
mother was raised Jewish and left Judaism to marry my father. . . . So
. . . there's a history of marriages that are not within a cultural group.
So I think that probably in some very broad sense that affected things.
(Virginia)

Precedents do not necessarily mean that a family is open. In fact,
some family members may condemn the precedents set by other
family members.

I'm from a fairly racist family. We've had interracial relationships in
the family quite a lot. I can remember when I was a kid it was brought
up because someone who would be like my third, fourth cousin . . .
married a Japanese woman. And that was an issue. . . . It was never an
issue in the sense of pushing the person out of the family. They're still
very much of the family, and the woman was welcomed into the family,
but there was the kind of knowing looks behind that this isn't going to
last, and it didn't. . . . My mother's oldest brother, . . . three of his . . .
children . . . have white wives, and it's become more of an accepted
thing in the family. (Emmett)

AFRICAN AMERICAN PIONEERS

Although some African Americans had precedents in family or community for their interracial relationship, others seemed to be pioneers in entering an interracial relationship. In fact, quite a few of those pioneers had been pioneers in other ways. Their entry into an interracial relationship was of a piece with their other precedent-setting acts.

The world I was raised up in, see, I was always the token black, or the first black in my endeavors by geographical location or wanting to pursue something that other black people didn't pursue. Like being a member of the International Youth Symphony in [name of city]. I mean, it was me and one other black guy in this. We got to travel and do things and you're 14, 15 years old. (Gregory)

Through all my education, I have been very much the one black kid in the environments I've been in. . . . Other than my kindergarten, the first time I had a black classmate was my junior year in college. (Emmett)

I started off going through [seventh] grade in all-black schools. . . . Going completely into being the first time a minority student . . . you have to develop sensors . . . in that situation, although I was probably better equipped than a lot of other kids because I also played piano and I went to conservatory. And I was the *first* black kid there ever. . . . [Integration] was new to the [junior high] school, and my family was the first family, and, of course, I mean, there are lots of things about being the first that come along with that too, but you do (sighs) learn to try to monitor certain things in how people react. It's pretty subtle though. I think there're, you have to say tools, or how you develop that skill. I think it has to do with going to those places and being exposed. (Wanda)

HUNGER FOR DIVERSITY

Just as some African American partners saw in themselves pioneering dispositions that may have contributed to their entry into an interracial relationship, some white partners saw in themselves a hunger for diversity. That hunger predisposed them to look for friends and lovers among people different from their own group.

It's a conscious choice on my part to seek out people of color and to seek out situations that are different from what my experience was beforehand. (Roger)

I looked at my own dating history. And almost every time I had dated someone who was very much like me, [it] didn't go anywhere. And I had been engaged to a Jewish woman at one time. And my first love was a Native American woman in South Dakota. And . . . I was infatuated with a number of Saudi Arabian women. So I thought, "Well, it looks to me like this is a long-lasting pattern." (Gary)

The type of young people that we were growing up, we were . . . very inquisitive and interested in differences, and to that extent, I would say we were the personality types that would not at all shy away from this type of relationship. . . . Certainly, on my part there was a . . . naïveté. . . . I mean, we were certainly interested in broadening our experience with all types of people, and I was certainly very interested in racial issues and those kinds of things. But . . . it wasn't like I was seeking out a black woman either. . . . I just think we were more open. And still are. (Adam)

THE CIVIL RIGHTS MOVEMENT
AND THE VIETNAM WAR PROTEST

A few of the couples in the sample got together during the time of Martin Luther King, the Black Panthers, the first wave of school desegregation, voter rights laws, and the enormous increase in white attention to civil rights. It was also the time of the Vietnam War protests. It was a time when old barriers were being broken down and when quite a few young people challenged taboos on interracial relationships.

The era in which we grew up probably had . . . much . . . to do with it because it was the 60s and the early 70s and I was in political movements, and that kind of thing probably actually had more to do in terms of contact and ideas and all that than my immediate family. (Virginia)

FEELING SECURE,
CONFIDENT, AND AUTONOMOUS

Some people said that feeling secure, confident, or autonomous was a foundation for being partnered interracially. Feeling that way, they were not affected by the disapproval of others. Instead, they felt a sense of empowerment to make personal decisions and to question those who opposed interracial partnerships. Feelings of security, confidence, and autonomy are probably not necessary for getting into an interracial relationship, but as indicated by the many people quoted next, such feelings facilitate entry into such a relationship and persistence in it.

I can remember a time when we were really young, I mean, we were 17 and . . . really concerned about what people think. We went to [a] really multicultural [high school], and I never dated Bayard because he's black, but it's probably something I was acutely aware of . . . but I think a lot of that is tied more to self-esteem upon my part. You know, the more self-confident I become, the less I think about it or notice. I think it's just growing up. (Ann)

As I matured and grew more self-confident and cared less about what other people thought about what I was doing, but my own life, I dated a couple of black women. (Tim)

I think it was sort of the openness of thought and . . . the allowance, the empowering aspect of being in a family that allowed you to be exposed. Now there are real good ways to close people off from doing anything that you don't like, and that's just by not giving them the opportunity to think that it's OK. I don't think that there are different specific [empowering] activities necessarily . . . , mostly just the feeling that you have the power to be an individual when you go out and away from home, and that makes most of the difference. There's always the fake power that you think you have. I mean, I'm sure that people experience that, and then that's generally when you tend to go back and

find that no, you don't have that power and we're telling you this is
not OK. But I think ultimately the power was really there. . . . We'd
be the person in the family they'd say, "Now, who would do something
different?" . . . and point at us. . . . I mean, . . . I would have been
pointed to for who will do something different. (Wanda)

As I look at my younger siblings, they're much more concerned about
what other people think and parental approval, and so they get much
more wound up in that kind of stuff than we have. And maybe this is
all saying something negative about us, and something good about
them. I don't know, but in this particular situation, whether it's really
the most optimal, healthy state or not, it's served us to get by.
(Christine)

I think it more has to do with how I nurtured myself. . . . I questioned.
. . . I can remember going to Sunday school . . . and *I* knew . . . that
this was a bunch of hogwash. . . . I questioned everything. (Rosemary)

I am so unlike what [my mother] wanted me to be. But at the same
time, I have her and my grandmother and my grandmother's sisters,
who were incredible role models. They were very strong women. They
were independent. [They] had their own opinions. And my mother
wanted me to be, and I think still probably would prefer that I was a
little bit more demure. . . . She used to say to me, "Nobody's ever going to marry you, 'cause you got an opinion about everything." She
said, "You don't talk when men are talking. You're not supposed to
have an opinion. That's just not the way it is," although she herself
wasn't like that. . . . My grandmother would say, "That little piece of
red flannel in your mouth," meaning your tongue, "is going to get you
in a *lot* of trouble." Or she'd say, "You'd argue with a sign post." And
my mother was just saying to a friend the other day . . . , "Patricia was
a trick untried when she was a kid," 'cause I didn't take what people
said as the absolute truth. I was curious, and so I think that part of that
is that independence that allows me to now say and to make that decision that "I'm marrying Gary, and it's nobody's business." (Patricia)

I've always felt like kind of the odd one out in my immediate family,
plus my relatives plus the closed community [in which I grew up]. . . .
It's a beautiful sweet town. It's very clean, but there was something
about it that I had to get out of there because I knew there was more

of the world out there. I guess I just had an attitude of "If I stay here . . . all I'll do is get pregnant and have to get married," because that's what happens. And I think it was just a process of listening to something else within me. I guess a different person within me that wasn't touched by those prejudices and those kind of closed ideas and the restrictions of religion. (Nora)

I've always thought that I was different; I don't know, I've always felt if you believe in reincarnation (laughs) that I might have been somebody else in another time, and I came back. I've always felt I was different than other people. And I have a lot of thoughts . . . that I write down about the way I feel, so I have my own strength inside of me. (Flora)

I've always been real outspoken and opinionated and have done things the way that I was going to do them. Anyone who knew me very well knew that. So this was not a big surprise I don't think. . . . I very early on decided that I was very different than everybody else in my family, and so I'm certain that there was an element of rebellion at least in terms of that I was going to make up my own mind about things. I don't think that it's the stereotypical, "I'm going to show my family up," but it was more of, I would not let them influence me on certain key decisions. (Virginia)

[I had a] very strong independent streak that was both accepted and nurtured by both of [my parents], made me feel from a very early age that I was just going to do whatever I was going to do and kind of make up my life as I went along. (Lorenzo)

When I was in high school I would go out with women who were other than black and I would get read the riot act. Of course I didn't give a shit; I wanted to be different anyway. So it was kinda like, "Say whatever you want; I don't care." . . . My sister, the militant Afrocentric American that she is, would read me the riot act. My mother wouldn't say much, because she knew I'd do the exact opposite of whatever she said anyway. But from other black girls in the high school, I went to a predominantly white . . . high school . . . and the black girls being very much in the minority and the black men the same, they seemed to feel there was some property value to black males. No one else should touch them because they are ours. So I'd get it from them. But then of course, I would just tell them, "If I wanted to go out with you I would be going out with you. Obviously I don't want to." (James)

My mother's pretty open and accepting. I think that gave me a vantage point to be open and accepting. . . . We couldn't say the big "N" when we were kids; we could not say N-I-G-G-E-R. Other kids could say it, but we couldn't! Maybe a sense of sort of like some pride of who I was, pride in my ancestors, pride in my heritage. I think that if I didn't have a pride in who I was as an African American, and some kind of understanding of my history, I don't know . . . if I could be in a relationship with someone of a different culture, different nationality. I mean, I do know about my history, and I know about my background. My mother gave me an early understanding about the pride that one has about who they are as a person. . . . I think you really do need to have that kind of feeling of security in yourself. . . . I think these types of relationships generate enough paranoia as it is. . . . If you've got a slight amount of paranoia, and you get into an interracial relationship, it's just gonna kick your paranoia up a notch. (Gregory)

The autonomy people had was not only an autonomy to go their own way but also an autonomy that allowed them to feel good about themselves when in contact with those who thought negatively about them because of their interracial partnership.

Whites Growing Up Hostile to Racism

Some whites had objected to racist things said in their families and communities. In having the confidence and autonomy or the moral outrage to oppose racism, they were more free to explore relationships with people of other races.

My grandma and grandpa . . . we would always get into arguments over black people. I can remember when I was 17 years old, very vivid. I'll never forget it as long as I live. My ma and dad went on a vacation. My grandpa and grandma were over, staying with us. And always into fights. "How bad black people are. They're the only ones that cause problems," da-da da-da da-da. And I would [say], "Grandma, the only reason black people are so bad is 'cause that's all you hear. There're just as many bad white people as there are black people, if not more. But you're not going to hear about it, because they're white." . . . And my mom and dad walked in the door from their vacation. The first thing my grandma said was, "She's going to marry a nigger." I was 17 years old. I had no intentions. I mean, I went, "You're nuts! I'm not going to marry a black person" (she laughs). And, hah, lo and behold (she laughs), I married a black person. (Olivia)

I decided from when I was really young; . . . I'm sure I was under 10 when I decided that I would never marry someone that was prejudiced. And, unfortunately, in my town everybody was. And guys that I grew up with in high school, they couldn't understand me, and I couldn't understand them because I just felt, and I told my mother, "I just will not marry someone who is prejudiced against people of other races." . . . 'Cause I am a Christian, I think it was because God wanted me to be that. And I didn't know at a young age that I was going to marry a black man. But like I said, I knew I couldn't marry someone that was prejudiced or had hate. And I think when I met my best friend, she's Korean, when we were in fifth grade I met her, and she really opened my eyes too, because she had experienced discrimination. She was adopted . . . and raised in a white family. . . . That really struck me. How in the world, why would she face discrimination? . . . When I saw her struggle, that made me even more so believe that . . . you can't dislike someone because they look different. (Eve)

With white people, certainly not all, you're never really really sure what their feelings on race are. So . . . I probably would not ever end up with a white man. I can only imagine what a horror it would be to marry a white man, to form a relationship with him and years down the road have him refer to someone as a black jerk. . . . My mother's family still lives in [the South], and we went every year. . . . This was in the 50s and I knew, I just knew there was something wrong with . . . water fountains for the colored folk. I wanted to drink out of the blue fountain. . . . And, of course, she and my aunt just thought that was so terrible. I remember one time there was a big store down there. I got lost and I met up with a little black girl who also had lost her parents, and we decided to have a high good time. And I had on a bright red sweater and she had on a green sweater and we . . . exchanged. And we were just very pleased with ourselves, and we were having a good time, and here came my mother and aunt, . . . and my mother just

(indrawn breath) and in fact my aunt was falling all over us . . .
because we had changed clothes. And then I got a lecture on the way
home, "Well, honey, you mustn't change clothes with a colored person." . . . I must have been maybe 6 at the time, and I can remember,
I couldn't put it into words in my mind, but I remember a sad feeling
that I knew that wasn't right. . . . I remember one time we came to
Minneapolis, and . . . there was a black family. [My dad] made a derogatory remark about them, and that was the first time that I ever
spoke out. And I guess I was maybe 10. And I said, "How can you feel
that way? How can you say that?" . . . I remember one time . . . [in]
Louisiana, . . . we had walked through puddles . . . and our shoes were
all wet, and we went into a shoe shine parlor . . . up in the high chairs,
and the man that ran it was so nice. He said, "Your feet are cold because of your shoes being wet," and he wrapped my feet in newspaper
. . . while he dried our shoes and polished them. And I still remember
what he looked like. I was just gazing at him . . . because the whole
thing was so interesting, and I truly don't remember thinking it was
terribly interesting that he was black, but I thought the whole thing
was interesting. And I remember my dad said, "You'll have to excuse
my . . . daughter. We don't have any colored people where we live."
He assumed I was staring at the man because he was black. And maybe
I was. I don't know. I thought I was just fascinated with the whole
thing. And I can still remember the look on the man's face. . . . He was
just as sweet as he could be, but now remembering that look on his
face, I realize that my father had humiliated him. (Dot)

I don't even really know what [my mother's] ideas are based on. It's
just kind of the habit of thinking a certain way and not varying from
that. I think it's just a weird prejudice that races should not mix, which
I guess I just don't understand. . . . It makes no sense to me. And there
were just things that I grew up hearing her say . . . things like, ". . . So
and so came home after living up in the cities, and she has a half black
kid." She would say things like that, and I would say, "Well, what do
you mean, half black? Why do you say that? Why don't you just say
she has a baby?" (Nora)

Presumably, it is relatively easy for whites like those just quoted,
people who reject racism, to explore a relationship with a black
person. A white person who has not rejected racism may still be
attracted to black people. But it seems much easier for a white person

to start a relationship with someone who is black if she or he opposes racism.

WHITES LEARNING THE
CONSEQUENCES OF THEIR OWN PREJUDICE

Two whites talked about learning in childhood how hurtful their expression of prejudice could be to another. For them, perhaps one impetus to move toward nonprejudicial relationships with African Americans was their experience of the consequences of their own prejudicial words.

I don't [think] that this has anything to do with what's going on, but it's something that happened to me as a child. And it happened because I was a product of a racist father. . . . I was playing in kinder-garten with a black kid on the merry-go-round. And he did something that I didn't like and I called him a nigger, a blackie. . . . And he looked very hurt, and the look on his face, it crushed me. I felt so bad that I had done that. And I think that from that point on, I just felt like I never wanted to do that to anybody ever again. And so I think that [was] the beginning of my open-mindedness, if that's what you want to call it, about different races. (Tim)

Once . . . my sister said to me, "I'll give you all of this,"—she had 11 cents; I'll never forget it, a dime and a penny—"if you'll say, 'Hi, you dumb nigger' to that woman over there." . . . I still remember my thought was that would buy a lot of candy. And I said, "OK," and so I hollered it, and I'll always be grateful to this woman. . . . This woman had every reason in the world to be afraid of a 6- or 7-year-old girl hollering at her. And the easiest thing for her to have done was to have kept right on walking. And this woman was so courageous! She stopped, she looked. . . . And she went like that, meaning "Are you talking to me?" She looked around. She was the only person there, and now I realized my sister had run. . . . And she walked over . . . and she said, "Come here." She says, "What did you say to me?" And . . . she repeated what I had said. And she said, "I know that you don't know what nigger means. I just know that. Do you?" And I went like that. And she said, "Well, you do know what dumb means." She said, "I'm going to tell you what nigger means." And this lady gave me a little lesson in racism there, and I don't actually remember the exact words she used. I don't remember her definition. I'm real grateful to her. I didn't recognize courage until I was older, but that also added to my sense that something wasn't right. (Dot)

WE TWO ARE SIMILAR

In a study of 29 black-white interracial couples in the Los Angeles area, Kouri and Lasswell (1993) reported that the large majority of the people they interviewed said that they were attracted to their partner because of similar values and interests. We did not question people about how they were drawn to each other, but one woman seemed to feel that the basis of her relationship with her husband was that she and he were very similar. In talking about her similarity to him, she seemed to be saying that racial/ethnic differences are trivial in comparison to other factors.

I . . . really believe that part of the reason we were able to come together and to stay together is that in some ways we're *very* much alike. We're both fairly independent; we can deal with being alone fairly well; and we're *both* pretty hardheaded, and so it's pretty hard to talk us out of things once we decide what we're up to. (Christine)

Other people also talked about their similarity to their partner, but it is hard to know whether that was a basis of coming together or an after-the-fact observation.

We have so much in common. And we're like soul mates. (Rosemary)

I realized we were so much alike, and I was real surprised with such different backgrounds [that] we were so; I always felt we were a lot alike. (Ann)

If you're really looking at who out of all the people I ever dated is most like me in terms of values and what we want to do with life, Patricia is more like me than anybody I've ever known. (Gary)

Acknowledging how much one is like one's partner of another race is a recognition that sociocultural processes have focused society on racial differences that are only of significance because society makes those differences significant, that the crucial factors in relationship compatibility are matters of values, personality compatibility, and the like (see also Johnson & Warren, 1994).

THE CHEMISTRY OF
RELATIONSHIPS THAT CANNOT BE

Sometimes the relationships that become most solid are ones that start out with no future. One couple said that their relationship started out as a friendship because they assumed that their racial difference meant that they could not and would not become romantically involved. They found, however, that starting out as friends can build a strong base for a long-term relationship.

GARY   It felt to me as if the first time in my dating relationship I'd ever been with someone that I could frankly, openly talk about ideals and things that I believed in, and that there was a kind of a connection, an ambition of things we wanted to do. . . . We certainly had a romantic and sexual attraction, but . . . this was over and above that. It was *very* different. It was the first time I'd ever experienced that . . . combination of being *very* attracted to someone for reasons in addition to sexual attraction. It was a very powerful combination for me. So we talked; we wouldn't just go to the movies. We'd go sit places and talk. . . . I had dated a woman when I was in college, and we'd become engaged, and we had kind of a stormy relationship. . . . I sort of formed this idea in my mind that really good relationships just don't exist, that . . . the best you can get is a relationship that is occasionally OK. And that was also based on my sense of other families I knew that I grew up with, that I didn't really know many relationships that were consistently good. They were bad a lot of the time. There'd be a lot of arguments. And then, after we broke up, I was not with someone for quite a while, and I discovered I could do OK alone. And I remember that that's how I was vulnerable. . . . I thought, "I'm not interested; I don't have to be with anybody. I'm absolutely safe here," and I didn't want to get into a relationship. . . . I was taking courses, doing a master's program . . . at night . . . , and I was very interested in that. I didn't want anything to get in the way, and the safest thing in the world was going to be to see Patricia sometimes. . . . There was no way I could get entangled.

PATRICIA . . . I've had good relationships and I've had some bad relationships, and the last one was very bad. And I thought, "I don't want to cook another dinner. I'm not buying another set of candles. I'm not; this is it." So going out with Gary was safe. . . . I remember . . . my roommate [saying] . . . , "Good Lord. Are you going to look like that?" And I said, "What does it matter?" You know, it *was* safe, because I would never marry somebody anyway. And I remember . . . when I first met Gary, my roommate . . . said, ". . . You never can tell when you're going to be sitting there and your husband's going to be there." And I . . . remember looking at Gary when I met him. He was sitting across from my desk and laughing, [and I was] thinking about what [she] said. . . . And I thought, "Boy, this sure isn't it." . . . So it was like not being on good behavior at all. It was like, "This is who I am." And I think the relationship grew because it was OK who I was, this stubborn and sometimes cantankerous and independent [woman].

GARY . . . When we first became friends, it was a great shock to me that friendship was changing into a romantic, sexual attraction, because . . . Patricia was my first black female friend. I had black male friends and had female friends of different racial backgrounds. . . . I was in a distant way attracted, but it was so tabooed that I didn't pay any attention to it. . . . When it happened, it was a tremendous shock. This is the real thing. This is as attracted as I've ever been to anybody or more.

CONCLUSION

Although people talked about many different factors that might have influenced them to enter an interracial relationship, there may be other factors that they did not mention—for example, the relative size of African American and white populations in their immediate community or the gender balance of African Americans and whites who were available to date at the time they met their partner (Barron, 1972; Spickard, 1989, pp. 6-7; Staples, 1992; Staples & Johnson, 1993, pp. 147-149). The accounts people offered were also after the fact, what people said long after they entered their relationship. Their accounts may represent only a part of what was influential and may be affected by the history they are trying to explain. Perhaps all relationships have their real bases in the accidents of random getting-to-know-you processes. But it still seems that people who reject racism are more likely to enter any kind of interracial relationship, and such people are more likely to be free from the constraints of those around them who are critical of interracial relationships.

Although what people had to say about the bases for their entry into an interracial relationship may be only part of what influenced them, their comments have a ring of authenticity. Some talked about family and community values of racial tolerance, whereas some whites talked about up growing up with an indifference to matters of race that comes with living where everyone is white. People talked about mixed-relationship family precedents, and some African Americans talked about growing up as pioneers in various interracial situations. Some people talked about a personal hunger for diversity or about the affect of maturing during the civil rights ferment and the Vietnam War protest of the 60s and 70s. Some people talked about growing up with a secure, confident autonomy, and some whites talked about growing up hostile to racism or about being strongly affected in childhood by the reaction of an African American to their racist words. People also talked about the special chemistry of their relationship, a sense of great similarity with their partner, or the magic of a relationship that succeeded even though it seemed it could never be because it violated taboos.

5

THE WHITE PARTNER'S FAMILY

WHITE FAMILY MEMBERS WHO
SUPPORTED FROM THE BEGINNING

Families in Which All Close Relatives Were Supportive

A few white families were accepting from the beginning; racist concerns were not raised by anyone in the immediate family.

> Roger's family . . . are a really, really loving, accepting family. And I've always felt . . . [a] lot of support for our, I mean, Roger is his mother's favorite son, and that helps a lot. . . . They think we're great. (Barb, who is black)

> TIM My family. . . . was perfectly happy with Flora. Matter of fact, probably happier with Flora, ... as a person, because of the person that she is . . . versus anybody else I'd ever dated. . . .
>
> FLORA His family has been supportive.

TIM My family never said, "It's OK that you guys are interracial."

FLORA They never talk about it.

TIM The topic never came up. It was just . . .

FLORA They have been supportive. Like a family.

TIM She'd always been accepted as my partner, my wife, the mother of my children.

However, even when the immediate family of a white partner might be accepting, there could be other relatives who raise concerns.

ANN He wasn't the first black person I dated. My family was always real accepting; I didn't have a lot of issues there. I wasn't rebelling. I didn't have to sneak around. . . . I grew up in a real liberal-to-the-core family. And I always knew it wouldn't matter, and I was real happy when it didn't matter. And the only thing my mother ever said was that marriage always had its problems, and that you will have more problems as an interracial family. You just need to be strong.

BAYARD What about your grandma? . . . Your one grandma disowned us for a while, didn't she?

ANN But that's because we were living together. She said, "Oh, heavens no. It would never be because he is black." I mean, she was fine with everything until we moved in together, and she flipped out. And as soon as we got married, it was like she found my number. And it was like a . . . week later. I've just been real lucky. I think my mom's parents didn't like it. They tried to give me money so I would go to a different college so we wouldn't be in the same place. . . . I remember my grandpa telling me . . . that you, he would never be able to . . . "travel in the same social circles." That was the phrase used, and they just thought that I should get out of it, that it would be hard, and it just wouldn't work.

INTERVIEWER So was it more protective than it was really racist?

ANN I think so, because they've always been great ever since. And they seem like really good people. . . . A lot of it was probably fear of the unknown. I mean, here's a guy they didn't know; here's this guy with a big 'fro. And they didn't know any black people.

Supportive Members of Families
in Which There Was Opposition

Some white partners had family supporters from the beginning even though other family members opposed an interracial relationship.

> My natural mother is very supportive. I don't think she thinks about the race business at all. . . . Interestingly enough, my foster mothers that I had when I was in high school, it's not even an issue or anything for them. I mean, they're OK with me; they're OK with Robert. If he's with [me], well, then he's gotta be all right. (Kate, who reported opposition from other foster parents)

> My middle sister . . . is . . . an environmental activist and she's always been very verbal about things she believes in, and she was OK with it. I think she at one time said, "Are you sure you know what you're getting into?" that kind of thing. (Nora, whose mother was initially upset over the interracial relationship)

> When we were first together, . . . my one sister, who I'm really not . . . very close to, although, well, I don't see her a lot, but I imagine, I guess we probably could be closer, just have busy lives. But initially, my sister went way out of her way to be supportive. She'd call me up with the latest developments. . . . (laugh) She went way out of her way to be supportive and still does that. . . . She made it very clear early on that race was not an issue, and I think probably almost instantaneously you guys got along. . . . [My brother] would be very outraged if he heard anybody in the family say anything against us. He [is] protective in that way. . . . The broader family there were some surprises. I had uncles, a couple uncles in particular, who not only were supportive but truly liked Lorenzo and thought he was wonderful. . . . They *really* like him and would be very insistent that we come to bigger family events and would call and give special invitations and . . . stuff like, "We don't care what anybody else says. We want you there and we'll kind of protect you if you come." (Virginia)

When family members are divided and feelings are strong, there is potential for family difficulties to snowball. The divisions mean that coalitions are formed and secrets are shared with some people and kept away from others, resulting in patterns of communication that can be challenging for all family members. In such a situation, some people may feel caught between family members to whom they feel strong attachment. It is heartening that in some families in which strong opposition was expressed to an interracial relationship, there were people who were supportive of the relationship. But one can feel concern for everyone in the family because strong divisions can put enormous pressure on some family members and make family relationships tense, dishonest, or otherwise less than optimal. It is also possible that the turmoil that was reported in some families existed long before the interracial relationship began. The interracial relationship may simply be another stimulus for the expression of preexisting family patterns of coalition, secret keeping, and triangulation.

OPPOSITION IN MOST WHITE FAMILIES

Similar to findings from an earlier study in four communities in the Midwest and South (Porterfield, 1978, p. 116) and from a more recent study in Britain (Tizard & Phoenix, 1993, pp. 134-135), some members of the immediate family of the large majority of white partners were at first hostile to or fearful of an interracial partnership.

> My mother . . . thinks everybody in the community, *everywhere*, thinks that us being together is very wrong. . . . My mother has been the problem. . . . She has been anything but supportive; she has been nasty. (Donna)

INTERVIEWER What kind of support have you received from your family or friends about your relationship?

ROSEMARY Absolutely none. Absolutely none from my family. . . . I told [my dad], and then he called me constantly, trying to convince me not to be involved with Ed . . . because of the cultural differences, all that kind of stuff. He was just panic-stricken. . . .

ED . . . Our relationship is threatening to their status as Lutheran.

ROSEMARY (interrupting) Oh, that's bullshit. That's their, that's my, especially my dad's fear. That's his worst fear.

My father . . . looks at people just for their basic goodness. He doesn't make any other kinds of judgments. . . . It was a difficult thing for me to first introduce the idea that we had met, and we went down to Jamaica on our first date, and I had these photographs . . . , and I had told my mother that I wouldn't be having Christmas that year because I was going on a trip to Jamaica, and she assumed that it was with a tour group because that's how she traveled (small laugh). And so I didn't say, "No, it isn't," but when we came back and visited her a few weeks later and showed her the pictures of our trip in Jamaica, and I said, "Well, that's the person I went with," and she just sort of started flipping these pictures over and saying, "Well, your dad always said he doesn't ever want his daughters to marry a black man!" (imitates an exasperated voice). Which, of course, my father never said, but that's my mother's idea. And so she was not real calm about the whole thing. (Nora)

[My father] said, "For the first time in my life . . . I am glad that my own parents are dead so that they don't have to see the shame that you've brought on me." . . . And we had no communication after that at all until he was dying and then he asked for me, a few years later. (Dot)

My dad, when he asked my dad if he could marry me (she laughs), my dad just got up and walked away from the table. But that's the way my dad deals with things. (Eve)

In the two excerpts that follow, it seems that part of rejecting a family member's choice of romantic partner is not to allow the partner into one's house. Maybe it is simply a matter of some white family members being too racist to allow an African American into the house, but it may be something more. A white family member's choice of partner is a choice of a relative for everyone in the family. By opposing the choice and not letting the person chosen into the house, other members of family may be saying, "We do not accept this person as a relative or potential relative." It may not only be that some members of a white partner's family are intolerant of the choice but also that they are opposed to counting someone who is black as in the family.

> When Isaac and I first met and started going out, my ma and dad didn't know about us. And then I did tell them, and they were not pleased. . . . It wasn't until a month before we got married that Mom and Dad and the family officially met Isaac. He was not allowed in the house. (Olivia)

JOHN We got a racist response from the sister-in-law. . . .

LIZ My brother too, 'cause my brother, I said we were coming and my brother left.

JOHN He left, yeah. . . .

LIZ Well my sister-in-law is really the perfect hostess, and she didn't invite us in, and I had stored some furniture, and she had it out in the yard waiting for us to pick it up. . . . [My brother] would . . . corner me when I'd go out to be there, and . . . he would call me a nigger lover then and make black jokes and stuff. . . . I just told him I don't think that's funny, and I just quit dealing with him. I haven't been out there to his house, I haven't seen him in many years.

Members of a white partner's family who were opposed to an interracial romantic relationship not infrequently tried to withhold information from neighbors and other family members. They may have been concerned about the racism of those others, but they may also have been concerned that the others would start counting the black partner as a family member. Withholding information may be a way of maintaining an image as an all-white family. Presumably, maintaining that image protects the family members who were opposed to the relationship from losing status and privilege with other whites who consider a family relationship with an African American to be a sign of low status (Johnson & Warren, 1994).

> My parents lost their minds temporarily. . . . My parents are . . . very southern, raised with calling a black person "nigger." It was OK; that's what you called them. My parents didn't put that on me, but that's how they were raised. When James first came to the house, he had red

hair. . . . We're talking flame red. . . . And being that he was . . . black and working [in a black part of town], that was bad, bad. Not only was it considered not appropriate for their daughter, they didn't want to meet him; they didn't want to know anything about him . . . , which was very hard for me because I respect my parents . . . , a very hard thing to go through, trying to, I guess, win their approval, because that was so dear to me, that they accept him. It took like 3 months. . . . [My mother] was the type of person who, "Don't let the neighbors hear," you know, "Don't tell the neighbors." She was concerned about how the neighbors would view [things]. You never tell your grandfather; you never tell your grandmother. They would just never understand. (Jill)

Once a white partner feels the rejection from close family members, the white partner might reject more distant family members—both because of fear of their racism and because it may seem inappropriate to connect with more distant family members when close family members have cut one off. Unfortunately, not connecting with more distant family members means that one cuts oneself off from relatives who might not be racist and who could be supportive. In fact, in the following excerpt, the white partner talks about an aunt who was not invited to the wedding (because closer relatives would not come) but who offered support for the interracial relationship despite having mixed feelings about African Americans.

Initially . . . it was like [my] choice to sort of cut us off from some people. . . . My parents didn't come to our wedding, [though] my sisters did. . . . My mother's . . . very prejudiced, very cutoff from other cultures. So I . . . prepared myself, and . . . what I did . . . was just not invite these kind of family to the wedding. . . . Because she wouldn't come, I couldn't ask anybody else, except my sisters were there. They're . . . very accepting people. . . . [My aunt] called. This is my dad's sister who lets everybody know everything that's going on (laughs). And Gregory answers the phone! And she went, "Oh, who's this? Why don't I know about him?" And she . . . spread the word. And actually, then she called my mother a bigot, which was not very good; I mean, it was not helpful to [their] relationship. And she lives on the north side and will sometimes say to me, "Well, I don't know about all these black people moving in." And I mean, it's like there's kind of a duality for her. It's like she really loves Gregory, but then she still has these . . . fears and stereotypes. (Joyce)

Family Opposition to Women's Interracial Connections

Opposition by immediate family members was reported in almost all of the white families in which a white woman entered an interracial relationship. Perhaps parents are concerned with protecting daughters and controlling their choices. One could say, "white parents," but, as the next chapter shows, black families typically raised opposition to the interracial partnerships of daughters. The reason we discuss white family opposition separately from black family opposition is that the roots may be somewhat different. For white families, the roots may include the racism of a dominant group and fear of loss in status. For black families, the roots may include the fear and pain of being connected with the oppressor.

Why daughters might be allowed so little leeway in relationships is discussed further in the next chapter. One can speculate that daughters may be protected, may remain close to their parents and siblings, may be seen as at risk if a child is produced in a relationship that subsequently falls apart, or may be seen as vulnerable to being a victim (of a man's chicanery) in a sexual relationship. It may also be the case that daughters are more controllable than sons.

OPPOSITION EVEN TO AN UNCOMMITTED RELATIONSHIP

Even when an interracial relationship was not a committed one, some white family members acted as though it was and seemed extremely upset. What was understood by the young couple as casual dating or a relationship with no likelihood of a committed future brought the white woman's parents to talking about marriage and children.

We had just been dating for a while, and [my parents] just sort of hopped up here without calling, which is very unusual for them. . . .

So they just sort of met him. And my dad was fine, and my mother was shocked . . . and . . . in great turmoil. . . . She was calling me; she was being threatening; she was really mean and nasty. And she got my dad all upset; and it was wrong, and "You're wrong"; "Society will reject you," and "My God! The children!" "Mom, we're dating. What children are we talking about?" . . . My one brother that I'm not very close to . . . made a comment to my other brother, probably 4 years ago now. He had no interest whatsoever in getting to know Henry or wanting to get involved in the whole situation . . . and . . . he wasn't gonna have mixed nieces or nephews. (Donna)

Even when family members of the white woman in an interracial couple seemed at least somewhat tolerant of the relationship, they could still be upset when the couple took a step toward greater commitment. For example, if the family came to accept a dating relationship, they might be floored when the couple moved in together or became engaged.

My dad was not happy about [our seeing each other]. He basically, he didn't forbid me to see him. This was after I graduated and moved back home for a short time. And he said, "I think you need to get out on your own now." . . . My Mom's always been very love your neighbor . . . , so she was, as far as I could tell (laughs), very accepting of [our dating]. Well, when we announced our engagement, my mother just lost it. Her concern was, "What about the children?" I don't think she was thinking about us or about her. I don't know exactly. That was her first thought, and then so she said she cried all night that night that we announced our engagement. . . . It was kind of like, either what will the neighbors think or what about your kids? . . . I was upset with her. I thought she had been watching too much Oprah Winfrey or something. You know, these little scare stories they have, like biracial children [having a] bad experience or something. And I think she probably saw one of those shows or Phil Donahue or something, and she gets concerned about that, and she still is concerned about that. I have to keep reassuring her, we're OK, we're OK. . . . She's afraid for our unborn children, maybe that they wouldn't identify with either culture or race, I don't know. We haven't really gone into that. (Shirley)

Even after a couple made a commitment to each other, members of a white woman's family who seemed accepting might become upset when she became pregnant. It seems that sometimes hidden under apparent acceptance lies a hope or expectation that the couple will break up, that the white daughter or sister will come to her senses or her African American partner will follow through on the white family's expectation that he cannot remain committed.

OPPOSITION FROM FAMILY MEMBERS WHO HAD SEEMED TOLERANT

Decades ago, social scientists studying interracial relationships observed the paradox that white parents who seemed fully committed to tolerance and racial equality could still be strongly upset by an offspring marrying a black person. Hugo Beigel (1966), for example, reported how white parents who were strongly in favor of legal equality of the races opposed the interracial union of a daughter or son. Similarly, in the present study, white partners reared in homes that fostered tolerance found that there could be strong family opposition to an interracial partnership. For example, when Adam described his father's opposition to Adam's relationship with Wanda (see the quotation a bit later in this chapter), Adam also said that he had grown up in a quite liberal household.

WHEN FAMILY REACTIONS ARE DIVERSE

When the reactions of the members of a white partner's family are diverse, the white partner can be buoyed up by the support from a sister or other family member who accepts the relationship. She or he can also find in that support hope for the future, a sense that there are family allies for efforts to win the approval of family members who are opposed and a sense that she or he is still connected and accepted in the family, that there is not total estrangement.

The diversity of white family attitudes to an interracial couple can be troubling when dealing with major family events. Attending an event when opponents are present can be painful; backing out of an event even though allies are present can also be difficult.

OLIVIA I backed out of my brother's wedding, 'cause of his very
degrading remarks against Isaac. And I just felt I could be
happy for them getting married, but I couldn't feel good with
myself to stand up with how they were treating Isaac.

INTERVIEWER So it wasn't just your brother but his new wife too?

OLIVIA His wife was very supportive of me, so she felt very hurt when
I backed out. . . . She fought against my brother and my
parents for me. So she felt like I should've been in the
wedding because she helped me. . . . And I guess I didn't
think that way when I did back out. I just didn't feel I could
do it.

THE LANGUAGE OF WHITE OPPOSITION

In America, there seems to be a standardized discourse against
interracial relationships (Frankenberg, 1993, p. 71). As evidence of
that standard discourse, the same six reasons came up repeatedly
when white partners spoke of the reasons family members gave for
opposing an interracial relationship: (a) societal, community, neighborhood, or family disapproval; (b) issues of safety and well-being;
(c) the alleged clannishness of African Americans; (d) problems the
children would have; (e) the likelihood of a poor economic future;
and (f) "problems" (with the problems not named). The following
are descriptions of family opposition that include illustrations of the
elements of the standard oppositional discourse.

> My mother never did what my dad did, which was not talk to us for
> years. I remember being in constant contact, with my mother being
> there while [our daughter] was being born, and she was involved with
> us before that, came and visited quite a few times. But I do remember
> my mother continually saying, "Are you sure you want to be in this re-
> lationship? It's going to mean problems. I don't want you to have prob-
> lems. . . ." I just could see her with visions of lynching and cross burn-
> ing. (Janet)

MANNING Her father was very overt and engaged in a real verbal
lashing of her about how we African Americans stick together

and . . . you don't know what you're getting into . . . [and] if you bring any brown babies home. . . .

CHRISTINE My mother would . . . call, like late at night on the weekends, bawling and being, real carrying on. . . . "It's never going to work." . . . She's never known a black person in her life, and she had all these pieces of advice to give me about how they were going to treat me, and what they're going to do with me. And he would stick with his family, and then when the time came he'd abandon me and go back to them. "So that's the way black people are." I mean, it was like *every* weekend it was some new crap. . . . I'd listen to her as long as I could, and then hang up. And that went on for, a couple of years?

EVE I think my mom's main concern was that . . . if I married a black man . . . my income level, statistically, your income level goes down. . . . And I don't think that my mom really meant it in a bad way. But I told her that that really didn't matter to me.

INTERVIEWER When did she say that to you?

EVE Long before we were married. . . . It might have just been, too, that he . . . was [struggling economically], so I think that she thought that he was going to have a hard time, and he wasn't going to school yet. . . . But now I think her views have really changed, because . . . it doesn't have to be true. And she sees that, because he's a hard worker, a good husband, a good father.

The most important [objection] that was raised by my family was, "While this might be something that you two, because you . . . are educated people, you can buy your way out of discrimination. Your children can't." And that it's going to be difficult for them at the dating stage; they're going to be forced to make a choice about what race they are. Or it's going to be made for them. And there was a lot of consensus. Everybody thought that. . . . My mother and family had no conception that we could ever live anywhere where it *wouldn't* be a major problem. (Gary)

ADAM [My father] was very upset. He was dredging up stuff like . . . this would have upset my mother. . . . He was struggling. He was grasping for some way to deal with it himself and striking out at the same time as best he could, by, you know, "Shame, shame. Your mother would turn over in her grave." . . . I think he regrets that. . . .

WANDA Mostly, the concerns probably for either family would have been kind of just safety and well-being. . . .

ADAM At least that's the way it was voiced. . . . What I was describing before was literally an immediate emotional reaction in a 24-hour period. After that . . . there was a much more thoughtful approach to things. . . . It was still a great resistance, I would say, and it began again to be voiced pretty much along sort of a party line of, "Well, we're concerned for you."

INTERVIEWER What were the concerns? Did he say?

ADAM That we would be hurt. That there are enough difficulties getting through life these days without putting additional burdens on yourself. What if you had kids? What about the additional burden on them? . . . I felt that it was sincere. I would say that on a percentage basis . . . it was still sort of 70% that and 30% some other things too, . . . if they were being honest with themselves in the way that *I* try to be honest with *my*self when I'm faced with a situation that I'm responding to real negatively that I think there's some other sort of more personal things.

VIRGINIA One of the first things out of my mother's mouth was the one about the kids. This was long before we had kids, and so that, I think . . . was easier for her to be openly concerned about children than it was about anything else. She certainly didn't acknowledge any of her own stuff, so that was kind of the focal point. And then I think actually when my family— and it was really my mother more than anybody else in my immediate family—adjusted, she somehow got it in her head that we weren't going to have children, and so then she had to go through the whole readjustment process (laugh) again when I was pregnant. But that was the one that was voiced most often.

INTERVIEWER Do you have a sense of the concerns that weren't voiced or that were sort of underneath what she focused on about children?

VIRGINIA Well, I think that probably there was a concern that I was
          making a decision that would somehow make the rest of my
          life narrower rather than broader and that I would never be
          able to do certain kinds of things. And I'm not sure she really
          knew what they were, but it didn't fit what her vision of the
          future would be. . . .

LORENZO [Her father] had blood family who wouldn't have anything
         to do with us, wouldn't come to the wedding. . . . So you
         know he had to talk about it . . . and deal with it.

Presumably, the language of white family opposition reflected the
stereotypes family members held. For example, there were white
family members who assumed that all blacks were poor and from the
inner city, so the arguments they used against an interracial partnership were based on their assumptions about the consequences of a
partnership across enormous differences in wealth, education, and
other aspects of social class.

PATRICIA I think [his parents] didn't envision a [middle] class in the
          black community. They simply thought everybody lived in
          . . . the inner city, in the ghetto, that people were poor. . . .
          Somebody [in] the family said I was probably a member of
          the Black Panthers and I was going to take Gary's money and
          use it. . . . The feeling was that not only was he marrying
          somebody black, he was marrying out of his class. He was
          marrying beneath him, because I had to be poor.

GARY This was typically people who hadn't met you. . . . Those who
      had just had this tremendous shock of, "She's not like what
      we expected." . . . She's . . . educated.

Some white parents also saw the choice of a black partner as a sign
that they somehow failed in raising a daughter. For example, Olivia
talked about her father asking her where he had gone wrong in
raising her.

It is difficult to know what to make of parental concern about
problems that their son or daughter or grandchildren would have.
The language of concern can be an honest report based on what the
parent knows to be true, an accurate reflection of the racism that
white family members know a person in an interracial family would

experience in the white family member's own social world. But it can also be a language that conveys or hides racist sentiments. It can be difficult therefore to decide what to make of parental concern. But even if words of concern express or mask racist sentiments, those words may still speak to realistic possibilities in an interracial couple's environment. In fact, some of the concerns family members of white partners raised about societal racism were concerns a white partner in an interracial couple might also raise.

TIM I don't think anybody's ever directly said anything . . .

FLORA Your mother did.

TIM . . . to me about; she might have asked the question, but that question was already in my mind. I do have concerns; I have concerns about my children. I already hurt in my heart for the pains that they may feel from somebody, some jerk's comment in the future. And I'm about ready to cry because I really feel very strongly that people are people and that their race should have nothing to do whatsoever with the way they are treated as a person. That they should be treated as people.

FLORA When we first met, I asked Tim what did his family think about me. He said, well his mother said . . . that if we had children we had to be concerned about them growing up.

Disowning and Disinheritance

A few white parents said that they were "disowning" or "disinheriting" an offspring who had entered an interracial relationship.

[My parents] were going to disown me. They said that. They would've had to push me out of their life. . . . "We'll disown you." (Olivia)

I went home and said I was going to be getting married. And I swear to God . . . the whole house just came unglued, and my father went through all, I mean, the drama of throwing me out, disowning me, from what I don't know. It's not like he's got money or anything, just, I, I don't know what he was disowning me of, forbade me to come home (voice shaking a little). His rationales were that this was immoral and that I must be doing it to hurt him. He couldn't figure out what he did for me to want to hurt him so badly. All my brothers were going to grow up to be deviants because I would be such a horrid influence on them, and they were at a very formative age. . . . And then he said horrible things about if we ever had children, and . . . so I just left (voice shaking a little) and came back here. (Christine)

That a white family's response might be disowning or disinheritance can be taken as simply a statement of strong feelings, but it might mean that there are some acts that are considered so offensive that the only way to deal with them is to cut off relationship with the offender. Perhaps, too, some white families want to avoid acquiring black kin. Although the anthropologist David Schneider (1980) wrote that many Americans do not count in-laws as relatives, some white Americans do. They use kin terms in addressing and referring to sons- and daughters- and siblings-in-law, invite such people to family gatherings, claim their successes for the family, and enact certain family obligations to them (e.g., giving them gifts for birthdays). An in-law may be a provisional relative in the sense that an end to the linking relationship through death or divorce may end the relationship (Rosenblatt & Karis, 1993-1994), but the in-law still seems to be a relative for many people. So it might be that by marrying a black person, a member of a white family is forcing other family members to become relatives of the black person. If the members of a white partner's family think that way, they can avoid becoming relatives of the black person by ending their family relationship with the white partner.

THE AFRICAN AMERICAN PARTNER'S REACTIONS TO WHITE FAMILY OPPOSITION

If family members communicated to a white partner in a couple that they were opposed, the opposition always reached the African American partner. African American partners were not neutral or uninvolved about that opposition.

Messages Directed at the African American Partner

African American partners might feel the sting of opposition especially strongly when the opposition was communicated directly to them by members of their white partner's family who opposed the relationship, perhaps as a strategy to persuade them to break off the relationship.

> His mother . . . was very kind, and she just said, "This is really hard for me." She wasn't rude to me or anything. She was very kind, and she started crying. And then I said, "God, I don't want to do this." (Patricia)

> We'd have family gatherings, and [my mother] wouldn't stay in the same room with him. She wouldn't give him eye contact; she went through all that. And I thought it would get better, and it got worse, and it got worse, and it got worse. (Donna)

Donna's partner Henry, talking about his mother-in-law's reactions from his perspective, said,

> She didn't even talk to me. She said my name once by accident, and . . . surprised herself, and I really believe that it did surprise her, because she let her guard down. And it was a really simple thing. We were passing by each other in the doorway, and she said, "Excuse me, Henry," and then almost like tried to snatch my name back into [her] mouth, because it was like she had displayed something that she wasn't supposed to, and then she even withdrew further.

Christine also talked about pressures from a member of her family directed at her black partner.

> My little sister was real angry at him . . . when she first met him, because she . . . felt that we hurt our family. And I think she felt that he hurt her, and so she was kind of a little bitch to him at first. She used to stare at him and look mean. (Christine)

Feeling the Partner's Pain

In couples in which the white partner had to deal with strong family opposition, African American partners could have strong empathic reactions to the pain and discomfort felt by the white partner.

The pain is deep. I've seen the pain. Pain, I feel the pain. . . . She *loved* this man. He was her father! She had nothing to do with it. She loved the man; she had no choice whether to love or not. She loved him. (Wilson)

Both the pressure felt by a white partner and the empathy felt by an African American partner could lead to questions about whether to continue the couple relationship.

The stress on her was also stress on our relationship, in not knowing if it was worth what she was having to go through. (James)

Countering the Opposition

With such strong opposition from the white partner's family, sometimes the black partner felt the need to create competing pressures, to make it clear that the relationship could not continue if the white partner went along with her or his parents or continued to be unsure about making a commitment in the face of parental pressure.

INTERVIEWER Have you, as a couple, experienced any internal or external pressure to consider splitting up because of the interracial part of your life?

OLIVIA I guess when we were going out, yeah . . . with my family, and with Isaac saying, "You're going to have to decide for yourself. You can't let me tell you what to do. You can't let your parents tell you what to do. You have to decide within yourself what you want to do." And so I had . . . to figure out, am I going to let my parents run my life, or am I going to stand up and be my own person. And I decided I was going to stand up.

Welcoming Honesty

Racism is often under the surface. Racists can be polite, even congenial to one's face but think, say, and do hateful things behind one's back. In some white families, there were such instances of hypocrisy. Given the possibility of hypocrisy and back-stabbing, a person who was honestly open about racism could be much easier to deal with.

JANET My grandmother was most refreshing though. She came up and would talk to Charles right from the start. Wasn't she the most honest of anybody?

CHARLES Yeah, I said "Hi" to her in her native language. That had a lot to do with it.

JANET I think so. . . . I remember when [our daughter] was born, "Oh, she's not so black!" She was just so blatant about it. "Oh, well, he looks like her," and she was just right out there about not really liking black people but just talking about it.

Her father . . . probably was the most overt about it, which was very good for me, because I can deal with overt people. At least you know where they are coming from. . . . I respected your father more so than my mother and your mother from the standpoint that at least he got it out, said what was on his [mind]. Early on he dealt with it. Now he doesn't see very many differences. The relationship is regardless what color you are, and that was good for me because *I* in fact had a lot to do with changing that behavior. . . . He said some things and got it off his chest. More probably concerned about what *society* thought of the situation, and really how it would affect his family in general. And I respect that, and even though he had some real bad racist feelings I still respect that. What I don't respect is the covert things that occurred with your mother and my mother, and *they* probably are harboring more concerns even up until *today* . . . through 16 years. (Manning)

OPPOSITION OUT OF LOYALTY TO OR FEAR OF ANOTHER FAMILY MEMBER

In some white families, there were people who went along with somebody else's opposition, apparently out of loyalty or fear. In fact, frequently, it seemed that one person's strong feelings, leadership, desperation, or potential for nastiness drew other people along. In some white families, one family member would speak of being willing to accept an interracial relationship but also of being unwilling to offend or disagree with another family member who was strongly opposed.

My father, . . . before we were married and I was visiting them, . . .
said, "I really wish you well and I love you; it's OK with me, but I
can't come because your mother's not coming." . . . She's the dominant person in the family. I felt like he really had accepted it but just
couldn't be assertive about it. (Joyce)

My mother . . . had never written a check, never paid a bill, had no
idea what [my father's] salary was. What he said, she did. She snuck
around. She would write me letters that he didn't know about, and I
wasn't supposed to write back. My mother viewed interracial relationships differently than he did. . . . My mother was raised in [the South].
She was raised to love colored people as individuals and to despise
them as a race, and she despised anything interracial. She referred
for years to my marriage as "Dot's tragedy" (laughs). . . . However,
she couldn't quite give up the idea that she was my mother. So she
would write these letters, and she would address them, "Miss Dot
_____." The line was blank. And she would send gifts through my
sister. (Dot)

THE WHITE PARTNER'S
REACTIONS TO FAMILY OPPOSITION

White partners were not neutral in their reactions to family
opposition. Just as Porterfield (1978, p. 118) reported for white
women in his study in four midwestern and southern communities,
quite a few of the white women in the present study experienced
family opposition as traumatic. Their feelings were often a blend of
pain, anger, frustration, desperation, determination to dissuade family
members from opposition, determination to make the relationship
work, and a cold distancing of family members. Unlike what Porterfield
reported, however, few white women in the present study reported
continuing alienation from family.

Pain Over the Loss of Parental Love

For some, parental opposition and distancing was felt as the loss
of parental love.

I've kind of quit crying right now, because it does (tearful), I'll tell you what hurt the most. At the time, my dad, I guess you've gathered, was never a real warm, come-home-and-play-in-front-of-the-fireplace kind of guy. He had, I don't mean to say there was nothing good about him. He was a . . . good provider. We always had a roof, a meal. . . . My mother was the same way. So for them to withdraw their love . . . because I was going with a black man was not a real surprise. It wasn't a shock. But I did make my choice, and I have never regretted it, and it hurt the most when [our daughter] was born. Because when she was born, and (pause) I don't know (crying), I knew immediately that there was nothing that we could do that would win their love. And . . . so I realized how . . . frail their love was to begin with. (Dot)

Interracial Relationships Fueled by Family Opposition

In looking back over their experiences, white partners did not usually report family opposition as a source of motivation to maintain or escalate their interracial relationship. Only Christine talked about family opposition fueling her relationship.

CHRISTINE See, with our personalities, when families threaten or push, that's just like fuel to the fire. I mean, it's like (snapping sound); that just vulcanizes us.
INTERVIEWER Yeah, so you probably do the opposite.
CHRISTINE Yeah.

Trying to Change Family Member Opposition

White partners tried many different approaches to persuade opposing family members to accept an interracial relationship. They often tried confrontation ("This is the relationship I'm in; you have to accept it") and rational argument, but they also tried the silent treatment, tears, working through third parties, and an assortment of threats.

I had to tell my mom that they were sick. They'd been through AA. My dad's been through treatment and Alanon. They have learned through all this that what's right for them doesn't have to be right for

me. I'm not doing this intentionally to hurt anybody. I'm doing this because I love this man, and I want to spend my life with him. You don't
have to accept it if you don't want to. That's what the serenity prayer
says. (Olivia)

The boycott helped, and then when we got to spend more time with
[my mother] I felt she really got to know Gregory, and liked him. Then
I think when we had children, . . . that made a big difference. (Joyce)

I brought him home, and I wanted him to meet Mom and Dad and the
happy-go-lucky-type life, you know, come on in and sit down, and they
were like, "No, uh uh." And it's like . . . you either decide between the
parents, make a stand, or tell him to leave. And it was, "I love you very
much, but he's a part of my life now, and this is how it's going to be."
And kinda just laid it out there on the table, not quite sure what was
going to happen. (Jill)

A few family members wanted to reconnect in some way with a
daughter (it was always a daughter) whom they had cut off, and in at
least one case, the daughter's response was that she would not travel
without her partner, that they had to connect with her partner as well
as with her. Dot talked about a time when her mother invited her to
a reconciliation meeting.

I was pregnant at the time and I wrote back and I said we're going to
have a baby in the spring. And because you are a mother and because
you have had a baby I'm sure that you can understand that we are a pack-
age deal, and I won't come without my husband and the baby. (Dot)

Perhaps most of the time what seemed to change family member
opinions was the expression of pain.

We used the silent treatment a lot (laughs). [And] I did cry. We were
working on the barn. I was doing some work for [Dad]. We were working together. I think I just kind of finished up my project and, ya know,
crying. I don't think I said much. . . . I remember being really emotional. I think I just basically bawled about it (laughs). I remember
'cause I was crying on the couch and he came to the door. He was,
'cause we were all mucky, he came to the door and kind of shouted in

the door, like to come there. . . . He looked at me in the eye . . . , "I'll love you no matter what." (Liz)

DOES FAMILY OPPOSITION WORK?

This study is only of intact couples. There may be many white people who had a black lover at one time but who left in the face of strong family reactions. We lack data on opposition that blocked a committed partnership, although Beigel (1966) reported instances among clients he had seen. Family opposition, even if quite obviously racist, may have an effect. Family opposition may build on the doubts that almost anyone might have about the future of a potential committed relationship. Moreover, to go along with a relationship that is opposed by family members requires a willingness to risk emotional and social divorce from family, recurrent personal pain, and hostility of family to any children one might have. Small wonder that some of the people we interviewed could talk about people they knew who had broken off or avoided escalating interracial relationships.

> A lot of my friends have dated black men, but . . . none of my friends are interracially married. . . . They would date a black man, but they wouldn't bring them home . . . for fear what their parents would say or do, or what other people would say. (Eve)

Some white partners also talked about how heavily the opposition of a parent weighed on them.

> In the beginning for me it was a heavy weighing of our relationship . . . by my parents. . . . I didn't worship my father but pretty close, and he was very, very important to me, and to disappoint him. . . . My mother you know, could spank me. My father would look at me and I was history. So for me, weighing the odds on our relationship and wondering, "Are we ever going to make it through this? Are my parents ever going to let this be OK?" It was a big thing for me. (Jill)

> There was a time when I had gone on a foreign study [trip] . . . , and we had stayed close and stayed corresponding, but I had come back and thought that maybe we shouldn't do it, maybe pressures were too

much. . . . This is when we were still in college. . . . It wasn't we were talking marriage at that point. It was more a matter of just questioning, and I think most of my concerns were based on the pressures and the input and what I saw as the societal barriers, and . . . [thinking], "Maybe my parents are right. Maybe we will just be causing ourselves trouble." (Adam)

In asking about the effectiveness of family opposition, we can also consider whether pressure from more distant relatives, friends, and coworkers on the immediate family of the white partner has an effect. Given white antipathy toward interracial unions, parents and siblings of a white partner may experience pressure from people around them to oppose the relationship. How much of that pressure is effective cannot be determined. There were certainly instances in which a couple was aware of the pressures on the white partner's family.

My mother's half sister, her husband banished my mother from their house due to our relationship. (Jill)

With my folks . . . this would have been a highly unusual kind of relationship . . . in the community we live[d] in. . . . Pretty conservative white views, . . . and they didn't have to deal with this kind of a thing. And so to have a son who was involved who would bring his wife or wife-to-be or girlfriend or whatever to that community, was . . . also part of the reason for that reaction. They did have to justify; they had to talk about it. Who knows? It might affect their careers. I mean, it could have influenced the way people would look at them. (Adam)

I have a memory of [my mother] saying things about particular friends, people who I did not know very well but who didn't approve and thought that somehow my parents should have done something. (Virginia)

The opposition directed at members of a white partner's family failed in the sense that the stories come only from couples who entered into a committed relationship. But one can imagine instances in which the pressure a white partner's family might have felt from others would have helped to block the development of a long-term couple commitment.

RECONCILIATION

Similar to findings in Los Angeles (Kouri & Lasswell, 1993) and British (Tizard & Phoenix, 1993, p. 134) studies, in every white family in the current study in which there was opposition, the opposition declined. At least some family members who had been opposed moved toward greater tolerance and acceptance. Sometimes, the process of reconciliation began almost immediately.

> My dad told me that if *I* ever did anything like that, referring to my neighbor getting married [interracially], he would never talk to me again. . . . I cried, and I told [him] then [about my own relationship]. And then he came back like a day later and apologized to me, and said he loved me no matter what. (Liz)

The "no matter what" said that even though he accepted his daughter's right to make her own choices, he did not fully accept her choice to have a relationship with an African American man. Even if reconciliation began almost immediately, it was not uncommon for the process to play out over many years.

> My mother . . . seemed OK with the relationship. My . . . aunt refused to see us for about 5 years. She refused to talk to us, and my father refused to have anything to do with us until we got married. Then he claimed it was because of this adulterous situation, the fact that I was married [to someone else when our relationship started]. . . . I think he was in shock, and he needed a reason, and it took him some time to . . . come up with that. When he saw that he was going to miss this whole grandchild's upbringing . . . he was open-armed. He changed from night to day. . . . First [my aunt] met our kids, and then she just decided she didn't want to get left out anymore. So she came about on her own after . . . I think probably 5 . . . years or something like that. (Janet)

> Her family, when she had [our son], and her dad, I wasn't even in the room when he was comin' in. I told him if he was a younger man he would have karated me, and he gave me one of those looks, and I gave him back a look. And now we get along beautifully. We interact real good now. I think it's the initial shock of the stereotype that they have

of peoples. . . . God knows what else their mind run past, their visions. [Now] . . . we sit down here and talk just like we're talkin' right now. Like, they like the Bible . . . , and I know the Bible. So that surprised them, 'cause they would figure that I would be a total scalawag. (John)

Even after apparent acceptance, family members who had disap-proved of the interracial relationship might still feel discomfort when with friends or neighbors who might have negative attitudes toward the relationship.

I get the sense that [my parents] don't want us to be seen too much, like when we visit them we stay home, and we don't go, I don't know if that's really a conscious thing or just the sense that they don't want us to be seen too much. (Joyce)

Now [my mother] loves him. I mean, when we go drive down to [my home town] . . . , she rushes up and hugs and kisses him and things like that. But I'm quite sure with her friends she almost apologizes for it. . . . I can't expect her to really not be any other way, considering the environment that she was raised in and where she's allowed herself to remain. (Nora)

The concerns about what others would think might also help define the process of coming to terms with the interracial partnership of a family member. Crossing the threshold to acceptance might involve publicizing the relationship in the community.

GARY I can remember the years when we'd first go back to visit my family in [a town] where there's very, very few black people.

PATRICIA But the community had all heard about our getting married.

GARY Everybody knew about it.

PATRICIA About the [family name] boy.

GARY And how important it seemed to me that my mother at some point made a decision that she was going to stand behind us and instead of hiding us in the home, would just insist that we go out with her.

PATRICIA Yes.

GARY Everywhere.

PATRICIA Everywhere. We'd go to church. We'd go to the country club, and it was like once . . .

GARY Every friend whom she would see, they would not have the opportunity to turn away, but she would bring us up and introduce.

PATRICIA Yes. She wouldn't leave anybody guessing about it, but I remember the first year we were there, and the town was just all abuzz with this marriage. And I was at the grocery store, and this woman says to me . . . "You must be new in town." And I said, "No, I'm just here visiting my in-laws." And she said, "And who are they?" And I said, "Well, you know, the [family name]." And she said, "Oooh! You're *that* [family name]!" And (laughs) everybody at three checkouts stopped and looked at me. And then she [asked] to see my ring. And then she said, "Oh, what a beautiful ring." . . . And then I'd walk down the street; you would see people come to the front of their shops, looking, because it was like, "OK, here I am." . . . We went to a big party [there] at Christmas time. . . . I remember Gary's brother; I think he was scared to death. And I think he thought I was frightened. So we were at this party, and he just takes me by my hand, and he stands in the middle of the room. All these people come by. It's like he's holding court, and all these people come by and say, "Hello." And I'll never forget that, because he was shaking. He was holding my hand so tight. He was shaking, but he was saying that, as sort of the head of the family now, "Here is the message."

My grandmother [is] an extreme example of how it's changed and, well with someone who [grew] up after the turn of the century it really is quite a significant shock for her to be introducing Wanda with great joy as the wife of a grandson . . . to her old friends. . . . That's a pretty significant change. (Adam)

The move toward acceptance also might involve some sort of signal to the black partner that the family was now more tolerant.

Over the years, . . . they would go out of their way to point out that they had a black friend here now, and gee, they just got a new teacher in the school, black, you know, and that was fine. I don't think we ever reacted negatively to that. They were trying. That was a part of reaching out to us, reaching out to Wanda. (Adam)

Sometimes the move toward greater acceptance involved family members' realizing that their expectations of negative consequences from the partnership were not confirmed by events.

There were predictions on both sides of the family that this was a disastrous arrangement, if not for ourselves, then definitely for our children. And those were from people who cared for us, and so they were of great concern. But we found so few of those predictions to have any reality that over time . . . on both sides of the family, they had come to accept this marriage as a very strong one. (Gary)

It helped, in some white families, that there was a family member who was more knowledgeable about interracial couples and about environments in which they could live with minimal difficulty.

My sister had a big influence, because my sister was living in New York. And she said to my mother, "You may not believe this, but there are places where interracial couples live. And, actually, they do OK." And that the two of us being educated were likely to be able to have some choice in where we live, and we could probably do all right. So I think it had a real influence on my mother. (Gary)

Even after white family members got over their initial opposition, there might still be misgivings.

My ma and dad would just give the world to us. They're there when we need them. They would do anything for us, but I still think sometimes in my dad's eyes that he doesn't like it. . . . They're learning to accept it more and more every day, but I can still see the hurt in my dad's eyes every now and again. (Olivia)

It's like jumping into the cold water. The . . . attitude is, "OK, we're here; we have to deal with it; we'll make sure that *we* are not the problem." They'll bend over backwards to welcome the person into the family, but at the same time, there's just that little bit of tension of, "(sigh) I don't want to make a mistake." (Emmett, who is black)

In another case, a family member who was accepting of the relationship was not willing to accept a similar relationship involving her own child.

TIM   [My sister] has no problem with our relationship; however, her daughter is dating a black man, and she is freaked out about it. . . .

FLORA   She doesn't like him because he's black. I said you're wrong right there. You gotta stop lookin' at this guy 'cause of his color. . . .

TIM   If he's screwin' up, he's not doing well in school, he's out partyin' at night and raisin' hell, there's the reason to be upset. Not because he's black. . . .

FLORA   It stunned me that she brought this up, 'cause I always liked her.

When family members are accepting but also leak misgivings or disapproval, it is difficult to know whether what is involved is a step toward complete acceptance or an end point. When the crucial players are still alive, one can hope for eventual full acceptance. If a crucial opponent has died, no one can know whether there would have been more complete reconciliation had the person lived.

When [my father] was dying, he asked to see me. . . . He was in a nursing home. . . . I went alone to see him, and he thought he was dying; he wasn't actually dying. Then the old boy held on for ages, but he had a big stroke. And so I went to the nursing home, and at this point I hadn't seen him since, oh, about 1969 . . . and that was then 1981. . . . He wanted to leave the nursing home and go for a Dairy Queen. So they got him into the car, and we went to the Dairy Queen, and he said, "Drive by Mother's place." So we drove by the apartment where my mother lived, and Wilson and [our daughter] were in there. And he told me, "Pull up into the parking lot. . . . I want to see the baby." . . . And I said, "Oh, OK. I'll go get her." And then as I got out of the car, he said, "I'm not ready." So then the next time I saw him, I took [her] with me. He wanted to see her, and I still remember she . . . must have been 3, and it was like she knew something. It . . . was like she was the adult and he was the child, and I have a picture of them, my sister pushing the wheelchair and [our daughter] hanging on to his hand, walking alongside, and she just was very, very kind to him. . . . After I think my sister had taken her out to the car . . . then the tears were streaming down his face, and I'm saying to myself, " . . . He's had a change of heart." And he said, "That is a pretty hurtful [thing]." About my baby! When I got ready to leave, there was a nurses' aide in there, and he was by then very, very tired out and could barely speak at all from the day's events. And he was saying something. . . . They could understand him better than I could because they work with him every day. And the nurse says, "Wait; he's trying to tell you something." And she says, "I caught the word 'forgive.' " And I'm thinking to myself that this guy is, he's going to say, "Forgive me." And I suppose it's possible for me to think that anybody should ask my forgiveness or anything. But suddenly it frustrated him very much that we couldn't understand what he was saying, and he blurted it out, and it came out loud and clear. "I forgive you!" . . . And those were his last words to me. I went home after that. And sometimes I think about that, and . . . that really rankles with me. I do have anger at him, and I can't get it out because he's dead, and I know that for my own well-being I need to forgive him. And I, I work at that. (Dot)

Pain and Reconciliation

As the preceding quotation and other quotations throughout this chapter indicate, the process of reconciliation may be painful. Part of the difficulty is that there is often still a sense of rawness and pain when family members who claim to be trying to change fall short of 100% acceptance of the couple's relationship.

[My mother] just got nastier and nastier. And nobody was supporting her by this time; people were starting to tell her that she was really off base, including her sisters, who had never even met Henry. The whole family [knew] about Henry before they'd met him, and everybody was saying that; "You're off base. You're gonna lose your daughter," and "We can't blame her for walking out on you. . . ." And she just kept it up until last year. She had a heart attack, and she got nailed in the hospital by everybody. They just thought she was a captive audience, and she couldn't yell back at them (laughs). While she's there, people were going in there telling her that her lifestyle better change. And I wrote

her a letter in the fall and just said, well, kind of like, "Back up what
you say," because she said she'd try, and she'd try. And I said, "Well,
time for trying's over; do it or . . . we're out of here." Simple as that,
and she finally said, "OK!" . . . She knew she'd probably be more
relaxed if she did [it], because everybody else was fine, except my
mother. So she made this change, and invited us to dinner. We were
invited for Christmas. . . . So she's working at it; I can't say it's a
total turnaround yet, but she's getting there. (Donna)

There also can be pain when the acceptance is of the black partner
but not of black people in general, with a message something like,
"You are OK because you are an exception," or "You are OK, but we
still have feelings or misgivings about African Americans in general."

You come into the family, you become legitimized, *But* . . . it doesn't
transcend to other parts of the community. . . . Their familiarity with me
doesn't make them more familiar with other black people. (Gregory)

My dealings with Nora's family have been, I think, pretty positive. I
get a sense that especially with her mother I am some kind of an exception or a freak or something. (Emmett)

A lot of my broader family, aunts and uncles and . . . cousins were not
an issue, but I guessed wrong as to who was going to be supportive
and who wasn't, which was really surprising to me, because there were
people who I thought would never talk to me who were absolutely supportive, who were just wonderful. I think what they did is they made a
little exception for Lorenzo. They didn't really change their views, but
somehow Lorenzo was different than everybody else, and so therefore
he was OK. (Virginia)

There is also pain when the relationship is accepted, but a white
family member cannot see past the African American's skin color to
see the person as a person.

I was just saying how good my family is, except my Dad. I thinks he
notices [skin color] a lot. . . . I think my dad really sees us as her and
my black son-in-law. . . . He hasn't got past the fact that you are black
yet. It's a really strong part of how he feels. (Ann, talking to Bayard)

There also can be pain that there had to be a process of acceptance—that instead of unconditional acceptance of a family member's choice of relationship there had to be a process of acceptance, sometimes extending over many years.

> [My dad took] 10 years to apologize and say, "I'm wrong. It's OK that you married him, 'cause he's OK, and I like him now." . . . I'm grateful for that. . . . It's probably a major step forward for him. But I don't see that as like any major support. I mean, it's reassuring [to] me, but . . . if I went 10 years without his approval, I didn't really give a rip. . . . It's like, "So now you're going to bestow your approval on me? Like it's yours to give and take?" So I'm grateful for it, and yet I have mixed feelings, 'cause I don't think that's what parents should do. I think he should've loved me enough to accept what I did and not have to give and take approval. So I do not particularly feel supported, nor do I really crave it. (Christine)

Christine's family was like some other white families in not accepting an interracial relationship wholeheartedly but accepting it as a fact of life.

> I think both of our families wish we hadn't done this. But I think they've given up, I hope they've give up, hoping it wouldn't work.

Sometimes what hurt was that, even though a crucial family member had accepted the relationship, there was some other family member who was not fully accepting.

> From the way my parents were raised, and my father, I don't know if bigoted or racist or what, prejudiced or what the proper term would be. But in time, I know our relationship changed my parents' life a lot. And they would not now look, my father especially. They say people can't change. And for being . . . 45, 46, older than that, 50, when we started dating, and at first it wasn't going to fly, but after that . . . James calls my mom "Mom," and dad "Dad." It wasn't Mr. [name] or whatever. At first it was definite difficulty, you know, with them accepting it. . . . And I have an uncle that came up to visit my father a couple years ago. . . . We were watching—the shock of reality again, because like I said I don't put racism . . . in the forefront of my mind if I don't

have to—we were watching *Predator,* and they were sitting there watching and . . . [my uncle] is watching, going, "Go nigger, go." And I looked at my father like, I mean, I was in awe, my jaw dropped, I couldn't believe it, because my father approves [of our relationship]. . . . And my father previously told my uncle that in Minnesota you're going to be shocked; you can't talk like that, that whatever your beliefs are, you cannot . . . talk like that. And my father knew that I was really hurt, . . . but you can't change everybody. And so I walked out of the room. But, see, my father changed, as far as his attitude. And he knew, he, like, came to me and tried to console me and say that that's his ignorance. But he was raised by the same father as my uncle was. But [my father] changed. (Jill)

Seemingly Genuine Acceptance

Although it might seem that family members who were initially opposed never change, some family members and some families seemed to move to something like complete acceptance.

DONNA [My brother] and Henry just met at Christmas . . . , and he was extremely friendly, ya know. It was weird.

HENRY It was strange, 'cause this was the same man that said I would never set foot in his house.

When they realized that we were . . . getting married and that they couldn't change us . . . , [my parents] decided they'd . . . accept it. . . . And now they think that's absolutely wonderful. They've been there for us whenever we've needed them. They would take on the world for us. You couldn't ask for better parents in that aspect either. My family has been very supportive. (Olivia)

SHIRLEY [My father's] attitude just turned completely around . . . once he could see that we were quite serious. . . . As the months went by, [my mother's] attitude was, "He's going to be a family member now, and let's go with it," and they love him now and everything is just peachy.

INTERVIEWER Do you know what happened that your dad made such a turnaround?

SHIRLEY He admitted, I guess, that night that we said we were getting
        married, he said, "I guess I can call myself a bigot," but maybe
        he isn't really a bigot, because he's not anymore. . . . In the
        past year, he's gotten involved with, I don't know if it's an
        Urban League. . . . He's got black colleagues now, and it's
        opening up a whole new world for him, and he's seeing the
        light, and he's just been wonderful ever since. . . . And he
        and Shane go to basketball games together, fishing . . .

SHANE Yeah, cool guy.

SHIRLEY Whatever. It's his son-in-law.

It's all gotten better and better and better. I mean, my parents love
him, and Houston is their son-in-law, and they are almost overboard
now about their black son-in-law (she laughs). . . . They kind of like
him better than me (she laughs). . . . I knew that once they knew him
that it wouldn't matter what color he was. . . . We see my parents more
often, and they really've grown to love him and love us as a couple,
and they just accept it. I don't think they accepted it completely, but
they never showed me that they didn't. So it's just gotten, it's gotten
better. And, like I said, once they got to know him, the color didn't really matter. (Eve)

In Gary's family we're kind of like the model marriage. . . . A cousin's
wife said to his mother, "What do you think is a good marriage? What
makes a good marriage?" And she said, "I think Gary and Patricia have
a good marriage because they can laugh," and she said, "even when
they're fighting they're laughing about it." And she said that to me,
and it's like, "OK, you want to know about a good marriage. There it
is. Right there. Those two people." (Patricia)

My father's mother . . . didn't attend our wedding because . . . , I want
to be fair, she just couldn't handle it, basically. And now I'm fond of
saying I think she likes Wanda better than she does me. . . . In August,
we were there . . . when my grandmother had all of her dear friends
around. Wanda and I were upstairs. . . . [Grandmother] was calling out
all over the room, she's going, "Where's Wanda? I must introduce her
to so and so and so and so." She wasn't calling for me, mind you, not
the grandson (laughing), so we've come a long way. (Adam)

Sometimes the transformation of attitude toward the interracial relationship or toward the black partner included a general attitude change toward African Americans.

> I think [my father] changed [his attitudes] as a whole. It wasn't James, a special person; it was viewing the African American man, woman per se. Not the typical stereotype. I really do believe that his attitude changed. . . . I think he changed on a whole. He was a very honest clear-cut man. I don't think there would have been a hiding or a disguising his feelings as far as that goes. (Jill)

The Place of Children in Reconciliation

Some white family members moved toward greater acceptance when a couple had a child. It is hard to say whether it was the charm of the child, a realization that the relationship was likely to be a long-term one, a feeling of connection to the child as a blood relative, an unwillingness to be hostile to an innocent child, the importance of a grandchild as a descendant who will live long after one's own death, or something else; but in quite a few couples in which someone in the white partner's family had opposed the relationship and in which the couple had a child, the child seemed to help to move the hostile family members toward greater acceptance.

> Children make a big difference. . . . Their attitude changed—I should say Joyce's mom's attitude. I think that Joyce's mom is pretty accepting. And they came down and painted the house for us . . . after we moved from our apartment to a new house. They came down, painted the house, bought this carpet here. They've done a lot, and now when I go up there, [her mom] makes me blueberry pies 'cause she knows they're my favorite pies. So I think the early wounds are certainly healed over. (Gregory)

Failing Health Promotes Reconciliation

Some white family members who had opposed an interracial relationship made efforts to make peace when they felt they were dying. That is, serious illness led some people to try to tie up loose ends in life and to be more exemplary adherents to religious principles than they had been before.

> That kind of half relationship went on until when I was pregnant. By then, my mother's health was failing quite a bit and so she had written me and asked if I would come to [name of city], which was midway between here and where she lived. . . . She thought this might be the last time she would ever have the chance to see me. She felt she was dying. (Dot)

Full Reconciliation May Not Always Be Possible

Perhaps some people can leave the past behind, but there were people who said that they always would carry the scar of past family opposition, that there would never be a complete healing. For example, Dot, who was just quoted, talked about bringing her husband and child to meet her ailing mother.

> As an individual, [Mother] just thought Wilson was so nice. What's not to love? . . . She was a little bitty lady who was in failing health, and he carried her out to the back yard, and she made the remark to my sister that they seemed to have such a nice marriage, and that Wilson actually consults Dot before laying down the law. That's something she had never experienced in her marriage. . . . I wouldn't exactly say she came around, but she came around to that point. To me, . . . were she still living today, I'm sorry but that crack would always be there. . . . That plate was broken, and the crack would always be there, because I would have never been able to forget that it took a baby for her to want to see him. And I loved him long before I had the baby and loved him as much as I loved the baby.

SUMMARY AND CONCLUSIONS

Although there were white families in which all close relatives were supportive of an interracial relationship, in most of the white families, there was some opposition. The opposition was often not unanimous, but it was clearly present. (The lack of unanimity means that a white partner may find family support even when some family members are strongly opposed to an interracial relationship, but it also means that families divided about an interracial relationship may struggle with triangulation, secret keeping, coalitions, and other family systems patterns that block members from easy and connecting relationship with one another.)

An analysis of the concerns that white family members raised in their opposition shows an array of racist feelings, assumptions, and fears. But certain concerns were at the heart of the discourse of opposition: (a) societal, community, neighborhood, or family disapproval; (b) issues of safety and well-being; (c) an alleged clannishness of African Americans; (d) problems the children would have; (e) the likelihood of a poor economic future for the family member entering an interracial relationship; and (f) unspecified problems. Raising these concerns might camouflage a family member's own racism, but the concerns that relate to reactions in the larger society suggest that racism has a snowballing quality because it pushes people who might not be so racist to be cautious or fearful in ways that promote racist goals. In addition, some of the reactions of members of the white families seemed to indicate that some people wanted to block an African American person from becoming a relative, that part of the opposition was to acquiring a relative one did not want.

White families seemed particularly opposed to the interracial relationships of a daughter. Perhaps white families are especially protective of daughters, that daughters are perceived as relatively vulnerable, that daughters are relatively close to families, or that daughters are relatively easy to control.

Some white partners did not have strong feelings in response to family opposition, but many did. They might feel angry at family hypocrisy, particularly if a family member who was opposed was one who had previously espoused racial tolerance. They might feel frustration and grief at the loss of family support and at failures to understand them and their partner. They might work at trying to persuade family members to see things their way, or they might move toward greater distance from family members. We cannot determine how often family opposition works at bringing an end to an interracial relationship, but it was clear that many of the white partners felt the opposition as a powerful force.

In every white family in which there was opposition, the opposition abated. At least some family members who had been opposed moved toward greater tolerance and acceptance. Sometimes, the process of reconciliation began almost immediately. Sometimes, it did not move far or (at least at the time of the interview) was still in process. Sometimes, it involved a great deal of struggle and discomfort on the part of many family members. Often, the move to greater acceptance involved a communication of that greater acceptance, not only to the white partner but also to the black partner and to members of the white family's extended network. In some cases, the healing was incomplete—for example, because somebody died before reconciliation was complete, somebody had not yet given up all racist attitudes, or the white partner in the couple continued to feel bad about the earlier opposition and hostility that had been expressed.

6

THE AFRICAN AMERICAN PARTNER'S FAMILY

FAMILIES IN WHICH ALL CLOSE RELATIVES WERE SUPPORTIVE

It is not simple to compare family responses in African American families with those of white families, because who counts as "family" is not necessarily the same for the two groups. Stack (1974), for example, found in an economically depressed black community that many people had strong and significant relationships with "play kin," people not related by blood, marriage, or adoption. Although the community she studied was from another social class and from another time and geographic location than most or all of the African American respondents in this study, some black respondents in the present study had close relationships with play kin. Increasingly, social scientists are loathe to make pronouncements about what a family is but try instead to understand how people themselves define

100

family (e.g., see Gubrium & Holstein, 1990; Weston, 1991). From that perspective, it is important to note that to some extent, the family of white respondents could be defined differently from the family of African American respondents.

Even when focusing only on genealogically close relatives, white respondents may have been talking about different kinds of kin than African American respondents were. In the accounts given by African American respondents, crucial kin less often included fathers and less often referred to the extended kin network of cousins, aunts, uncles, and grandparents. Mothers seemed much more central or much more exclusively the relative whose opinion mattered. Furthermore, 15 of the black partners were raised at least part of the time by a single mother (or aunt or grandmother), but only two of the white partners were. At the time of the interview, more black partners than white partners had no father (step, biological, or otherwise). Those differences may help to explain why one's mother is more often the key player in the life of the black partner. Black partners were less likely to have a father available to react to an interracial relationship, and even if they did have a father available, the mother might be the parent whose reactions counted the most.

Given that to some extent who constituted family was different for black respondents than for white, blacks reported more often than whites that their family members were accepting of, or at least not openly opposed to, the interracial relationship. Similar findings have been reported in other studies of interracial relationships (Golden, 1954; Kouri & Lasswell, 1993; Porterfield, 1978, p. 116). Golden found that the families of African American partners in interracial relationships, in contrast to the families of the white partners, were usually willing to meet the white partner. He also said that African American families were much more able than white families to see the white partner as a person, rather than to react to him or her as representative of a category. Many of Golden's white respondents developed warm, close relationships with their partner's relatives. This was less common for the African American spouses in relation to the white partner's family. In a recent study, Frankenberg (1993, p. 98) also found more acceptance by the family of the African American partner than of the European American partner. In the present study, African American mothers, often the central family players, seemed comparatively accepting.

> My mother said, first question that she had about Joyce is, "Is she taller than [you]?" "Nope, she's white." My mother said, "Oh, OK." "No, actually she is taller than me." She said, "Oh." My mother's all of 5'1", or 5' even. . . . And I said, "She's white." And my mother said, "Oh, is she nice?" And, "Yes, she's very nice." She said, "Oh, good. When are we going to meet her?" "Well, she's gonna come down this summer, and you can meet her then." She said, "Good, I look forward to it." . . . I think she was very welcoming of Joyce and befriended her in a lot of ways. I remember we [attended a public event] . . . , and they were asking people in the audience to name their children; my mother said, "I want you to meet my daughter, Joyce." My mother was very affirming of the relationship. (Gregory)

> I absolutely adore the ground [my mother-in-law] walks on. . . . I think she's the neatest woman. She's so funny. She stayed here this winter. And I . . . was devastated when she left. Well, Ed has, that was Ed's mom, and so he has different issues. I don't have all that stuff with her. And I have to remember that, because part of me wanted to jump in, because it would be like if my dad moved in here, he probably would get along with him just great. And I'd be just like, "Get out of here!" . . . [She] is pretty down to earth too, and I think that's why we get along really well. (Rosemary)

> I told Mother we were getting married, and she [said], "Great, she's a real good girl." (Shane)

> I sent my parents a picture. That's the way I did it, because I wanted to give my mom (laughs) some . . . time, and I didn't really think that she'd have any big problems with it. . . . Her only remark was that she thought that Adam's eyes were a really strange color, but that was about it (laughs). But that's because at the time he was wearing brown contacts over green eyes. . . . So in terms of my family's reaction, I feel fairly comfortable, and I think it's interesting because my mom . . . has become much more militant about her support of interracial couples. . . . Just the idea and more the right to exist than anything else. . . . The freedom. And I mean, ultimately, that's where my mom's . . . sympathies lie for anything. I mean, if somebody says that you don't have the

right to do it, that immediately puts her on the side of that individual (laughs), because that's with the rights. (Wanda)

LIZ   [John's brother and his wife] came and spent a week here after
      I had [our daughter] last summer and helped. Yeah, that's
      been real great.

JOHN And his wife has really been nice too, 'cause that one day when
      you all spoke to each other and you all both decided to go
      have the rhythm and blues. And y'all went out to this mall.
      So my brother and his wife, which is what I would consider
      my family, they have really been, I would say, supportive.

In some cases, the white partner was even accepted by family members of the black partner who were militantly black and who were opposed in principle to interracial marriage.

I have two cousins who're both in, one's a Black Muslim, and the
other one, well, . . . both of them are in African religions, so even
though they have a hard time accepting my being married to someone
white, they're fine with Kent on a personal level. (Gloria)

A black family's treating a white partner as an exception did not seem to cause the kind of pain that a white family's treating a black partner as an exception caused. When white family members accepted a black partner as an exception, they could be seen as still racist, whereas when black family members accepted a white partner as an exception, they could be seen as realistically aware of how common white racism is but also inclined to respect a family member's choice of partners. In Gloria's family, and in some other black families, the acceptance of a white partner did not mean that family members accepted whites in general or interracial partnerships. It was acceptance of the choice a family member made.

In my family once you're an adult you're pretty much on your own,
and there's little interference one way or the other, and especially in
our case since I was 30. (Gloria)

In my family because they know the type of person that I am, . . . they
accept Kate a great deal just based on the person that I am. And they

know that I am all right the way that I am, so therefore Kate must be a very decent person, regardless of [her] color. . . . My family hasn't raised any issue at all about that. I don't see 'em very much at all. [We] get home from time to time. When we go down there once every year or two, personally I never experienced any type of hostility or any type of animosity . . . against our relationship from my family. (Robert)

Both of our families have been really accepting, and I think my mother's . . . asked more questions and has also been . . . pretty understanding of things. I mean, there have been times when she has, just kind of a part of her culture is to make disparaging remarks about other ethnic groups (laughs). And so she'll say things about white people. . . . I've . . . never worried about that when she comes to town, but what I'm concerned about is when my daughter was old enough to kind of understand what she was saying. (Barb)

Surveys in 1972, 1978, and 1983 found a more or less constant 23% of black respondents not approving of interracial marriage (Schuman, Steeh, & Bobo, 1985, pp. 144-145). Surveys are not simple to interpret, but included in that 23% might be people who feel strongly that children, cousins, grandchildren, brothers, and sisters should not marry a member of the oppressor group but who might still be respectful and accepting of a family member's choices.

Supportive Members of Families in Which There Was Opposition

Even when there were family members who were opposed to the interracial relationship, there were supportive family members. It seems that, in contrast to some of the families of white partners who were interviewed, there was never a solid wall of opposition in a black family to an interracial relationship.

VIRGINIA Your family has been fairly supportive. Your father has been totally accepting and supportive immediately.

LORENZO Yeah, and my brothers. . . . I think if you ask [our children] with no strings, so they didn't have to feel threatened about it, who their closest relative is they would both say . . . the younger of my two brothers. . . .

VIRGINIA . . . And he still introduces me as his sister. . . . Yeah, that has been a very close family relationship.

FAMILIES TOO DISTANT
TO BE ACCEPTING OR OPPOSED

In some cases, it was not clear whether the couple's relationship was a matter of any interest for the African American partner's family. Issues of family acceptance or opposition did not come up because family members had little or no contact with the couple. They may not even have met the white partner. For example, during the couple's 5-year relationship, Donna, who is white, had not met Henry's closest living relatives, his father and brother. She had, however, developed a good relationship with Henry's two teenage children from a previous marriage. Her not meeting his father and brother may have had more to do with their geographic distance and the extent to which Henry had lived for a long time independently and at a distance from his father and brother than with antiwhite feelings in his family or his fears of his family's response to her. In fact, in a number of the families of African Americans who were interviewed, most relatives were geographically and emotionally distant, so they had no opinions about the interracial partnership, their opinions were not known, or their opinions were a matter of indifference to the couple.

WANDA I have such a large family, you know, I have the size of family that . . .

ADAM You may not even know what's going on with them.

WANDA Yeah, oh yeah, well there's some that you know, you kinda, "Oh really? That's what you think, huh? Who cares."

As I was sayin', my family, which is my brother, have been real supportive, ya know. Other than that, my family don't really interact with [us]. (John, most of whose family was 2,000 miles away)

My relationship with my brothers has been pretty much, we don't bother one another's personal lives that much. We're not that involved. Some people might have real close relationships with their family, and they might say things, or feel involved that way, but . . . I don't think my brothers said anything. (Gregory)

The distance an interracial couple might have from the black partner's family may be partly a matter of the cost of travel, telephone communication, or even written communication. The economic oppression of blacks in America means that it is difficult for a substantial number of black Americans to afford travel to visit distant relatives, telephone contact with them, or even correspondence with them.

> From Robert's family, we have support from them in their own special way. I mean, his sisters in North Carolina are very, very materially poor. So it's not like they're sending cards, gifts, letters, money. I mean, that just doesn't happen. But when there's some communication, it's very loving, real genuine. (Kate)

Another source of the comparative lack of involvement of black families was that all but 3 of the 21 black partners were living far (more than a 4-hour drive) from where they grew up and far from where many or all of their family of origin (and perhaps children by previous relationships) lived. By contrast, only 9 or 10 of the 21 white partners lived far from where they grew up and far from where many or all of their family of origin lived. In addition, some African American men in the study had established autonomy from their families years before the current relationship began.

> I had . . . gone out with white girls before and had dealt with those issues with the family then. And . . . I never really allowed my relationships to come under the scrutiny of my family or any of their associates. So that's like, my secrets are my secrets. They're none of your business. And you don't have an opinion about it, whether you know about them or not, because you have no right to that. Which is still how I feel. . . . At the beginning of our relationship, no one ever came out and said anything . . . directly about the fact of the difference in our cultures except for my militant sister. . . . But of course, like anything else she does, I just blow her off, because she's a pinhead. (James)

OPPOSITION IN BLACK FAMILIES

With black families, it was often much less clear whether there was opposition to an interracial couple. Whereas there was clear opposition by at least one person in the immediate family of most of the white respondents, there was clear opposition in the immediate family of fewer than half of the black respondents. In black families, the basis of opposition seemed generally to be different from what was reported for white families. The mother described in the following excerpt, for example, had a complex set of concerns, including the educational future of her son, the risks of marrying down educationally, the importance of a black feminist son marrying a black woman, and the rejection of black femininity that seemed to be implied by her son's choosing a white partner.

VIRGINIA I think your mother had more problems than she'll acknowledge. . . . With your mother, part of the problem when we got together wasn't just race but the fact that she assumed that Lorenzo was going to go on to graduate school. . . . I had dropped out of college, and I had no clear idea as to what I was going to do, and she thought we were too young, and my family was not educated. . . .

LORENZO The only concerns that I heard raised were from my mother. . . . I think that Virginia is pretty accurate in her assessment of why it was a problem, but I think the additional thing is that as a black woman who really tried hard to raise three avowedly feminist black boys, which is, there aren't that many women who can proudly say, "These are my sons and they truly like women and respect women." And even though she's very quiet about it and very unassuming, she did have sort of this sense of mission that she's sending out three boys. And she was certainly hoping they were going to find three suitable black girls. . . .

VIRGINIA But my bet is too that she, although she never voiced it to me and probably not to you either, I think was concerned that somehow this meant some rejection of her.

LORENZO Well, that's part and parcel of what I'm talking about. That is part of the psychological issue for black women as a whole. I think that for black women, I talk with some about the issue, that's exactly what it represents for them when they see, *especially* a black man who they know and care about with a white woman. It just feels like you've rejected black femininity in favor of not only a white standard of beauty but also, on a deeper level, that you have, by embracing a white woman, embraced white women and womanhood, you know, as opposed to black womanhood. And so they can personalize on some level every time they see a black man with a white woman.

There were instances in which African American family members were apprehensive about attacks from white racists that an African American (or members of the African American person's family) might experience as a result of a marriage to a white person. For example, the person just quoted had a brother living elsewhere who was at first quite fearful about possible problems stemming from the marriage. The parents of another man had visions of lynching.

My family was kind of a, "You know what you're doing?" (laughs) "Do you know what you're doing? Are you aware of what you're doing?" Because, especially in older black people, they have been raised in an era where black men have been lynched for much less then just marrying a white woman. (Wilson)

Some black family members were less clear about why they were uncomfortable with the relationship, although the interracial couple might have had their own understanding that the origin of the discomfort was connected to the sense that whites are the enemy—to a black version of prejudice that is rooted in centuries of white racism.

MANNING When I told [my mother], she . . . immediately thought you were black (laughs).

CHRISTINE Yeah, yeah, "Why would you marry her if she isn't pregnant?" (still laughing). Yeah, I forgot . . . about that. . . . (She is laughing now too.)

MANNING "Thanks, Mom, I can't be married to somebody. I have to knock 'em up or something." I mean, the term that she used. (They are still both laughing.) . . . Shows how much you think about me, too. Right.

CHRISTINE Yeah, so then we went there, after we'd been married a few months. . . . We get there, and we're tired. And we get in there and kinda start meeting everybody. . . . And we got there, and I swear to God we didn't have our butts in a chair and she starts picking at us. He was fat, he was bald, he looked old. I was fat. I mean, all this kind of bizarre stuff, just coming out of nowhere. . . . This went on for a while . . . and I looked at poor Manning, and I just lost it, and I said, "Cut the shit. This is not what this is about. And we didn't come this far for me to listen to you do this shit to us. And so I'm leaving, and I'm not putting up with this. And if there is something else that's wrong, you've got to talk to us." And so I went trotting off. . . . I guess finally . . . she apologized. . . . We made nice, but it's not, I mean, I could live without her.

MANNING Yeah. She never faced up to her own racism. . . . She kind of talked to me about it years later, but she still isn't facing up to the fact that, hey, you're no different than anybody else. You *can* be a racist on some issues. It's just as simple as that . . . , but she's afraid to face up to it. . . . [My mother] is trying to teach me one thing, and (laughs) I learned another, and that *hurt* me. That hurts me today.

The Black Partner's Own Issues

An African American partner might not only struggle with family concerns that he or she was sleeping with the enemy but also with personal feelings about sleeping with the enemy. Sometimes, such feelings were put aside until somebody reminded the black partner of a time when he or she had expressed such feelings. For example, one black partner who had in the past expressed strong opposition to white racism and strong apprehension about relationships of black men and white women shocked family and friends when he entered an interracial relationship. The shock expressed by others reminded him of the opposition he had voiced earlier.

The way the rank and file of my family, my cousins, or my friends thought about white people, that's how Kate got [stared at] when she went [to my home town in the South]. "OK" [people thought about

me], "what are you doing always speakin' out on rights for black people, stuff like that, and how we are always being trapped by a white
woman? . . . Don't you think you reneged on your philosophy and
your thinking about white women? And now you want to marry one.
How can we relate to that?" OK? That's what I was dealing with. . . . I
. . . made a decision, based on what is right, that you can't judge all by
what one may have done or what a selected few may have done. So I
came here with a whole radical approach to the whole essence of race
relations; I did. And I can tell you why. Because I had to change that
philosophical thinking about that, or I never'd married Kate; I
wouldn't even come close to talkin' to Kate, because of the [fear of]
trouble [when a black man has a relationship with a white woman]. . . .
We would talk, and we were in trouble. Don't do a thing with Kate;
don't come close to Kate or [she]'ll scream rape, and here I am in jail.
. . . When I came [North], I came to a whole new attitude about everything . . . in the race relations area. (Robert)

Parental Opposition and Offspring Gender

In black families, as with white, overt opposition seemed more
clearly to be to an interracial relationship involving a woman family
member.

My mother told me to go to the library and get a book (laughs). . . . It
wasn't any book in particular. Just go to the library and get a book.
You just take your mind off of this. . . . Go get a book. Find something
else to do. I mean, there's an expression, I don't know, maybe you're
familiar with it, "You just run out now" (laughs). You know what that
was? That was in that same genre. "You just run out, so go do some-
thin' else" (still laughing). . . . I think it's still pretty difficult for her.
. . . And somehow she blames herself, I mean, if she hadn't lived there,
maybe it wouldn't have happened. And then she loves Gary dearly. But
she still feels compelled to try to provide an explanation for people
about it. (Patricia)

Probably the concern I've heard most often, and I haven't really heard
it a lot, it's been voiced by my mother and then in the form of questions
from friends, is, "What about your kids?" . . . One concern is . . . do
you want your daughter to think of herself as white or black or mixed?

... And then ... who will be her group of friends? And will she be rejected by white and black, or will she have to choose one? (Barb)

FLORA My mother did not accept Tim. . . . His age was a [difficult]
thing for her more than his color. But she tried to make color
the whole thing. . . .

INTERVIEWER So, for your mother though, it was an issue of Tim was
white.

FLORA Of race. Umm hm . . . To rag on us. . . .

TIM [Her sister] was very adamantly against our relationship. And
tried to get Flora to date black men.

Black men, like white men, seemed more often than black women
to have considerable latitude in their relationship choices.

HOUSTON My family . . . they just look at it and said, "It's just a
family," so I don't think they see there needs to be any kind
of support. My father and mother, they see that I'm a
strong person already, so what more could they give me,
besides the money or something? So as far as my family, they
see that with my family here that I guess everything's under
control. . . .

EVE I think your family has been supportive just in the fact that they
just accept anything. I mean, his family is just, easy come,
easy go. They're really easygoing about it.

A case can be made that families protect young women more than
they do young men. In fact, all five black women in the sample seemed
to come from a relatively protected home situation. In this regard,
several black women talked about how much more their families
guarded and controlled them than their brothers.

I think that culturally . . . there are some differences in the things that
black females grow up with, and what they're told, expectations that
may be greater in some ways, I mean, because the male . . . is always,
and I sort of tease my oldest brother about being the prodigal son, he
can do anything and get away with it, and it's OK with the family. He
can not come home for 2 or 3 years, and it would not make a differ-

ence. But if I don't show up for some holiday. . . . So the standards are
very different. . . . There is a double standard there. . . . That's why
you maybe get more vocal anti-interracial dating from women, from
black women as opposed to men, because there's the sense of obliga-
tion. There's this sort of familial (laughs) heritage that you are to carry
on. . . . It's a harder thing to leap over because it goes back, it's much
stronger than the racial issue. Although it manifests itself in a way that
becomes racial, because (laughs) you even end up having people say,
"Oh, the reason we're doing this is because . . . if we're going to carry
on our race or if we're going to have this sort of purity and all those
kinds of things then, the female is responsible for that." And it's that
responsibility, and it becomes racial in that sense, but it's very cultural
and it's not endemic to one particular race. (Wanda)

It has been said that race problems in the United States are entangled
in matters of sexuality (Frankenberg, 1993; Hernton, 1965). One can
see evidence for that in the history of extremely brutal white control
in the United States of any contact remotely relating to sexuality
between a black man and a white woman (Staples, 1982, chap. 8).
Looking at that history, it comes as no surprise that some white
families are very concerned about a daughter's becoming involved in
an interracial relationship and that some black families are very
concerned about a son's becoming involved in such a relationship.
Presumably, how the culture defines women's and men's sexuality is
also involved.

VEILED OPPOSITION

Any time a couple relationship is formed, there may be veiled
opposition in the two families of origin. The concerns that family
members keep to themselves may be about couple compatibility, the
maturity of one or both partners, the possibility for violence in the
couple, the extent to which the partners seem to have communicated
about the matters that couples need to deal with, or something else.
In some black families, it seemed that there was veiled opposition
linked to matters of race, but the couple could not be sure that race
was the issue. With veiled opposition, one may sense the opposition

but be unsure about what is behind the veil. So some people who were interviewed talked about the *possibility* that a member of the black partner's family may have been opposed because of racial matters.

> Charles's parents were on the surface very welcoming and accepting and happy, although deeper down, and again I don't know if this is racial or if the fact that any woman that was going to take Charles away from his mama was going to get shit, so there was an underlying thing going on there, and there were some racial undertones. (Janet)

> My family's been very closemouthed (chuckles), and they continue to be. . . . I believe her father was very, well he probably was the most overt about it, which was very good for me, because I can deal with overt people. At least you know where they are coming from, versus my mother, who was very covert about it. And all of the beliefs that she raised me to believe, that all people were go-o-od, but it finally comes out that that's not the case (chuckles) all the time, especially when it happens to one of yours. (Manning)

In some black families, there was no direct statement of opposition to the interracial relationship, but there was so much anti-white sentiment that a white partner could not feel comfortable or welcome.

> His family is very hard to know. . . . And I know like in that instance that will be with me for quite a while. . . . We went over to their house where the women . . . get together. . . . And I was the only white person there, which I didn't have a problem with. I went gladly; I didn't even think twice about it. And as we were sitting at the table and conversation and blah blah blah and all of a sudden they have a problem . . . with . . . the director of . . . *Glory*, . . . white directors. . . . They were discussing that, and they were talking about that . . . and continu[ing] to say derogatory things while I'm sitting there. And (sighs) not feeling confident enough in getting up and walking out of her house, I just sat there. . . . I don't think that the attitude of his family will change very much. . . . It was really hard because I really wanted to be friends with his mother, but I don't think it will ever happen. (Jill)

CONTINUING RESERVE
ABOUT MATTERS RELATED TO RACE

In the families of some African Americans who were interviewed, even after there seemed to be an acceptance of the interracial relationship and the white partner, boundaries might still remain that reflect race relationships in America. In particular, African American family members might continue to be careful not to talk about matters relating to race in the white partner's presence.

EMMETT There are times . . . my mother on the phone will say, "Now, is Nora on the line? I don't want her to hear this, but," because there's a real sense of welcoming her into the family, but topics of race being such a sore point that we're not going to mention it in front of her.

INTERVIEWER What kinds of things might your mother say to you that she wouldn't want your wife to hear?

EMMETT Attitudes about white people, you know, something happened because it was a racial thing, the white people did this or that. . . . That's basically it. Any topics of race. It's like it can't be discussed or Nora might take offense.

RECONCILIATION PROCESSES

Processes of reconciliation were not commonly mentioned in describing relationships with the families of the African American partner, partly because there was less overt opposition to the interracial relationship in the first place. Sometimes, however, a militantly black family member who was opposed to the interracial relationship, although not changing in militancy, came to be warmly accepting of the white partner.

ED In *my* family, my brother, who's a black militant, who went to Howard University, who . . . spit on President Reagan's limousine . . . and has had this Secret Service inquiring about him because of his militant views, did not like Rosemary, because she's white. Despised it, just cussed up and down, "Why did

[you] marry her?" And right now in my family him and
Rosemary are bosom buddies. So . . . we won him over.

ROSEMARY . . . I can remember him just yell, I mean, he was just like
following us through the, wherever we were walking; I know
we were walking somewhere. And he goes, "Well, I suppose
you think you know what it's like to be black now?" (small
laugh). I was just like (small laugh), "How would I know what
it's like to be black?" But he was . . . going on and on and
on. And I was just really, I think he got, I mean, he didn't—I
don't know what the deal was or how it got better.

In some African American families, there was an initial shock of
opposition but no real need for reconciliation. The initial shock
melted quickly into a warm acceptance.

They were very nice to me. I remember his dad said, one time another
older couple was over and the lady, I don't know if she was deaf or
drinking . . . or what, but she said, "Well, Wilson, you married a white
woman." . . . And [his dad] said, "Well, they do that nowadays." And
she kind of sent what was meant to be a comforting look to me, so
they, regardless of how they felt, they were very nice to me. I felt accepted . . . by all of them and really, really welcomed by his sister and
brother. . . . We receive support emotionally from his adoptive father,
from his natural mother. . . . His natural mother's affection, I mean, acceptance of me, was absolutely unconditional. I walked through that
door and it wouldn't have mattered if I had a horn sticking out of my
head. This woman was prepared to care about me. And emotionally,
she's still that way. He had a woman who isn't a blood relative, she
was always a mother, like a mother to him. We call her Ma (name). . . .
I called her when my father died. She cried with me. She still treats
him like he's her baby boy. A birthday cake comes every June for him,
and she treats [our daughter] as though she were her real granddaugh-
ter. So that's a lot of support. She also has several children, and
they've been real supportive emotionally. His sister is my best friend.
Unfortunately, she's [800 miles away]. . . . So we've had a lot of emotional support that way. (Dot)

In a few African American families, there was a movement toward
greater reconciliation, but as with some white families, the movement

had so far fallen short of complete acceptance. A couple might differ about the meaning of the emotional distance but still might agree that there was distance.

MANNING [My family] is real supportive now.

CHRISTINE I disagree. . . . It's support relative to what? I mean, you're looking at it, and you have a right to, you're looking at it that they have evolved, and so they at least talk to us, and we're invited to some family occasions when we're tolerated and treated sociably nice. But that's not the same as being treated the way other people we know are involved in *their* families. . . . They're more accepting, and they're tolerating, and they try sometimes to be nice, but I don't feel like we had any particular support. They just stopped hurting us.

MANNING Yes. . . . And that's fine for me, but I can't do anything about the distance that's between Minneapolis and [where they live]. And I think perhaps if we were in [their city], things would be different. . . . I feel OK with what I'm getting here at this point in time in the relationship. . . . You have a valid point. Perhaps they don't, but I think [geography] has a lot to do with the situation.

CHILDREN FROM PREVIOUS RELATIONSHIPS

Five of the African American partners (all men) had children from previous relationships. In every case, the children from previous relationships had African American mothers. In one case, it did not seem that the children had much to do with their father's white partner, but in four cases they did, with frequent or extended visiting. There are reasons to think that an interracial blended family could have problems (Baptiste, 1984). Any blended family may have problems as rules are combined, resentment over the parental breakup plays out, relationships with now divorced parents are worked out, money issues are faced, and so on. With interracial blended families, there may be additional issues about a child's identification with a stepparent of a different race, about attitudes (not always in awareness) about people from groups other than one's own, and about an ex-spouse's (or that person's family) objecting to a child's having contact with someone of a different racial and cultural group who might at times act like a parent (Baptiste, 1984). But there were no reports of problems centering on the black partner's children or the reactions of those children to the white partner.

HENRY She has met my two sons, and I have one son who is 17 . . . and another son who is 19. . . . And almost from the beginning of our relationship they've been involved one way or another. They drop by here; one son was just by here yesterday, comes by for haircuts and the like, so I do that. . . . They'll come by and spend Christmas with us, or Thanksgiving, whatever—feel comfortable enough to call here. I don't think they've ever said a negative thing about our relationship. I know they haven't said anything negative to you.

DONNA They've been wonderful.

HENRY . . . They are different as night and day. They're very different, but they are consistent in the support that they provide this relationship and the way that they relate to us.

In the family in which the children had little contact with the interracial couple, when they were present, their father did what he thought would minimize their jealousy or antagonism.

I have never shown any affection or emotion in front of my kids to Liz. . . . Until I feel comfortable about it I just won't. . . . I want to get my life in alignment with my person . . . and I want to, like, establish who I am with them before I try and get them to accept who I am in any other circumstance. (John)

In the other four families, the children were described as accepting, and in some cases it was clear that the new white partner of the children's father had fully accepted the children.

There are a lot of stepmothers who don't enjoy the relationship with their stepchildren. When I met him, I was prepared to love them because I loved him when I met him. And now I love them in their own right. That's a special blessing that I wouldn't have, married to anybody but him. (Dot)

So not only were the families of origin of the black partners generally accepting but, when present, the children from a previous marriage were accepting of the white partner.

SUMMARY AND CONCLUSIONS

Black family members (more often than white families) were accepting of an interracial relationship but perhaps also more often indifferent and perhaps more often veiled in their opposition. The people who were interviewed spoke about racial-cultural militants in the families of some of the African American partners, and some militants were hostile to the white partner and opposed to the relationship. But close family members who were militant might still be accepting of the white partner and the relationship. How might the greater acceptance by members of black families be explained?

In many black families, mothers play the key role in accepting or not accepting an interracial relationship, much more than in white families. In white families, fathers were more often major players, as were siblings, grandparents, and other kin. Those differences may help to explain the greater acceptance of interracial relationships by black families. If women respond more often with openness and efforts to relate and less often with prejudice to the relationship choices of sons and daughters, then the fact that the crucial person in black families is most often a woman means there may be more acceptance of a family member's entry into an interracial couple. Also, with only one family member being the key to acceptance or rejection, opposition is less likely than when there are several family members in key roles. In white families, with so many more family members whose opinion could make a difference, it was more likely that someone would be opposed. If, for example, the chances are only one in three that someone might oppose an interracial relationship, if white families average five people whose reaction might count and black families average only one or two, the chances are much greater that opposition will appear in a white family.

The fact that the black partner in the couples studied was more often a man might also make a difference. Men in any group may be allowed more latitude by family members. Family members may feel less protective of men; men are more likely to be out of the house and launched; and families may have less concern about a man's entering difficult relationships because in American society if the relationship breaks up, it is the woman who typically has responsibility for children of the relationship.

Another source of the greater acceptance by black family members is that they may be more open about who gets counted as kin. Many black families have strong connections with people who are not literally relatives but who are counted as relatives. Illustrating the openness of black families, there were two accounts of a white woman partner being introduced as a family member's sister or daughter. That may partly reflect black usage of the terms *sister* and *daughter,* but it may also represent the greater openness in black families in who is counted as a sister or daughter.

Whatever the dynamics, there was less opposition from black than from white family members. The difference may reflect gender patterning in the couples interviewed or any of a number of other factors, but it also may say a great deal about the force of white racism in American society.

7

SOCIETAL RACISM

DISAPPROVAL
OF INTERRACIAL RELATIONSHIPS

Many Americans seem to consider interracial relationships taboo (Johnson & Warren, 1994; Mathabane & Mathabane, 1992, p. 10; Porterfield, 1982). Although survey data suggest that at least up to the early 1980s, there was more acceptance of interracial marriage among blacks than among whites, a majority of Americans up to the early 1980s disapproved of interracial marriage (Schuman et al., 1985, pp. 82-83, 144-146). Perhaps there is more acceptance now. There is certainly more than earlier in this century, when interracial marriage was illegal in many states, when an African American student in a predominantly white college might be asked to sign a pledge not to fraternize with white women students or a white woman dating a black man might be committed by her family to a psychiatric institution (Spickard, 1989, chap. 10). Many who were interviewed for this study said, however, that in their experience many people think interracial relationships are improper.

120

I know enough about interracial relationships to know that they are not socially condoned in America. (Gregory)

I think that, overall, people aren't really accepting of interracial relationships. And I think that my friends who are black and in black families have some prejudiced feelings against my family, but nothing that is really harmful. . . . You do have trouble being taken seriously sometimes because of the fact of being interracial . . . people having questions about your sexuality, and is that why you chose across racial lines. (Barb)

Of all the various couplings . . . the world at large likes this kind the least. . . . I've read some things that will take it back to the psychological reality of slave times, reactions to that, and they make sense to me, just that and enmity between black and white, that it's just so fierce; it's still so fierce, that it's the least comfortable alliance for the world at large. (Laura)

If I were to fantasize how the community thinks about us, I think that people see us together and, like if we go out . . . I notice sometimes people immediately look at my hand, and then they are horrified. They see the ring, and they, "Oh, my God. The worst I feared is there." (Patricia)

JAMES I . . . know that there are individuals who would not look upon this relationship as favorable. It's just a fact of life. . . .

JILL I still don't think it's acceptable in a lot of people's eyes. . . . I've been told, "It's OK that you do it, but I couldn't do that."

Along with disapproval comes a great deal of stereotyping and prejudice.

What the larger community thinks . . . I think they think, "Why, what is that about?" And a lot is . . . curiosity about it, a lot more curiosity based on stereotypes. . . . A stereotype is something that you don't really understand; it's a way to kind of characterize something, put in that pigeonhole. "Well, you married her because you think white women look better than black women." No, that's not the reason I married her. "Well, you married her because there's a mystique about interracial sex." No, that's not it either! (Gregory)

You don't fade into the background. For sure, people are always
aware of who you are. It's a continuum from people being thoroughly
disgusted and *assuming* that there has to be something deeply pathological, probably sexually pathological, and all of the stereotypes about
obviously this is a pimp-prostitute type relationship (laugh) or something like that. The other extreme is fascination, where somehow this
is a, although it's equally unreal, that somehow there's something very
exotic about our relationship, our family, and that somehow therefore
we must have the answers to all sorts of social questions. . . . The other
thing is that people often think that we are an exception because we
are educated, because we speak well. There's been numerous times
when people have made comments to indicate that they think Lorenzo
is not an American, that he must have grown up in Europe or some
other place. (Virginia is white)

What does it mean if an interracial couple receives poor service at
a restaurant? What does it mean if a neighbor snubs an interracial
couple? It is sometimes difficult to separate racism directed at the
African American partner from racism directed at the couple.
Frankenberg (1993, pp. 112-113) talked about antiblack racism
"rebounding" on a white partner, meaning that even though the
racism might be directed at the African American partner it retains
enough force to strike and hurt the white partner. There may also be
a number of versions of racism, some of which are directed primarily
at the black partner in a black-white interracial couple and some of
which are directed at the couple. When couples in the present study
were asked whether they had experienced discrimination, prejudice,
or racism as a couple, some seemed to find it easy to separate couple
experiences from the experiences of the African American partner.
But some saw the experiences as blended. For example, in response
to the African American interviewer's (Richard Powell) asking about
couple experiences, one black man said,

> Now, being an African American male and you being one, I know you
> face it every day. . . . We could really go by your experience, but mine
> will do. . . . Yeah, we face it every day. I mean, if it's not at the grocery
> store asking for nine different IDs. . . . It's just anything like that.
> (Houston)

For him there may not have been a clear line between his individual experiences and the couple experiences.

An interracial couple's experience of racism includes their awareness of racism directed at others.

> My girlfriend . . . that I grew up like the closest neighbor, she married a black man in a local church. . . . It was . . . the talk of the neighborhood. And I was staying with my parents that summer. So I kind of got to hear, too, some of the neighbors talking about it. . . . I was in the local tavern and heard the gossip. And one of the neighbors even said, "Well, how does she dare do that to her dad?" or "How could she do that to her parents and marry this black person?" And I was just sittin' there like, "Well, if they know about me." (Liz)

It can be even more unpleasant to hear gossip directed at oneself and one's own family.

> I was one of the few that would cross racial lines in terms of friendships and say, ". . . I like these people; I don't care what people are thinking about them being different or that's not the way to go; if I like somebody then I like them. And if their lifestyle is not what mainstream America deems as being OK, that's mainstream America's problem." Hey, that's easy to say! On the other hand, it still hurts when you hear people make comments about my family being different and that your kids are gonna have a real hard time. (Gregory)

A person in an interracial couple may also hear racist opposition in people's assertions of what they think is true about interracial couples. Consider the belief that interracial relationships are doomed to have serious problems.

> Everybody always tells me that interracial couples don't work. I always hear negative things. The children are mixed up. . . . So in that respect it *is* important to me that we . . . project a positive image for interracial couples. . . . The larger community, I still don't think that they accept it yet. But I think it's because they don't understand it basically. . . . I don't see the larger community as seeing us in a very positive way. I still don't think that people feel it's OK. I think a lot of people,

although they wouldn't say it to my face, . . . don't think it's right. (Eve)

Racist Incidents Were Infrequent

Despite the belief that there is a taboo on interracial relationships, most people said that they experienced only a few incidents in which racist acts or words were directed at them for being in an interracial relationship. This is a very important point. Although many people felt they were living in a society and a community in which there was considerable opposition to interracial couples, the number of incidents most people could recall was small.

> We've been real lucky, I mean, in 13 years we can probably count three instances of overt racism ever as a family. I mean, we've had just great experiences all the way through. (Ann)

> From my own experience, we've been treated well, really well. People surprise me sometimes. I will look at someone and think, "Oh, there's a redneck," and they turn out to be one of the most decent people. (Shirley)

> We don't get a lot of overt reactions in people, that I'm aware of, that question or that criticize. (Barb)

How can sense be made of the contrast between feeling that there is very substantial opposition to interracial couples and the experience of rather few incidents expressing such opposition? Perhaps the taboo against interracial relationships is not widely shared. Perhaps these couples are good at protecting themselves (see Chapter 9) from situations in which they would be targets of racism.

Even if people recalled only few experiences of racism directed at them as an interracial couple, some of the incidents were extremely hurtful or frightening. It would be an enormous mistake to equate reports of a small number of incidents with a benign social environment. People may have considerable evidence that tells them that there is disapproval of their relationship, even if they experience only a few overt incidents. Incidents of overt racism may represent an unpleasantly distinct edge to a vastly larger, if less easily confronted, mass of hostility toward interracial relationships.

Counting incidents and assuming that life is easy and stress free when people in interracial couples report only a few racist incidents may be a mistake in another way. Even a single incident in a person's lifetime may have serious consequences. It may take only one incident to make a couple cautious about every venture outside the home, to make every journey away from home tense, and to put a couple on the defensive everywhere they go. Here is the joking but macabre analogy suggested by one woman, after she had told of several unpleasant incidents:

> So other than that I guess we haven't had so much (laughing). "Other than that, Mrs. Lincoln, how was the play?" (Dot)

It is important to note that most incidents were remembered in vivid detail. That is evidence that those incidents are not to be dismissed lightly. People recalled the details because the situations were frighteningly or painfully memorable, an important piece of information for them about their social world. After an incident remembered in such detail, a person might always be on the defensive to avoid or ward off further incidents, always be on the alert for possible dangers, and constantly investing psychic energy in trying not to be affected by further difficulties or the possibility of such difficulties. We think it is important to describe the situations couples reported. Most if not all of the couples seemed to be living an upbeat and ordinary life, but the incidents they reported occurred in enough different settings and relationships that one can easily believe those who were interviewed who said that opposition to interracial couples is widespread. In what follows, the incidents reported are divided into casual encounters in public, racism on the job, threatening attacks, institutional racism, and reactions in the black community.

CASUAL ENCOUNTERS IN PUBLIC

Store Clerks and People Who Wait on Tables

Some people had experiences in stores and restaurants that meant to them that an interracial couple was unwelcome.

BAYARD One time we were in Rochester, and we went into this little corner restaurant, and we sat there for 25, 30 minutes, didn't even get a cup of water, I don't think.

ANN And they weren't even busy. It was right by the Mayo Clinic. I mean, this was right downtown.

BAYARD I mean, there was hardly anybody else in there. The waitress talked to one of her friends or something. She wasn't doing anything.

ANN I couldn't believe it.

BAYARD And we just got up and left.

When I first moved down here, . . . I used to wait for the bus at a PDQ and used to wait sometimes inside. And there was a [clerk] there that was very friendly toward me, "Hi, how are you?" and chat, chat, chat. And then one day, this went on for, you know, weeks, months, whatever. One day, Shane waited for the bus with me, and things changed after that. The guy was, "You can't wait in here anymore." (Shirley is white)

WANDA Like getting put by the kitchen. [A white male friend] and I went into Ciatti's downtown, and the hostess put us by the kitchen, and the restaurant was completely empty, and that from my point of view was an act of racism. . . .

ADAM (laughs) Yeah, you always speculate. You're left to speculate. What was that?

This hasn't happened for years because we don't do bar things anymore, but I remember when we were a lot younger, there were certain clubs downtown where either interracial couples or black couples . . . used to be required to have three . . . picture IDs. (Christine)

MANNING When we're at a department store, this has happened a million times probably, I'm over in one end of the store, and she's over [at] another end. . . . The salesperson . . . might be African American or Indian or whatever. . . . We come together as a couple to purchase something. The expression, the body language that we get is a tipoff that this shouldn't be the way it is, but it is, and it's different. So I guess in the perception of the individuals . . . they're uncomfortable with it. That's happened a million times, so I couldn't isolate one specific instance, other than to say that right now I really couldn't care less how they feel about that situation, or the surprise in the situation is kind of funny. . . . It doesn't irk me. . . .

CHRISTINE If it mattered at all at first, it mattered because we met with so much disapproval. I wouldn't describe it the way he does. I don't think it was quite that people thought it was different or funny. I just thought it was that they thought it was dumb or immoral. . . . And then I guess after the . . . novelty of that wore off, I went through a long period where I guess I was pretty blasé about whether it mattered or not. It didn't hurt too much.

Christine also talked about some of the times she and Manning were treated as an implausible couple.

CHRISTINE Every time we're in a grocery line together or a Target line, and, like, we'll be touching or talking . . . I don't think most strangers act like that. They're always like trying to separate our goods. . . .

INTERVIEWER As if you're not together.

CHRISTINE Yeah, yeah, it's like that happens a lot.

Some couples had an opposite experience, being perhaps better treated because they were in an interracial couple. That does not deny the reality of a taboo on interracial couples. Instead, it implies that some people go out of their way to communicate that they do not share the taboo by being supportive of interracial couples.

LORENZO We've had a lot of really good experiences with people [when we were] traveling. . . .

VIRGINIA Yeah, it really just comes back to people trying to make up probably for what they expect we're experiencing. I remember one time when we were in . . . Georgia, and a waitress coming, very clearly coming over to wait on us first (laugh). She was going to make sure that we knew that we were welcome and that she was going to do it. . . . That kind of stuff has happened far more than the negative stuff, which has happened too. . . . I think . . . [there] is a real concern about how we are being treated as individuals and concern that we understand that their whole community is not racist.

Motels

Although several couples talked about being careful in their choice of motels, only one couple talked about being turned away from a motel.

JOYCE We were traveling in Canada, and I went in to . . . get the room for the night; fine. Went back out to the car and the person in the motel looked out the door, kinda came back in and said sorry, you can't stay here. . . . We left. . . . I was just kind of in shock.

GREGORY . . . We were like a thousand miles from home and you're tired, you're pissed and you're tired; I'm gettin' out. I know if I go in there I'll just say some things that I don't want to say. So we say, "OK, let's go to another motel." . . . It still hurts. [But] there's only so many battles that you can fight like that. (Joyce is white; Gregory is black)

Words and Gestures From Strangers in Public

Another unpleasant, sometimes frightening, expression of opposition directed at interracial couples occurs when a stranger communicates hostility or disapproval. The majority of the couples had had such experiences.

We were in Sausalito a couple of years ago. . . . We were walking down the street, just sight-seeing, and doing what tourists do. And this guy's coming up the street, and . . . as he approached us, he kind of said under his breath, "White girl, wake up." (Henry)

One time we went on a vacation in South Dakota, to this cabin, and we were walking down the road, and this big semi comes pulling by. . . . Initially, I thought the guy was waving at us, and I started bringing my hand up but when he went by he was giving us the finger, and the truck just drove on. (Bayard)

I can count on one hand, in fact, we've had so few incidents. And like I said, none of them have been threatening. But [to Shane] you've been called "nigger" a few times when we're together, like in Taylors Falls, that guy that drove by screamed. . . . People think they can do anything when they're in a car. They can drive away. . . . The stares, the insults, whatever that I've gotten, or we've gotten, have always come from young white men. We've never been screamed at by white women, black women, old people. Always been about 20 to 30, rednecks that are threatened by us. . . . They come from their own little worlds. (Shirley)

One night we were driving . . . and these guys pulled up to us and said, "Hey, zebras. Hey, there's a zebra family." (Patricia)

EMMETT We were driving around looking for houses. So we would spend evenings just going through neighborhoods, trying to learn about neighborhoods, and we passed this truck about three times, and he realized that we were looking at the neighborhood, and he yelled something out.

NORA . . . We passed them as we . . . entered into the Seward neighborhood. . . . They were coming this way. It was Memorial Day. I don't know whether they were juiced up, looking for trouble, or what, but this one guy looked at us and was pounding the dashboard; you could hear, I mean, sometimes you can almost guess what they're saying to each other, and you know . . . the tone of what it is. So we were kind of driving back and forth looking for "For Sale" signs . . . and then we ran into them again. And I don't know whether they had been following us . . . , but this guy slowed down as he approached us and yelled . . . , "What are you doing here?" or something to that effect. . . . This was the first time that I really felt that kind of chilling feeling of, "These guys are scary; these guys are icky; they're creepy; I don't want to ever have to deal with them again."

EMMETT And we ruled out the neighborhood for that experience.

NORA . . . I would not live in that neighborhood because of that. Part of me says, "Yeah, but I want to move right next door to them," you know. I want to own them, put it in their faces in a way, but yet, you don't want to have hassles in your life. And I can understand how people have left neighborhoods

for the sake of protecting their children or themselves because of people like that.

We were leaving Target . . . and two young white pinheads in a car
backed up right in front of us out of the parking lot like they were
trying to run somebody over. As they pulled away, they yelled to Jill,
"Get a white man!" You know you say, "Well, they're ignorant.
They're foolish," or whatever, but it sticks in your head. Why, what
did you do to provoke this? By your mere presence you provoked this
anger. (James)

FLORA When we first came here, we didn't know where we were
going, and we were on a bus.

TIM And I can't remember what they said, but something like she
was a hooker and I was a john. (Flora is black; Tim is white)

ADAM Going to the grocery store and getting the looks. . . .

WANDA Having some guy come up to you and saying, "(tsk) Well, I
just want to congratulate you" (laugh).

ADAM Yeah, wanted to congratulate us for standing in the grocery
store line. . . .

WANDA We were in Boston, and we were walking around the pier
and had [our child] with us, and [the child] was sort of
swinging between the two of us, and [we] got remarks from
these young black males who were very young and sort of
questioning why I was with him. (Adam is white; Wanda is
black)

Probably the most intense thing that happened to me was not when
Lorenzo was around. . . . I was with his mother. And we had the children in the car, and my mother-in-law was driving. . . . She had pulled
into a . . . parking lot, and it was pouring rain. And there was a car
next to us with a white guy and his wife, in their mid-20s maybe. And
the guy hopped out of the car and was extremely angry and yelling,
and I thought he was yelling at his wife, who was driving—that there
was some problem there. It was at a shopping center . . . , and I got
out of the car to get the kids out, and when I got out of the car, I understood that he was yelling at me and not at his wife. And I mean,
this was incredibly vicious stuff. It was sexual and racist and just incred-

ibly vicious. And it was raining so hard the kids couldn't hear what
was going on, which was (laugh) a good deal, but my mother-in-law
was getting out of the car, and she heard what was going on. And we
just kind of both looked at [him], and I just bit my tongue because I
was intensely angry, but I was afraid of letting loose . . . because my
mother-in-law is very quiet and genteel . . . , and I just wouldn't use
the kind of language that I would've around her (laugh). My concern
for not getting her upset kept my temper in control, and we just got the
kids out of the car and into the shopping center, but it was extremely
intense and we were both really upset. . . . It was . . . extremely
vicious. That was probably the single most intense thing that I have
experienced. (Virginia is white)

Stares

In questionnaires mailed to couples in the Twin City metropolitan
area, Welborn (1994, pp. 91-92, 109) found that 64% of black-white
interracial couples reported experiencing some sort of negative public reaction, in contrast to 4% of African American couples and 7%
of European American couples. The primary negative reaction reported by the interracial couples in the Welborn study was hostile
stares. In studying interracial couples in four different urban areas,
Porterfield (1978, p. 101) also heard many accounts of stares. As in
the Welborn and Porterfield studies, quite a few people in the present
study mentioned being stared at by strangers. Some experienced
stares as benign expressions of curiosity or of reaction to novelty.

ANNE People are intrigued a lot.

BAYARD They are intrigued a lot, ask a lot of questions, especially
when they see . . .

ANNE Stare at the kids.

BAYARD Stare at the kids, like when they see me with [our older
daughter], as light as she is, they wonder what is going on.
Even if they see me and [our younger daughter] together,
they'll wonder. (Anne is white; Bayard is black)

There are stares certainly, but I don't find them threatening at all. I
think they just—sometimes they are just curious. (Shirley)

People who do work for you on your house, or people who sell you things and have to come into your household will look for a while—they'll look a little bit startled. (Roger)

Sometimes in restaurants, people just staring. . . . There really hasn't been any . . . kind of racially harmful things; it's been more just people's sort of awkwardness of staring, not quite knowing how to react. (Joyce)

More people experienced at least some stares as intrusive and perhaps an expression of hostility.

ED I think when we were out riding in the car that that's when I'm my most sensitive, or I get into a paranoid, eggshell type feeling of when I'm driving and I see other people looking at us who don't know us, and that makes me a little angry, the way they look. . . .

ROSEMARY I can remember one time, it was several years ago, and there was . . . [this couple]. They both, like, turned their heads and were just staring at us. And I was ready to go through the window. I just thought, "Ach! I do not appreciate being stared at by anyone." And . . . it was, like, "Why are they staring?" . . . I think most people are really fascinated by [us]. I really think we're kind of like this novelty to them.

EVE [Race] is always at the foremost in their minds. That's what they see when they look at us. Sometimes, they can't see past that. . . .

HOUSTON One thing we noticed, in the black neighborhood, she is very well, she's accepted by black people, but in the white neighborhood we are accepted, but we are watched more. . . . It's really kind of hard . . . in a white neighborhood, at least, for us both to be accepted.

WILSON The thing that I've really gotten a charge out of the past few years is like on a Sunday morning, like today, there's a nice sunny Sunday morning and [I] could be in the front yard maybe fooling around with the flowers or the lawn, and I just see these cars coming down the street, and I assume these people are going to their place of worship, and to see some of the looks. . . . I said, "Oh, my gosh. We spoiled these people's religious day" (laughs). I don't see how in the world they're going to go to church and . . . have any kind of spiritual relation with anything. . . . But the people in the neighborhood that I know of, personal basis . . . I think they're fascinated; I think they're surprised.

DOT Except of course for Mr. _____ (laughs). . . . He just hates us, absolutely hates us. . . . He just stands out there and almost throws up. (Wilson is black; Dot is white)

When we first started dating and going shopping and people were staring at us, and never being in an interracial relationship before, I was, like, "Is my shirt buttoned? Is my pants buttoned?" I mean, I didn't view it as . . . color, but it changes. You learn that that's what the looks are. And it's sad. I was naive; I didn't know to expect that as a part of the relationship with someone. (Jill is white)

Stares may be more common in places where interracial couples are less common.

GARY In New York, there were so many interracial couples around that it was a novelty for us. We just couldn't believe it. Every day . . . when we come home we'd talk about the number that we had seen and how it wasn't something people stared at in New York. And that was because when we were dating, it was at [an isolated military base], it was real different there. There was never a situation where somebody didn't stop and some way notice that we were an interracial couple. . . .

PATRICIA [A town in Oklahoma], I'll never forget. The small little town, we stopped to get some ice cream. It wasn't malicious or anything, but the *whole town* stopped. . . . It was like all of a sudden somebody froze them.

NORA Going into certain places, let's say restaurants . . . , heads turn. In small towns, you know, people kind of wonder. And a lot of it is just the attitudes of, "Black people should stay where they belong, and if you're a white girl and you're with a black man you're a slut or a whore." . . .

EMMETT I'm on the road a lot. And it's very interesting to be in other
    towns, where I [stand] out because I'm with Nora and watch
    people's reactions to interracial couples. It's . . . that staring
    of, "I don't understand this. What is going on here?"

Stares are open to interpretation. One person may interpret a stare
as communicating disdain, hostility, or shock that anyone would
violate the taboo against interracial partnership, whereas another
person might interpret the same stare as communicating curiosity or
supportive fascination (Porterfield, 1978, p. 130).

I find it intriguing when we go into restaurants, and they look at me.
. . . [Do people] look at me because I'm different; look at me because
generally they don't like me with a white woman; or look at me to say,
"There's another white trash married a nigger"? (Robert)

I think for some people we're a curiosity. They don't quite understand
it, but yet there's not really a sense of disagreeing with anything. It's
just that they . . . have no experience, and I think there's a lot of that.
. . . Initially, I [thought] . . . , "They're thinking we're wrong. . . ." And
over the years, I've realized that some of those people are also in interracial relationships (laughs), and they're watching to see what you're
doing. . . . Others . . . are just amazed that you're willing to . . . be different. Others truly think it's wrong. I can't say that as a rule that we
run into lots of those people, probably a handful in our lives that I can
recall . . . that have expressed it. . . . There are others that I'm sure totally disagree with it and try to ignore it and pretend we're not there.
But I think because there is a diversity of opinions, some people try to
be supportive. . . . [Maybe] it's this sort of real liberal sense of, "Well,
we should support these people, . . ." politically correct supportive
(laughs). What's really interesting is I've run into a lot of grand[moth-
ers] who ask questions. . . . But even when people . . . go out of their
way . . . to tell you that they have somebody in their family, . . . you
still don't know whether . . . they disagree or agree with that being a
part of their family. But there's something about your existence that
makes them feel somehow attracted and willing to open up and ask
those questions. (Wanda)

Some people said that they had started out annoyed with the stares
but then decided the stares could be shrugged off.

We still get stared at. . . . I may have reacted to people looking . . . in earlier years. I do less of that. I'm less concerned with it. (Flora)

OLIVIA If they don't like it, they don't have to look at us (she laughs). . . . I just finally decided that whether Isaac was black or white, he was the person I enjoyed being with, and therefore it didn't matter. . . .

ISAAC People always look . . . , "Geez, these go together." But it's like I told you, "Hey, that's their own problem." See, I have my own problems to take care of, but if you don't feel comfortable with me walking along the street with somebody of another race, you've got a problem. . . . It doesn't really bother me.

Some people had experiences that suggested to them that underlying curious stares there is sometimes a fascination that can lead to good things for an interracial couple.

VIRGINIA Most of the time when we've traveled in areas that other people are concerned about, . . . we've had wonderful experiences. . . . We were . . . on one of the Sea Islands of Georgia once when one of the young rangers took an interest in our family and like gave us a private tour of the island and it was . . . very positive, and that kind of stuff happens all the time.

LORENZO Other interracial families that we know have had the same experience where interesting folks who we would want to go out of our way to meet anyway will come over and strike up a conversation because they find us the most interesting people . . . on the boat or on the train or on the bus.

Lorenzo went on to differentiate friendly stares from more negative and intrusive stares in terms of whether the person staring strikes up a conversation.

People who are curious in a petty and potentially pesky way don't usually start up a conversation. They just stare . . . , and you really don't have to deal with them. They also tend to be quite embarrassed about staring, if you look back. It's just for the most part those people. Purely curious people are not a problem.

Stares are part of the environment of interracial couples. Stares can be ambiguous. They may represent hatred, curiosity, fascination, support, an interest in something that has nothing to do with race or other things. But there are enough signs of hostility, outrage, and opposition directed at interracial couples for it to be quite believable that some of the staring directed at interracial couples represents strongly negative feelings.

RACISM IN THE WORKPLACE

In contrast to the brief encounters involving stares, being at one's place of work involves repeated encounters with coworkers. One may never again see a person who stared in a shopping mall. But the people at work may be in one's daily life for years. Racism in the workplace can be especially burdensome because work can be a constant and important part of one's life. One woman talked about defending against racism at work.

> In the jobs that I've had, I would say it takes 4 months before they know that my husband is black. I would say that's about right, because I want to test people first. I want to find out what they are all about, and if they say something stupid before they know I have a black husband, I'll keep away from them. Like there is a guy I work with does not know I have a black husband, and he is a redneck. . . . He was talking about Detroit and all those "spear chuckers" and da, da, da, and I left the room. . . . I decided . . . not to confront him. I would have liked to, but I don't feel like having educated him, and I don't work directly with him anyway, so I will just greet him in the hall and that's it. We don't need to have any conversation . . . , because everyone else in the company knows . . . that my husband is black, and no big deal to them, but this guy doesn't need to know. (Shirley)

Racism directed toward interracial couples may show up at the time of a job interview.

> Shortly after we were married, I got a job offer in Duluth, and this was just kind of surprising to me because it was some of the earliest comments I guess that I had gotten. . . . As it turned out, . . . Nixon . . . cut

off all the funds for new programs . . . , and the job fell through. But I remember going on an interview up there, and their biggest concern was that I understand that Duluth was not Minneapolis and all sorts of dire kind of warnings and, you know, benevolent concern about what it would be like to be an interracial couple [there]. And these were *all* white people who probably had no idea what it would be like. But I remember finding that just kind of mildly offensive, because it was very patronizing kind of stuff. (Virginia is white)

Some of the racism experienced at work was momentary, a single interaction that indicated that somebody lumps one's interracial relationship into a category.

JILL   When I first started at work, I had a picture of James on my desk and (pause) I can't remember the exact wording but a girl came up to me and her wording was . . .

JAMES   Wasn't that the one that said, "Oh, you're in one of those relationships?"

JILL   Yeah, . . . and I just started there. I didn't know who that person was. She just kinda like hopped into my cube. (Jill is white; James is black)

Such a brief comment may be shrugged off, but it may also be a haunting presence in all dealings with the person who made the remark and in all one's days on the job.

Sometimes the racism experienced on the job was covert, with evidence that coworkers would say racist things to one if they did not know one was in an interracial relationship.

I think there is a sensitivity in this community that people know better than to be openly racist, most people. So a lot of stuff that goes on behind your back, you can never find out. It is interesting to hear Nora talk about some of the humor that she gets in the workplace, you know, very specifically racially oriented jokes until they find out that she's married to me. And then suddenly those are out of place. Well, that lets you know that in any other situation they would be very open about it. And in fact she's expressed feelings, and I think she's directly confronted people with it of, "Why do you think because I'm white that I would want to take part in this just automatically?" (Emmett is black)

One can also experience a categorizing from people who want to show that they are liberal about racial matters. Such categorizing can be taken as well-intentioned, but it also can be taken as a form of racism, of condensing one's identity down to being a member of an interracial couple.

> One of [my bosses] who I introduced to Lorenzo just casually because Lorenzo was dropping me off at work, and since then, he's down in my office a couple of times talking about broad (laughs) social policy that has to do with race. And I'm certain that that's why he's down there. . . . He's not asking me questions, and I'm not even certain that he wants to hear my responses. It's more that he wants to let me know that he is concerned. . . . I give it a very benign thing because I like him, and I think largely what he's saying is true. . . . I think he's exaggerating his concern in this really mystic kind of expansive [way], but I know that he would not be down there talking about those particular issues if he had not met Lorenzo. (Virginia is white)

ATTACKS

Hate Phone Calls and Hate Mail

Some people reported receiving very nasty and threatening anonymous phone calls or letters. There is no question of interpretation when people receive such messages.

> Somebody called and called me a nigger lover. So somebody out there doesn't like that. . . . I just decided not to be intimidated by it. Hang up rather than try to figure out who it is. (Liz)

GREGORY The guy that wrote the letters. I can't think of his name. . . . He had sent letters to a lot of interracial families, and we got a letter, must have been, what? 10, 11 years ago, 'cause we were on this panel. About 10 or 11 years ago, Minneapolis had a conference on interracial families and interracial relationships, remember? . . . At the old Radisson downtown. And I did a presentation there, . . . and we must have been interviewed by the paper, and anyway, this clown sent out letters to whole bunches of people. And we got a letter from him. And it was Xeroxed, and I think we ended up throwing it away, 'cause Joyce looked at it, and I looked at it, and I said, "Well, this is just stupid stuff. I'm not gonna keep it. I'm not gonna read it any further than I have." . . .

JOYCE . . . It was scary too, because it was so, it was like newspaper clippings put together; it felt like, "Who is this crazy person, and how does he know us?" I mean, it was like we didn't know where he got names.

INTERVIEWER Assuming that it matters to the larger community that you're an interracial couple, what do you think that community thinks of you or about you?

EMMETT Well, from my Elroy Stock file? (laughs) . . . There are the level of people like the Elroy Stocks and indeed I do have a file of things I have gotten from dear Elroy . . . , because . . . my name is in the paper. Your name is in the paper, and he sends you stuff. (Emmett) [Elroy Stock sent hate mail to hundreds of interracial couples in Minnesota.]

Hate Literature

One woman talked about hate literature she received from people who did not know she was in an interracial couple.

HOUSTON They didn't know she was married to a black man. . . . They gave her this pamphlet and it was in regard to interracial marriages. . . . They're like saying that interracial marriages are not biblical. . . .

EVE And they put on the picture in the front a black man and a white woman, of course. As if white men and black women are never together. And they called the children of mixed marriages mongrels. . . . They say that they are Christians. . . . This was at the Minnesota State Fair just last year. And I really feel bad about it. . . .

HOUSTON They were just passing these out to anyone and everyone. . . . That's right here in Minnesota. Don't let anyone tell you, "Oh, it doesn't happen up here; we're very liberal."

Physical Threats and Attacks

At the extreme were incidents in which physical threats were made or in which physical attack actually occurred.

INTERVIEWER Have you as a couple had experiences of prejudice, discrimination, or racism, and if so, what kind of things have you experienced and how have you responded?

VIRGINIA (small laugh) Yeah, we've had a few. Actually not as many as people would think. . . . They stand out because they've been unusual. . . . One time we almost got run off the road, remember, when we were driving?

LORENZO That's right. That was in Tennessee.

VIRGINIA The kids were asleep.

LORENZO We did get run off the road. . . . We just didn't go into a ditch.

I had an experience when I was with Gregory's mother, in St. Louis, we went to a, like, a Goodwill, . . . and somebody threw a basketball at me, and I didn't know where it came from. But it felt like it was somebody [not liking] me being there. . . . It just came out of nowhere; it felt pretty awful. (Joyce)

INSTITUTIONAL RACISM

Institutional racism is racism that is supported overtly or covertly by a substantial institution: a business, a labor union, the government, or a university. When one experiences racism in interaction with a person who represents an institution, one cannot tell whether the racism is idiosyncratic to that person or expresses a pattern that is supported by the institution. Diagnosing institutional racism requires data across representatives and situations. There are such data in the United States and in Minnesota for a number of institutions. In the news at the time of the interviews were reports of institutional racism in real estate sales and rental, in mortgage lending, in hiring by firms and public agencies, in the surveillance practices of the plainclothes security guards of a Twin Cities department store, in the actions of local police departments, and in the courts. This is not a study of institutional racism, but some people reported what they thought was institutional racism, and some experiences of racism (e.g., with the police) were reported so commonly that it is easy to believe that there was a pattern of institutional racism.

Institutional Racism in the Real Estate Business

Perhaps because of changes in laws or in public attitudes or because the Twin Cities are different from the communities in which Porterfield (1978) interviewed, fewer people in the present study reported difficulty obtaining housing than was the case in Porterfield's (chap. 5) interviews with interracial couples in four midwestern and southern communities. Nonetheless, two couples in the present study described experiences of racism in real estate purchase or rental.

> When we purchased this house . . . , we were at the closing. . . . I had gone to the bank prior to the closing . . . to pick up the check. . . . It was a bank draft. It was not a . . . personal check. It was not a certified check. But it was a bank draft. . . . So . . . we get to the part where they ask you for the money in order to continue the process of closing the deal. So I pull out this check and give it to this individual. They look at me, knowing good and well that when we got there this was an obvious interracial couple. . . . And this woman says, "Now you have to have cash or cashier's check." And I said . . . that "this check is as good as the paper it's written on. It's not a personal check, and [if] you're not going to accept it here at the closing, I will walk out this door." That, to me, was some indication of very institutional racism issues. I don't think they would have asked a white guy (laughs) about a cashier's check when this check was just as good as a cashier's check. It's printed on a bank statement. Obviously, there had to be money in the bank. A bank is not going to issue a check if there's not any money there. So that really kind of pissed me off. . . . I started to walk out. When I said that, everybody pulled back and started this nice patronism BS. . . . When I said, "You don't want to take this check; bye, let's go," immediately, they jumped up. [The sellers] even saw the racism in that closer. (Manning)

EVE We used to live . . . in [a suburb]. . . . We lived in the first
building, the one closest to the road. And there was a building

behind us. . . . The second building behind us was real quiet, and everyone [who] kind of looked like us . . . [was in the first building]. Everybody in the front building that we lived in was either . . .

HOUSTON Chinese (laughs).

EVE Hmong, black, interracial, or like . . .

INTERVIEWER Minority groups.

EVE Yeah. I felt like they had put all the misfits and . . . like the . . . younger kids . . . in there. We were all thrown into one building, and this second building was like a whole different world. This is all the same apartment complex, but the second building was the older, working class, quiet types. . . . That really bothered me, that they . . . separated us there, 'cause all of our neighbors were Hmong or . . .

HOUSTON young partiers. And maybe that was good for them. I don't have no problem with that. Maybe that was good for other people [who] were quieter. . . .

EVE But that means they were really looking at our application, and really looking at what we were when we stepped into that office, 'cause it was where we were put.

Institutional Racism on Government Forms

Governments at all levels seek to categorize people by race, sometimes because there is an interest in determining whether people of different races are being fairly treated. Some people resent the categorization, because it can be understood to accept a reality based on racist thinking. For them, governments that make racial categorizing important or that boil down the complexities of a person's background and identity to a simple category that is laden with racist overtones can seem to accept a racist view of the world. It is no surprise then that some people choose not to categorize themselves racially on a marriage license application (Welborn, 1994, p. 67) or census form.

Even for those who are willing to categorize themselves, the categories the government provides are so out of touch with how people define themselves that they can be experienced as racist. If people's own realities and the complexities of their identity and experience counted with the legislators and civil servants who create the forms, there would be either no request for categorization or a much more complicated set of alternatives than is usually provided (see "Federal Government Is Urged to Rethink," 1994, p. A9). Particularly for interracial couples, the message on government forms that a couple is either black or white is a denial of their own experience. Similarly, the absence of categories that fit the identity of a person whose parents were not of the same race is a racist (or at least an insensitive) denial of the reality of an interracial couple (see Kouri, 1994, for one mother's struggle over how her children would be identified on birth certificates).

Why does the Equal Opportunity Statement that we're working on not have a place where you can check off more than one race? Why do you have to choose on those kinds of issues? (Adam)

Then there's the institutional stuff. There's the fact that the Census doesn't allow for you to put down that your child is of more than one culture or whatever. Those are probably the things that anger me the most. . . . That even goes to schools, and that's why I try to be involved in schools. . . . There are lots of kids out there who are aware of interracial couples, . . . have friends or have parents or have whatever at some level, and yet within the school, that's not something that's put out there. (Wanda)

Institutional Racism at Church

One couple experienced a rejection from a specific person in a church setting, but the church experience that seemed most to involve institutional racism was when a preacher publicly interpreted scriptural passages as expressing divine opposition to interracial relationships.

It was at church. They were talking about once again the big question, which is blacks and whites and marry. And they always try to use that verse, that you shouldn't be on an unequal yoke. (Eve)

That more couples did not report experiences at church that might represent institutional racism may be a result of the efforts of many of the couples to find a church that welcomes interracial couples.

When we got married we were looking for a culturally diverse environment in a church setting. . . . We have a multiracial church. . . . What attracted me to that church, the congregation is very warm, they are multiracial. We feel like we want to bring our kids up in an environment that don't speak to one or the other, but an environment that speak to the whole. (Robert)

The Police

The police are in many ways the most visible representative of government. The reactions of police can be taken as a representation of opinions shared by many influential people in and out of government. The opinions may be that people of color need to be controlled, that interracial couples are potentially a problem, or perhaps (the racism of neglect) that interracial couples and people of color are not important enough for police chiefs, city council members, state legislators, newspaper editors, and business leaders to exert much effort to see that they are treated with the same care, politeness, and application of laws as white couples.

Seven couples talked about experiencing racism from police, and the police forces involved represent a number of different communities.

CHRISTINE We lived in south Minneapolis until we moved here, and we had started to be stopped, just kind of like . . . driving . . . you know, Saturday morning; we're dressed casually, we get in the car, we are going to drive to the lakes to go for a walk. And we get stopped for no reason.

MANNING You're talking about being stopped by police officers?

CHRISTINE Yeah. And the funny part about being out here [in the suburbs] is like I don't think that will happen, and that's a benefit, is that there are so few African American males that I think they know who they are and where they live and so, I mean, that's kind of a bizarre advantage . . . here, but in south Minneapolis everything has gotten so tense, and everybody was suspect, and we lived in the Powderhorn neighborhood, and so for us, we driving around in nice cars . . . it was suspicious to people. So I was not liking that feeling. That kind of stuff really makes me angry or really hurts me.

Christine talked about similar experiences with the Wisconsin Highway Patrol.

When we first got married, he was in [a town in] Wisconsin. And I lived here, and I had started working, and I had a car, and so if we were going to be together on the weekend I would drive over after work on Friday, and we'd drive back together. And we got stopped for speeding. . . . And we would get tickets for, like, 3 miles over [the speed limit]. . . . At the time, it was angering and frustrating, but . . . because I don't want to be looking for racism in every situation I thought . . . "It's those wackos in Wisconsin. They're just out to make money." But then I remember a few years later . . . he's in school. I'm just starting my first job. Then we had to get high-risk insurance, and I mean, you know what that does to your budget. So we had to pay that, for several years, but then . . . there was an article in the paper about how, in fact, the Hudson [Wisconsin] police had finally been repri- manded for stopping either African Americans or mixed couples at an incredible rate. (Christine)

One time . . . we stopped in this really small village . . . where my mother's buried. And we went into the cemetery, and the . . . people next to the church called the police immediately. And we weren't do- ing anything. And it was because Ed was, I'm assuming it was because Ed is black. So, yeah, there are situations, and I was absolutely—I have never been so angry in my life. (Rosemary)

DOT Police pulled us over. I was driving, got out. Him and [my stepson] had to put their hands up, and I had to show my license and [the officer] said [we] could go. Now I have had enough experience . . . with the police that I didn't even question that man. We came home, and I called the . . . police station. And I said, "You know, you have to understand that a certain amount of humiliation was suffered here. At least two neighbors drove by and looking at the [name] family with their hands on top of their head." And the man said, "Well," he said, "the thing is there has . . . been a rash of stolen checks cashed and," he said, "it is a black man and a white woman in a navy blue Cadillac or Lincoln. . . ." And I said, "Well, we were a black man, a white woman, a black boy in a black Oldsmobile. And I understand the police have

to do their job. I want them to do some soul-searching too."
But we looked suspicious, and the thing that identified us as
suspicious was once they heard that it was an interracial
couple driving around with these checks, it really didn't
matter if it was Oldsmobile or Pinto. . . . [Another] time, we
were stopped by the police. They took us in separate cars,
put a gun to my head. . . . I was subjected to many, many,
many horrible remarks on the way downtown. . . . When
deciding which car to put me in, they used the "N" word
repeatedly. . . . Then on the way down there, they just said
horrible, icky, ugly things about our [being] interracial. . . .
[They were] looking for drugs. And they didn't find anything,
of course, but at any rate, you had to come home by some
other method. In a police car or . . .

WILSON They lost the keys. They towed the car, and then they took
the keys, and then they couldn't find the keys, of course, so
we had to go home and get another set of keys.

DOT So you came home, and at any rate, we were separated again.
Wilson came home, and then the man who had been nice to
me, which then later I realized that was a game, you know—
the uniformed policemen was quite mean—and then they sat
me down with this man who was just in regular clothes, and
he was very, very nice to me. And the idea, I think, is by then
you're so grateful for a kind word you tell it all. I had nothing
to tell. At any rate, the nice guy was bringing me home. And
I said to him . . . , "I understand the guns being out. I
understand if they really had, assuming that they're sincere
in their belief that we were involved in a robbery, then I
understand them taking us to the police station. I understand
the guns out. I even understand the gun at close range,
although touching my head with it was pretty tough." I said,
"I know the police have a job to do. I understand all that. I
understand maybe some not quite polite remarks on their
part because maybe that's the way they're supposed to do it.
But," I said, "I don't understand . . . all the horrible names
and . . . I don't understand being made to fear. I want you to
tell me why that occurred." And he said, "Police deal in
deployment of society all day long, all week long." . . . He
attempted to justify that. And I don't know if it would have
been different if I had been a white woman with a white . . .

I don't, but I know that I was treated as though I was not warranted of any kind of respect. . . . I was treated like I was nothing. And I don't know if that would make a difference or not. I think it would have been different.

JILL Tell them about the DWB.

JAMES Oh (laugh), that.

JILL We call it, "Driving While Black." We have a . . . nice car. So we got pulled over for a DWB. . . .

JAMES We were coming back from Lake Harriet, where we like to just go and walk and talk or. . . . And I think Jill was about . . . 7 or 8 months pregnant. Anyway, we have the top off the car, and we're driving down Plymouth Avenue because it's pretty much the fastest way to get back. . . . Well, I see a cop in the same lane we *were* in, and he's coming along rather fast, and I think, "Well, I have a feeling he's coming for me." . . . We get to the light, turn on the signal, make the turn, here comes the cop, turning from the wrong lane. Now I *know* he's coming for me. So I pull over and pull onto a side street and here he comes. He says, "Are you in a hurry?" . . . And he took my license and registration. He goes back to his car, and he comes back and says, "You didn't use your signal when you turned." . . . I say, "Yes, I did. I always use my signal." What did he say, that I, am I calling him a liar or something like that? . . . I said, "I'm just kinda confused about the whole setup." And he said, "Well, do you move around a lot?" I said, "No, I've been in the same location for I believe the last, oh, 7 years." And he said, "Well, we have three warrants for your arrest."

JILL Which you know is a lie. The law is that if there was, they would have had him out of the car, cuffs on, and in the back. And it's a straight out lie. You know it's just harassment. . . .

JAMES And I had listened to the police radio when the policeman called in my license, and I heard the dispatcher say "No warrants, no warrants." So I told him he was wrong!

JILL . . . They told him, "If you want to discuss it, we'll take you downtown now."

JAMES It's a Friday night. If you go downtown and you're booked in, you're there till Monday. . . . But I was, of course, rather heated now, because I know they're lying. They're bluffing. Well, I'm going to call the book. But of course, in the real world, it's unfortunate that there are police abuses that go on, and it's possible that I would have never made it downtown. Would have ended up battered and bruised somewhere. . . . The bottom line in the situation is . . . that I'm a young black male driving in a relatively bad part of town in a nice car with a white woman in the passenger seat. . . .

JILL Their last thing was, "We'll be watching you." . . . And there wasn't nothing there to be taken care of.

JAMES . . . There was never a ticket issued.

> The police in this neighborhood, they treat Houston differently. Like one night, we had to call the police because our window had got broken in our house, and these two white policemen came, and he was in the alley with the three white kids that broke the window, and the policemen pointed their guns at him. . . . You don't want to believe that things like that are true, but they are. And I think that situations I have seen like that have . . . just made me more aware that it's not any better. . . . The black man and the law. He has to deal with that every day. I never had to deal with legal issues. I never even saw what that's like. And just being a black man on the streets, he could be hauled off at any second, just because of the color of his skin. (Eve)

ADAM We were in [Chicago] and walking through a particularly bad part of town that we found ourselves into near [downtown]. . . . And it was a white friend, a man, with us, and it was the three of us. . . . We looked radical I'm sure, but we walked out of the neighborhood, and as we walked out we were followed by a couple of plainclothes policemen. . . .

WANDA They thought I matched the description of some young woman who had been kidnapped. . . . Actually, I think all they were saying is that you don't look like you belong together.

REACTIONS IN THE BLACK COMMUNITY

Although most of the examples discussed so far in this chapter are of white reactions to interracial couples, there were also reactions from blacks who seemed critical of interracial relationships. In the 1970s, Porterfield (1978, pp. 145-149) argued that interracial relationships had become less acceptable in the black community than in the past. Although we cannot speak to historical changes, it is clear that at the time of our interviews (1991) a number of people could recall stereotyping and opposition in the black community.

Black Assumptions About
the Couple's Economic Relationship

One man talked about stereotyping (of whites, of blacks, of interracial relationships) by black acquaintances.

> Even with black people, especially black males, I noticed when they come over to . . . our apartment, they just assume everything is my wife's. That makes me sick (laughs). They just assume . . . she provides everything; I am not supportive at all. . . . Growing up, there's a lot of myths between us. We all used to think, "Oh, all white people got money." All white people do not have money. And another thing is, . . . at least where I am from, all the black guys say, "Get you a white girl. White girls have money. Get you a white girl. They will buy you everything." And the fact is that did happen to a lot of my friends. . . . It didn't happen to me. . . . So they just assume that that's what our relationship was. (Houston is black)

Black Women Resent the Loss
of Black Men to White Women

Much has been written about the concerns many black women have about romantic relationships between white women and black men (Collins, 1990, pp. 189-192; See, 1989; Spickard, 1989, p. 304; Staples & Johnson, 1993, pp. 148-149). In the present study, by far the most frequently mentioned reaction of African Americans to interracial couples was resentment on the part of black women to partnerships between black men and white women.

> There's a thing that happens when you go out in society and you run across, like especially black women. Whenever they see an interracial

couple, I don't know, maybe I'm totally off base, but they give you the impression that they look at you in a certain way, like they say, "Why you with that woman?" (John is black)

I had one instance in a bar. This is with a black woman. I went in the bathroom and waited in line, and the . . . lady says to me, "Are you with a brother?" And I, you know, you can take me out of North Dakota, but you can't take North Dakota out of me (laughs). I said, "No, I'm with my boyfriend." And I was just so proud to be with my boyfriend (laughing). She said, ". . . Are you with a brother?" And I said . . . "Yes." They didn't like that too well. . . . They suggested that I take my business elsewhere. (Dot)

The most negativity towards me personally because I was dating and am now married to a black man comes from black women. There seems to me this kind of thing of like, "Well, you've taken one out of circulation, and that means there's one less good one for me." (Nora)

The resentments seem to stem partly from a sense that there are not many black men available as marriage partners.

When we first met . . . I always felt like black women looked nega- tively at us. . . . I hated having that feeling. . . . [But] I had maybe only a couple of encounters with black females in a negative way. . . . I had one African lady asking me why I wanted to marry a black man. And I said, "Well, I don't know that I necessarily wanted to marry a black man. I wanted to marry him." And then she had said to me, "Well, don't you know you are taking all our men?" And I just said (laughs), "Well . . . if you really want him you can have him." . . . I try to keep it kind of lighthearted. . . . I don't like to fight with people about things like that. (Eve)

For more than 50 years, there have been more single women in the black community than single men. Moreover, the many factors blocking substantial numbers of black men from earning a decent wage have markedly decreased the pool of black men whose earnings make them viable partners by their own or by a black woman's standards (Dickson, 1993). So one might well imagine why a black woman who would like to be married might be upset when a black man who is earning a decent living marries a white woman. This is not to say that black women necessarily see things in those terms or only in those terms. Some may see the higher rates of interracial marriage by black men as a rejection of personal identity, as a rejection of black women's beauty, as a failure to acknowledge and reward the support that black women give black men, or as a betrayal of the black community. One black man who had felt the pressure of such attitudes talked about his marrying a white woman.

> I think probably the more politically correct thing to do would have been to marry inside the race. . . . Joyce was with me one time where the woman said, "Well, you took the cream of the crop. . . . Why did you marry one of our brothers?" Or people sayin', "Why'd you go out-side the race?" . . . Maybe if I'd waited around and stayed single longer I would have met the African American woman and settled down, and that would have been the politically correct thing to do. . . . But then on the other hand, I look and think, "I've always been sort of different in terms of how I thought about who I was." . . . I like people to like me, but if they don't like me, I don't go out of my way to change it that much either, so I do what I think's best for me. And, certainly, in thinking about getting married to Joyce, I had a number of friends tell me, "No, that's not the thing to do. . . ." And I certainly told (laughs) Joyce that in the beginning, too. ". . . You think you want to marry me, but no, this is not going to work, and here are the reasons, and this is the way racial relations are in America." (Gregory)

Some black men talked about color as less important than what a relationship provided. For example, one man said that he had been "down and out," and it was only the white woman he eventually married who had been able to see his potential and help him to become what he has become.

> If people say, "Well, how come you didn't marry a black woman? Weren't they good enough for you?" I says, . . . "When Rosemary met me, I wasn't as prosperous as I am, or settled as I am now." I was down and out, in reality. And there weren't no black woman around wanting to take me up by the hand and say, "Well, come along." . . . But she

was the person that was there, and because of our relationship and our children, I'm able to have a stable and clear path in life. And it's not because she's white that that happened but because we just happened to chance upon each other . . . and it's worked out. It's been rough, but it's working. . . . Color has nothing to do with it. Sometimes, we can chin and talk about it, about, oh, she's . . . white and I'm black. But . . . that's not the real thing. (Ed)

Similarly, another black man felt that black women who insisted on marrying a black man were making a mistake. From his perspective, the right thing to do was what he had done, to search for the best possible partner, regardless of race.

I watched a show . . . last night. The topic was, where are the black men? . . . They were interviewing a lot of educated black women who can't find a palatable educated black man. . . . When I see shows like this on TV, because I am involved in a biracial relationship, do that make me sad to see these intelligent, beautiful black womens out there can't get me because Kate got me? . . . When I saw that show, I said to myself, ". . . lookin' for a black man, you may gonna find a problem; you may not find a man you lookin' for." But if we are out there lookin' for a person, a man, who I want to be a part of my life, who fit all those *A, B, C, D,* and *Es* out there, then you surely gonna find that man. . . . There is some who want to marry within their race; there are some who don't care because they are lookin' for a decent relationship. That's the way I was. I's lookin' for a decent relationship. . . . All I'm tryin' to say is that we have to be open; we have to believe in ourself, to say, OK then, there're 35 black mens out there; I want one of them got to be with me. I'm gonna get that one there! He may turn out to be, because you so much lookin' for someone, turn out to be just the baddest thing you ever touch upon. (Robert)

For some black men, the issue of freedom was also involved. To bow to pressures not to take a white partner would be to give up some freedom.

Black people have a lot of negative things to say about a black man with a white woman. I would like them to know that I am seeking my freedom all the time, and I will not be limited if I can help it. (Wilson)

Some white women who were interviewed resented the reactions of black women toward them.

> The other thing that's happened recently for me that I think he thinks is funny, but (snort of laughter) I've gotten kind of angry about black women and how rejecting they are of us and how hostile many of them are. (Christine)

Other white women seemed to be more tolerant of the reactions of black women and also to be able to maintain good relations with black women who had such resentments. One white woman talked about her understanding of the resentments and her efforts to get along with close women friends who were black.

> I have some very close women friends who are black, who early on in my dating black men had to struggle with the issue and [didn't] care for it and have come around out of love for me, really; simple as that. Adopted a wider view about it. . . . [My friends] explained that they just found it really hard to deal with. . . . They felt abandonment by black men choosing white women, and I remember one of them was describing once that it just Uggghhh! She didn't like to think of it! It made her shudder to think of the coupling, . . . but I think the abandonment issue was the biggest. And the enemy factor. . . . If white people are to be perceived by black people as enemies in any way, shape, or form, then (laughs) this is a strange coupling. One friend laid it out as plainly as she could and pretty much these were the things she was saying, then had to couple it with, "But I love you, and I don't know what I'm gonna make of this, and I think you make good choices." (Laura)

She also talked about the possibility that there is not widespread resentment by black women, only a myth of such resentment. The following statement, from a black man, echoes the idea that what seems like widespread resentment may be a myth perpetuated by the mass media. He also saw the possibility for black women's resentment being that there were far more black-white interracial couples involving a black man and a white woman than involving a black woman and a white man (something noted in Chapter 2). With such an imbalance, if nothing else were going on to remove eligible black bachelors from the partner pool, there would be a shortage of black men.

> The black women that I deal with and work with are very questioning, and not on a personal level. It's just because of the media and the fact that interracial relationships generally go the man of color and a white woman that they do question a lot. . . . They won't hide that kind of conversation out of deference to me. You know that is being discussed; it's going to be discussed. And there is a sense of not being confrontational about it. It's just, . . . we as black women want to know why. What is there that this happens? Is it a personal insult? But that I don't consider as having to do with *my* relationship, and I certainly feel much more comfortable when those discussions . . . go on in my presence and . . . I can take part. . . . I think it's just the nature of the friends I've had. I mean, I've been raised in a very intercultural environment. It would be different if I worked in southside Chicago and somehow had snuck out to Highland Park and met someone. . . . I know that there are couples that are in the *Jungle Fever* kind of situation. That's not where I'm coming from. (Emmett)

Two other black men talked about the resentment of African American women being based not only on the disproportionate number of black man-white woman interracial couples but also on the shortage of educated black men with a decent income.

> I know there are feelings that aren't verbalized by females in my family . . . because there's this attitude, and I don't know where it comes from, but there's this attitude that says . . . "Black men are the property of black women. There are not enough black men to go around." Well, that's not exactly true. There's not enough well-schooled, well-employed, upper-middle-class black men to go around. (James)

> I think there's probably some individual black women out there that are real resentful and feel that all the quote unquote good quality black men are dating white women, but I don't think it's an overall feeling. I work with black women; I know some black women, and they all know I'm married to a white, and I don't feel any hostility from them. They don't treat me any different once they find out that Ann is white. . . . So I think it's a lot of stereotyping and preconceived notions that go into that, and I think it's unfortunate where a couple

of people have been able to express their views on the topic and all of sudden become spokesmen for all black women. I have seen black women who have looked at us and kind of turned their nose up and rolled their eyes . . . , and you don't know what they mean, and you should ask them, but you can pretty much guess that they don't like the relationship. . . . My sister has told me that a couple of her friends that saw me . . . asked if I was married. She [would] say, "Yeah" and show them a picture, or somehow they would find out that Ann was white. They'd get angry, and my sister would say, "Don't talk about it that way; that's my brother's wife. She's a real nice lady." (Bayard)

The perceived shortage of desirable black bachelors may also underlie feelings of competition among black women. One African American woman talked about her dating experiences while attending a college where there were few African American men.

WANDA I dated both [black men and white men]. . . .

ADAM I was just thinking again there weren't that many black guys around (laughs).

WANDA No there weren't that many around. Got me into trouble because other women were always fighting over them.

Whether or not black women compete for black men, it seems that interracial couples involving a black man and a white woman must come to terms with resentment by some black women. Although the resentment is far from unanimous and may not always be verbalized, it is significant in the experiences of some people.

Black Concerns About
Joining With the "Oppressor"

In contrast to the gender-patterned concerns that some black women have about black men who join with white women, some people in the black community are concerned about any black-white interracial relationship. A major factor in that concern is the feeling that it is inappropriate to choose as a partner somebody from the group that has been oppressing African Americans.

I do get anxious when we're in an all-black situation, just because I feel like people aren't gonna accept me because of my husband. . . . Some of my friends give me a hard time. I mean my black friends, but not so much because of Kent per se, just because of he's a white person. . . . They'll . . . tease me about it. . . . I guess that's my concern when I meet people who don't know I'm married to someone white, is whether they'll still talk to me or accept me as a person or my husband as a person. . . . I have a black male friend . . . ; it's not like he stopped talking to me, but he kind of gave me a hard time. . . . "Oh, you don't like the poor black man, huh?" (laughs). I mean, he talks like that and saying I have to take responsibility for the fact that some people aren't going to like me. See, I have this problem of still wanting to be liked despite being in an interracial marriage. And I think that gets me into trouble. I need to realize that there are going to be people who just aren't going to like me, and that's that, and there's not anything I can do to change their mind. (Gloria)

I've had women say to me, "How could you do that? You know, these are the men who raped and pillaged . . . our mothers. How can you do that?" (Patricia)

We went back to Chicago for Christmas, and she met my mother, guys I grew up with, and saw a lot of my old friends [from] high school. But she didn't meet everybody (laughs), because I knew there were people who wouldn't like it, no question about it. I wouldn't feel obligated to explain myself . . . ; I'm too old for that, but there are such folks. (William)

CONCLUSION

One of the challenges of being in an interracial couple is to navigate an environment in which racist opposition is always possible. Although the choice of an interracial partnership is, in a sense, a choice not to be fettered by racism, the racism is still present so that in some ways, an interracial couple may act to restrict their freedom as they defend against, wall off, or otherwise deal with racism.

It is, however, not a simple matter to evaluate the racism reported by couples in this study. Many of the instances were not clearly directed at interracial couples but were ambiguous reactions against black people, interracial couples, or people who are in some way out of the ordinary. For example, regarding reactions of store clerks, coworkers, and the police, it can be difficult to tell whether the racism is directed at interracial relationships or at the black partner. Perhaps the issue is trivial, in that both members of an interracial couple can feel stung by an incident whatever its underlying source. But the issue is still important to understand from the perspective of efforts needed to neutralize racism.

Many people said that they experienced few difficulties, and many said that most or all of the difficulties they had experienced were behind them. As Chapter 3 indicates, many couples see themselves as ordinary people living not unusual lives. It would be dishonest to deny their experiences of racism. But it would also be dishonest to blow their experiences out of proportion. Interracial couples can and do live normal lives, centered on the everyday joys and challenges of living together. That the couples who were interviewed experienced as little difficulty as they did suggests that many Americans are tolerant or even actively supportive of interracial couples and that some who think badly of such couples do not express their opinions in the presence of an interracial couple. It is, however, possible that the comparatively few slurs, stares, incidents of police harassment, and the like that were experienced may be quite enough to pervade the lives of some couples with concern, caution, and defensive efforts missing from a more privileged existence. In fact, even if a couple has not directly experienced police harassment, discrimination in mortgage lending, or the like, the knowledge that such things are possible may put them permanently on the defensive, may make them permanently constrained in their daily lives, or may force them to put enormous amounts of psychic energy into trying to think and act as though the threats are not present.

As this and the next chapter indicate, many people felt the pressure of the negative reactions, were affected by them, and worked hard to avoid, deflect, ignore, or neutralize them. It is also possible that what is reported in this chapter underestimates the amount of opposition in society to interracial couples. The couples knew how to avoid difficulties, and they often tried to ignore other people's negative reactions. It is also true that it may take only a single negative experience (or even a report of the experience of another interracial couple) to create profound barriers to happiness. But as a kind of subtext to many of the accounts in this chapter, one can see that these couples were not letting the negatives undermine their happiness. Some stories in this chapter were told with laughter, and many were told with a kind of detachment that said the events were now in the past. Interracial couples can leave unpleasant incidents behind and get on with the joy of living.

8

DEFENDING AGAINST RACISM

Even if a couple could recall few incidents of racism directed at them, they might still feel the pressure of societal disapproval. The experience of racism, the knowledge of racist disapproval, and the possibility of an encounter with racism were part of everyday reality for all black partners and most if not all couples. Their experience, knowledge, and awareness of possibilities could make everyday life more difficult and could add to the challenges that all couples face in living together. Some people felt the pressure and were determined not to let it affect their relationship.

> I'm not going to allow the bigoted attitudes of individuals to affect our relationship. . . . There's enough problems you can have in a relationship without that. (James is black)

European American partners have had much less experience than African American partners detecting and dealing with racism. One white partner in an interracial relationship talked about the strain

and second thoughts she experienced in thinking about the extremes
of racism.

> Sometimes I just wonder if things would be easier if we were the same
> race. I guess a lot of it again is probably my own fears about his safety or
> our safety when it comes to the madmen out there or whatever, but I
> guess I have to push those ideas out of my mind, because, hopefully, there
> aren't very many of them. I guess it's just the kind of thing of, "Would
> my life be easier as far as certain things if we were same race?" (Nora)

Although experiences of racism can come as a shock to a white
partner who has had little or no experience of racism and can place
additional burdens on a couple's relationship, dealing with those
difficulties can make for a stronger relationship.

> I think often the white person in an interracial marriage is not used to
> being . . . on guard. . . . White people don't realize how free they are.
> And then to suddenly be in a situation—oh, I guess with the marriage
> it wouldn't be sudden because you would have gone together before—
> but when you first begin an interracial relationship, the change, where
> you are suddenly aware of people looking at you and maybe wishing
> you harm, maybe in fact intending to do you harm, must be very, very
> stressful. And that might be the reason for the fact that interracial mar-
> riages sometimes don't last very long. . . . I think that interracial mar-
> riages that do last are stronger than . . . same-race marriages. . . . It
> takes work for any marriage, but if you're willing to take all those
> regular problems plus a little bit of bad attitude from the outside
> world, I think you really have something solid. (Dot)

Another person who talked about the strain put on an interracial
couple by racism agreed that dealing with racism can strengthen a
couple.

> I think that . . . the best message to give if you got to give any message
> to society at all is just keep on ignoring, 'cause the more that you can
> work on building family and relationship and the less you have to
> worry about where you're allowed to live and whether or not people
> are going to accuse [you] of things or talk to you bizarre ways at work,
> the longer those family structures can survive. . . . I think struggle

strains families. I mean, having to struggle with society's conventions is bad for families. I suppose it's probably good also. I mean, having to struggle's probably always good. If people can let those things happen and leave them alone long enough so that nobody makes a lot of big deals out of it, the more likely it is to succeed. (Roger)

Women and men in interracial couples often hear from people around them that the partners in an interracial couple are unlikely to stay together, that they are fundamentally incompatible or are unlikely to be able to cope with the additional difficulties of being in an interracial couple. One couple experienced that as a societal desire for them to fail.

HOUSTON We knew there's going to be people that were going to say a lot of different things. That's what people want. That's what they want. Society wants us to be apart.

EVE They want us to fail.

HOUSTON Right, they want us to fail. See, and we know that we can't listen to them. If we listen to everybody else we would have been drew apart the first hour or so . . . after the wedding.

How are couples affected by the racism around them and how do they deal with it? In this chapter, we explore how societal pressures can put interracial couples onstage, can make them permanently wary, and can weigh them down with concerns about the vulnerabilities of their children. We then go on to outline some of the ways couples defended against racism.

ONSTAGE TO SOCIETY

Some people felt onstage, in part because society will take any failing of an interracial couple as evidence that all interracial relationships are flawed.

I think sometimes when feeling kind of like depressed and maybe a little bit reclusive, I get a little bit maybe paranoid. And then I think . . . that if we're screwing up over here and anybody knows about it, you know how you can think, "Oh, the neighbors are going to know. We've had a fight." That's when I think, "Well, they're going to think it's because I'm white and he's black." (Rosemary)

When people feel onstage, they may work to perform well. For some people who were interviewed, that meant that clothing and other aspects of appearance were considered important in confronting racism.

With [our son] . . . I'm just a perfectionist when it comes to how he looks . . . when he goes to school. I don't want anybody or the teachers thinking that because he's a biracial child that he comes from this, like, single-mom home. And I'm real aware of wanting Ed to participate so they know he has a dad. 'Cause that is a stereotype that I think society has put on biracial children . . . that usually they come from a single-mom family. And it's just irritating to me, but I'm buying into it. . . . He's scrubbed to the hilt, and I . . . sew a lot. And if I can't go out and buy more, I'll sew him just like these great clothes, and just make sure he looks like a million bucks. . . . We're not poor, but we're struggling sometimes. So sometimes the issues are not . . . race. . . . It's more a class thing. . . . It's like you don't want anyone to know. . . . I would no more let [our son] go to school, like, with a hole in his jeans, even if it's the style. (Rosemary)

I'm very careful about how I dress when I'm with Gary, because I think people will make an assumption that I'm a whore. . . . When I go out or when I travel, I dress in such a way that I get the least amount of crap from people. . . . And sometimes I've said to Gary, "I don't want you [to] look like that if you're going somewhere with me." And I say to [our son], "People . . . judge you by the way you look anyway, and if you have dark skin that's an extra you have to deal with. And then . . . you're not likely to get crap from people." (Patricia)

Other people who talked about feeling onstage said that they wanted to show others that interracial families are wholesome and do well. The efforts to perform well could include self-conscious work at keeping their relationship intact.

People [will] believe that if my wife and I divorce, we did not divorce because we are having money problem or child problem. They will say we divorced because we are different race. So for that reason . . . if my wife and I [have a problem], I will try everything within my power to make sure it's resolved. I will carry on just for that reason, that they will think we divorced because of the different race. I repeat, I will prevent that. (Isaac)

For the same reasons, some people felt bad when they saw an interracial relationship come apart.

I feel a twinge of disappointment when I see [an interracial couple] break up. . . . I would say I feel a special twinge . . . because I know that if I go back to, say, my parents' first reaction, . . . it's more fodder for that kind of a shock at the relationship. . . . "It will never work because look at these people. It didn't work, and they broke up" . . . which of course may not have had anything to do with their race. (Adam)

However, some people saw efforts to impress society as a trap. They felt that one had to live one's relationship in itself and not for an audience, that living for an audience would undermine a relationship.

To start with . . . I was going to prove this was going to work. And then I finally had to get past that. "I'm not going to show anybody anything! I have to do this because this is someone I want to live with. I can't show the world or prove to the world I'm going to do it." . . . Yeah, at first it was, "I'm going to make it work. I'm going to prove that this is going to work." (Olivia)

One can imagine other ways in which efforts to persuade society that interracial relationships work would be a trap. Frankenberg (1993, pp. 117-118) mentioned a woman who apparently did not confide in others about experiences of abuse, in part because she did not want people to think badly of interracial relationships.

GOING THROUGH LIFE FEELING SUSPICIOUS

Given that interracial couples can be targets of racist hostility, it is not surprising that some people in interracial couples would talk about being suspicious of strangers.

ISAAC If people see my wife and I walking along the street, and they
         smile, so I am always suspicious. Are they just smiling to let
         me think they approve? But right inside they resent it; they
         just don't think it is appropriate. So that is why right now
         I'm always full of suspicion. . . .

OLIVIA I guess at first, when we go to a new community, I kind of
         wonder what kind of reception we're going to get, because I
         have heard of other interracial couples getting nasty letters
         and things like that. And at first, I'm always leery if I'm going
         to get that or not.

If suspicions about strangers can make a couple wary, a move to a
new neighborhood can be quite frightening.

I'm very paranoid about being an interracial couple, when it comes to
where; I was scared as hell to move into this neighborhood, when Rosemary first told me about this house that she found, and where it was
at. And I knew that on the other side of the . . . creek was the dominant black neighborhood, and on this side was the liberal white neighborhood. I didn't know how these people were going to receive us,
and I was really scared. (Ed)

DEFENSIVE TACTICS

Given the experiences recorded in the preceding chapter and the
issues of being onstage and of going through life being suspicious, it
is not surprising that people talked quite a bit about how they
defended against societal racism and prejudice.

Being Prepared

A first step in defending is to be prepared, to be alert, to know the
environment, and to be prepared to react to things that may happen.

ROBERT It just seems to me that in a biracial relationship, unless you
         are prepared every day, because I know society sees me as
         different . . . , I've got to deal with society. . . . So every day,
         mentally, emotionally, and spiritually I prepare myself for

that 8-, 9-, 10-, 12-, 24-hour deal. Day after day, week after week, year after year, I prepare myself for that. That's what I do to myself every day, and unfortunately, biracial couples have to deal with that; but that's what we have to do. Otherwise I think you settin' yourself up to have a very dysfunctioning relationship, one that, when the issue comes up, you're not going to deal with it because you . . . don't know how to deal with it.

KATE Or you don't even recognize it. Or denial. You just said, "Oh, well," ya know.

ROBERT Absolutely. . . . They are in for a real big setback. . . . Every time you get into it, you quarrel with each other; you take it out on each other because what it is, you have the thought, you're feeling guilty about yourself, maybe it's because I marry him or marry her I wouldn't have these problems. . . . You have to deal with yourself every day, when you get up. Every time you go outside, you go out as a couple, people are going to see you as different. Believe me, 25 people, 22 may feel OK, but the other three may feel that way. So you still got to deal with that.

Perhaps fearing that preparation to deal with racism can undermine everything else he would like to be doing, the man quoted next talked about not dwelling on preparation to deal with racism. Yet he also felt rage that racism exists and that he must be prepared to deal with it.

When we're here, it doesn't matter [that we are an interracial couple], because I don't have to answer to anyone, and I don't have to worry about anyone pointing a finger and saying, "Look." But when I step outside the door, I have to realize where I'm going. . . . I have to be alert to certain attitudes. . . . Just going to the mall, shopping together, you may get stares from [someone] who's not used to seeing [interracial couples]. So you kind of set yourself into a mode where, either I'll respond or I won't. But I won't be surprised. I'll be ready to follow whichever path I want to go on as far as I want to stare them down or I'm going to confront the situation or I'm just going to blow it off. But it's not something that I dwell on. It's not something that I allow to impinge my life. It's not that important. It shouldn't be that important to anyone else as far as I'm concerned, which I suppose brings out *some* outrage if I was to get any direct response from someone just because we are together. (James)

How One Carries Oneself

If people feel onstage and work at presenting themselves in a favorable light, surely an important element of that presentation is how they carry themselves. Some people talked about that and said that they believed it made a difference in how others reacted to them.

JOHN I don't have in myself as the type of person that you want to come up and . . . express racism to, unless you want me to slap you or some shit if you disrespect my woman or something. It isn't any kind of a thing whereas I'm out there sayin', "Oh my God. I wonder who's gonna be racist today," 'cause they sense that; those people would sense that you're uncertain about something.

INTERVIEWER Right, so on a certain kind of energy level they pick up on that and . . .

JOHN Yeah. . . . This vibration just comes in, especially when you know you're in a place where it's more likely to happen.

INTERVIEWER Is that a conscious thing you do . . . about your energy, or is it who you are?

JOHN No, it's being black for [44] years, OK? You don't consciously know when, where you're at. It's a kind of a thing whereas like if you've been black all your life you know when you're someplace; you just know. You're always aware of yourself.

I put myself above things, above being whatever they would want me to be. Even with . . . black people, if they want me to just be this black dude after white pussy, I'm above that. With the white people, if they just want me to be, the pimp personified or whatever, I'm above that. . . . That message is deliberate, quite frankly. (Ed)

[Nowadays] I just don't care that much, and I'm really confident, and I don't walk around thinking that people are staring at me like a lot of people do. I just don't even see it. I think if they're looking it's because we are such a great looking family (all laugh). I do. I don't perceive that people are looking down at us. I just don't even see it anymore. I mean, I just have a pretty generally positive outlook about it. I think it's just like a maturation thing. I was a lot more insecure, and so I was really tuned in to. I'm a real people pleaser. I want people to like me. And the older I get, the more I like myself. It doesn't really matter. . . . Bayard is like that to the core, and I respect that in him so much. He's so great about that. He just doesn't care what people think, and I just admire that so much. It's good for me. (Ann)

When we decided we cared enough about each other and had enough respect for each other and love, we decided we wanted to get married. I just made my mind up that this is what I want to do, and society be damned (laugh). You can accept it, but it's not that simple. You're always working on your own emotions, and attempt to maybe change somebody else's mind, because there seems to be a stereotypical attitude [toward] couples who are mixed races, in a derogatory way. So I attempt to carry myself in a manner as not to embarrass Dot or my daughter. . . . And that's OK, I can handle that. It's just, I don't seem to have enough (laughs) power to change some of these narrow-minded people. (Wilson)

Carrying oneself was an important part of the socialization of biracial children of some couples.

VIRGINIA [Our children] both have wonderful social skills. . . . They get along with everybody, and I think that they . . . feel the freedom to act out in the world, [and] the kinds of trouble that a lot of kids get into, they just don't at all.

INTERVIEWER So in a sense, you are saying they're like ambassadors for . . .

VIRGINIA Yeah.

INTERVIEWER promoting or sort of dispelling myths that might be there around interracial families.

LORENZO In a very low-key way. . . . They're not caped crusaders . . .

VIRGINIA Yeah.

LORENZO who make this a conscious game plan, but it is in fact what they do.

VIRGINIA Yeah. . . . I think that they are conscious of there are a lot of people who are very willing . . . to make negative judg-

ments about the family, and they're not going to give them
the fuel to be able to do that.

Circling the Wagons

If interracial couples are subjected to racism and the constant
threat that somebody will stare or in some other way suggest that
there is something taboo, wrong, or odd about their relationship,
small wonder that some people felt more comfortable at home than
in public. In public, there is always the possibility of difficulties. In
private, they can be themselves—two individuals or a family with
ordinary, comfortable relationships. Thus, some couples said that
they try to minimize their contact with the public and with people at
work.

> One of the things that I don't do is I do not involve myself in any so-
> cial activities with my family at work. That's just a choice I made a
> long time ago because the job's hard enough for me to come by I
> don't; it's not like people don't know that I'm in an interracial mar-
> riage. . . . They do. . . . But I have my own personal life, and I have my
> own social life. We have our social life, and it's not in any way con-
> nected with my job. (Charles)

WILSON We really don't have any friends. . . .

DOT I have more of a need for friends than Wilson does. . . . And I
      guess that's taken care of at work. I'm real chummy with
      those people, and we have a good time. But, yeah, once I get
      home from work, we're pretty much [alone]. . . . We had
      some experiences years ago, and so we've kind of learned not
      to go here, not to go there; so rather than go to nightclubs
      or whatever, we manage to entertain ourselves at home.

When a couple has children, circling the wagons draws the children more tightly into the family. Sometimes, that seems to make the
children less rebellious, more loyal to their parents, and guarded in
relationship to the outside world.

VIRGINIA I think that [being a biracial family] has a big effect on how
          we identify ourselves as a family and probably a pretty

significant effect on how I view myself as an individual. I think in terms of relations within the family, it's not a big deal. It's a bigger deal doing the dishes and things like that (laughs). On a day-to-day level, I don't know that it matters that much. It certainly makes a difference in the kind of things that we talk with our kids and how we interact with our kids, and I think actually in a pretty significant way it has affected how our kids deal with us and the larger community. I haven't really put all the stuff together, but I think that when I was their age I was much more rebellious and much less . . . willing to relate to my parents. . . . With the kids, I think that they feel more of a kind of a bonding with us and a need to protect the family unit from the outside world.

LORENZO Yeah, in a mild way it's us against the world.

Shutting Out Racism

Some people talked about shutting out racism, trying never to notice it. Shutting out may work often, but it can also leave one quite startled when racism gets past the barriers one has put up. That may be why some people talked about situations in which they used their "radar," a perceptual alertness to racism, a mental preparedness that allowed them to navigate around racism or to deal more deftly with it.

VIRGINIA I think through the years I just have, I don't know if it's thick skin or just a lot of what the broader community expects where it really impacts me personally, I basically have shut out. It's just too much bother to, takes too much energy out of the day, to even think about it or worry about it, so every now and then when it intrudes, it sometimes surprises me.

LORENZO . . . I went out to breakfast with a . . . female friend . . . 2 weeks ago, and I noticed that I had my radar cranked way up, higher than I normally do when it is just Virginia and me. . . . If you can imagine a graph where the bottom, say, 40% of responses shaded in terms of intensity, well that shit, I just tuned it out. I don't even see that anymore. But I noticed with my friend that I was picking up the whole image again because . . . she has lots of black friends, but most of them are female, and I think she was kind of taken aback by how incredibly much attention we were drawing just by walking into a room to eat some goddamn breakfast. Give me a break. So I think my natural desire to do the male buffalo thing and protect was like it used to be when we were first married. . . . For those first couple of years that we were together, I was very intense and I found myself doing the same thing with her.

Minimizing

Some people minimize racism in the sense of trivializing it. This may be a way of keeping pain to a minimum and making it seem that the threats are not dangerous. It is also a way of not feeding racism, not giving racists the idea that expressions of racism have a power to injure or control.

> One night we were driving . . . and these guys pulled up to us and said, "Hey, zebras. Hey, there's a zebra family." And we laughed harder than they did, which just put them out of their misery. . . . We have certainly seen people looking at us, and we joke about that. We'll laugh about that later. (Patricia)

Careful Choice of Places to Go

Another part of defending against racism is to know the environment and to be careful in choosing places to go.

> Being a person of color [racism is something I've] experienced myself lots of times; I'm very much aware of it. I do make a point to avoid situations where I can see there's going to be problems either for her or for me. (Charles)

> I think I probably have the same type of relationship internally, inside the home, if I was married to an African American woman. But if I were married to an African American woman, then I'd have a greater range of access outside. I mean, there are certain places that, as an interracial couple in either the black or the white communities, you don't go there. (Gregory)

You have these sixth senses. Maybe you don't want to pull into that particular restaurant 'cause you see another crowd going there before you. (Ed)

We tend to keep to the main thoroughfares, I think, on a lot of things, and [if] we're gonna go somewhere and stay somewhere we typically don't go to a small mom-and-pop resort, [where] people are going to be fishing and hunting. . . . Maybe go to something much more staid and placid, where people are just gonna be able to walk around the lakeshore. So what you do, I mean, you get a sixth sense about how the world works. I think that if we go up to the North Shore, . . . if there's a lot of people [at a resort] the chances of running into bigots is increased. Oh, there's only a few there, . . . let's go to that one. (Gregory)

Some people said that they refused to restrict their travel. A couple who refused to let racism limit their travel options might still use their protective radar, however.

VIRGINIA We've never made a verbal decision, but we've basically made a decision that we're going to do whatever we wanted to (laugh) and that we are not going to limit ourselves. I have friends who are in interracial families who would not, for instance, go camping in northern Minnesota. . . .

LORENZO . . . I remember interracial friends when we were still very involved with the interracial family workshops just tripping . . . that we were camping in North Carolina. . . . We were so nonchalant about the car breaking down in rural Alabama at 2 in the morning. . . . We dealt with it, quite fearlessly, actually, but there were reasons for that fearlessness. . . . Unlike the households that a lot of my friends grew up in when I was a kid, my father was such a relentless hard-ass about race and racial issues and often went to jail when I was a kid because he refused to accept that there was no service; he refused to accept that we couldn't go in. My poor mother. I grew up listening to her saying, "Joe, Joe, please."

VIRGINIA Yeah, he's lucky that he's survived, actually, yeah.

LORENZO . . . I think for me, that was good, because . . . that was a good model for me because it never occurred to me that I shouldn't do anything, you know, in my obeisance to the fact that . . .

VIRGINIA It's got to be uncomfortable or might be uncomfortable.

LORENZO Yes, or even potentially dangerous. And I trusted that radar too. I could usually see trouble coming a long way off and just do the smart thing and avoid it.

Being Open About
Being in an Interracial Family

Another approach to entering a situation in which racism might be expressed is to warn people in advance of entering a situation that one is in an interracial couple. For example, in warning a clerk when one is making resort reservations, one gives the resort personnel a chance to prepare and also creates a situation in which the reservation may be denied without the inconvenience that would be experienced if one's family were turned away from the resort only after presenting themselves at the check-in desk.

> Choosing a vacation spot, being in the middle of the boonies . . . that's . . . when I really feel it. . . . I guess I have stereotypes about parts of the country . . . and just know if I'm going to stay at somebody's resort I want to know that they are comfortable with our family so that we aren't feeling any hostility so we can have a good time. I think I'd probably be real frank with somebody on the phone. . . . When I was applying . . . to do day care, I put ads in the paper and was getting lots of calls, and I felt like people were coming into my home and they had talked to me on the phone, and they were . . . surprised when they found out that this was an interracial family, and I just decided that I was going to tell people right up front on the phone that we're a multicultural family. . . . Most people were real nice; "Oh, no, it doesn't matter." (Ann)

Later on, Ann said that she was not only trying to head off situations in which she would have to deal with racism but also trying to protect others from the embarrassment of having said something inappropriate.

> I always tell friends right away [about my interracial marriage] because people I care about I don't ever want them to . . . say something stupid and later feel really bad about it.

Some people who had no interest in telling people in advance that their partner was of another race told stories about what can happen if one does not tell people in advance.

> People say to me, "Why didn't you tell me?" And what is there to tell? I'm remembering a really nasty incident. . . . We were moving. We just bought a house, and this woman said, "Oh, I'll come and help you move." And I really didn't need that because we hired professionals, and she said, "Well, let me take you home." And so she took me home, and she met Gary, and so she said, "Gee, can we talk?" And I said, "Sure." She said, "Oh, I couldn't [have] my husband . . . , ask him to come help you move . . . 'cause he's not going to be coming to help no white man move." . . . I was *so* angry. . . . She was trying to cultivate a friendship with me, and she thought she could do that by helping us move. But it just ended once she met Gary. (Patricia)

Sorting Out Associates

People who feel onstage may play to audiences, and they also may be selective about their audiences. Quite a few people talked about sorting out friends, coworkers, neighbors, and so on, dropping people who seemed racist and building relationships with people who were tolerant.

> In my earlier years . . . I may have been more careful . . . about . . . who I associated with. But at [42] it doesn't matter, because I refuse to let it matter. I refuse to let people make decisions about what's so personal and private to me. It's really none of their affair. And that doesn't mean I'm not . . . sort of vigilant about what people think. But I'm less likely to let what people think influence my behavior or what I do or where I go. A couple of years ago . . . I did a TV program, and the host of the program was saying he was appalled that people would marry somebody that their family didn't like. And I was appalled that he would say that. And I said to him, "People marry people all the time that their families don't like." And so for me, it's like a continuation of that racism that the world can tell me what I can and cannot do. And as I said, it feels so private to me that I don't think it's anybody's business. So that's my stance at age [42]. I don't really care anymore. And I don't associate with people where it does matter. I simply just exclude them from my life. (Patricia)

Finding Tolerant Communities

For some couples, the selection of associates and environments extended to selecting a community—friendship groups, organizations, churches, neighborhoods, and cities. People talked about efforts to find tolerant communities. For some, the key was to find an urban area in which there was a great deal of openness to interracial couples, a place that gave them the freedom to play, work, shop, and so on with few worries. Parts of the Twin Cities were seen as open in that way. In fact, some couples had moved to the Twin Cities because they had heard that the area was a good one for interracial couples.

> We wanted to live in a northern-tier, . . . relatively liberal city. . . . That's how we ended up here, and . . . I feel very comfortable with this city. This city has its problems, certainly, and I have days when I feel the pulse of expected racism. . . . But overall it's a very good place to live. . . . [People] are fairly accepting, and the people that are not leave it alone. That is to say, I know that there are people out there who don't like our relationship, but . . . [here you can more often] expect tolerance, compared to the rest of the country. (Charles)

> I think our community here where we live in . . . there's plenty of interracial couples around, so I don't think it's that big of a deal around here, Minneapolis, and certainly this neighborhood, the church we go to or had gone to in the past. We have interracial couples who are friends, know other interracial couples. I don't think it makes that much of a difference. I think society in general . . . still has a hard time dealing with the races . . . intermingling. There's a lot of stereotypes and racist beliefs. . . . The society at large sees an interracial family, they start wondering, "Well, why are they together?" (Bayard)

> We feel we can't live anywhere. That's why we're in the Cities, because we feel accepted here. But I do [feel] very resentful of that, because we can't go just anywhere and be comfortable. We have to think really hard about where we're going to take our vacations, and it bothers me because we have to think that far ahead. And we can't live wherever we want, like some people can. (Shirley)

[Being in an interracial marriage] influenced most of the major decisions we've made in our lives, about where we would live, about what
kind of occupations we'll have, what parts of the country we'll be in.
. . . Part of why we've been able to make it is because we were educated and because we have had independent incomes, and we've been
able to choose where we live. (Gary)

Because I travel a lot, I notice how extraordinary Minneapolis is in
terms of anywhere else in the country in the predominance of interracial couples. It's unbelievable, the difference between Minneapolis and
any other city I've been in, including some of those that I consider the
more liberal, like Seattle. (Emmett)

This community is becoming more enriched as there are more children
from interracial marriages, as there are more interracial relationships
out there. . . . We were fortunate enough to be able to move to a community *here* 10 years ago by choice. Knowing that we'd see other people like ourselves . . . , and still being able to find jobs and all those
kinds of things. So [we] picked an environment where we would feel
comfortable . . . raising a family. (Adam)

The racism people had experienced in the Twin Cities—for example, with the police or in renting or purchasing a place to live—is
apparently less than what at least some who were interviewed would
expect in other parts of the country. Also, consistent with what people
said about the comparative safety of the Twin Cities, the examples
given in Chapter 7 of the experience of racism included quite a few
experiences out of town—while traveling, while living outside of the
Twin Cities.

Confronting Racism

Although a great deal of what people said about dealing with
racism had to do with avoiding, deflecting, minimizing, or sliding
away from it, some people talked about confronting it.

INTERVIEWER I'm curious about your talking back to the woman at
      the fair. Were you hoping to change her mind? [This refers

to an incident, discussed in Chapter 7, involving the distri-
bution of hate literature.]

EVE . . . I brought Houston back [to the fair], and then when we got
there, I didn't want to go. . . . But he really wanted to, he
wanted to confront these people. . . . I came home, and I was
all mad about it, and he right away was, like, "Well, let's go;
let's go talk to them." So he did; he pushed me into it, and
then once he did start talking with them, I was glad. . . . It's
good that we both shared. And we went away from those
people, they liked Houston. . . . We had been able [to have]
a nice conversation. It wasn't an argument. They really sat
there.

White partners can be on edge when they meet new people because
there is always the possibility of having to decide whether to confront
racism that might be expressed when someone finds out they are in
an interracial relationship.

Sometimes I wonder if I'm strong enough, if I'll be strong enough if
I'm ever directly confronted [by racism]. A lot of times when I meet
new people or I start a new job there's that kind of thing that you start
talking about families and things like that, and I guess I assume that
everybody assumes that I'm married to a white man. . . . And . . . I
reach that point where I have to reveal that we are in a biracial marriage. And it's hard to figure out how to do it. (Nora)

Sometimes it may seem wise not to confront but to let something
go by. One African American woman talked about how she chose not
to reply to some young blacks whom she didn't know who were
commenting on her being with a white man and her biracial child.

It's not worth responding to. I mean, if you get into a debate with people it gives them some credence. (Wanda)

SUMMARY AND CONCLUSIONS

Societal racism adds additional burdens to interracial couples.
Some people at times wondered whether it would have been easier

to be in a same-race couple. Others resolved not to let the pressures undermine their relationship, and some even felt that dealing with the pressures strengthened their relationship. Living in an environment where people communicate a sense that their relationship is likely to fail and living in an environment of racist hostility led couples to feel onstage, as though they were always being watched. It led at least some to be suspicious, especially in encounters with strangers.

How did couples defend against racism? People talked about being wary and about being careful about how they carried themselves. They talked about isolating themselves from others, about trying to shut out racism by not noticing it, about minimizing it when they did notice it, and about being careful about where they went. A few people talked about warning others that they were in an interracial couple. Most talked about being selective about the people with whom they interacted and about efforts to find relatively tolerant communities. Although people might not enjoy confronting racism and might work hard to avoid getting into situations in which confrontation seemed necessary, some said that confrontation was one of the ways that they had dealt with racism.

As is reported in Chapter 7, many people said that they experienced very few difficulties, and many said that most or all of the difficulties they had experienced were behind them. As Chapter 3 indicates, many couples saw themselves as ordinary people living not unusual lives. Their experiences of racism are not to be denied. That they experienced as little racism as they did may say that many people in the society are tolerant and others are tactful about when and how they express their racism. It also suggests that the approaches couples used to reduce their contact with racism were rather effective. It is, however, possible that the comparatively few slurs, stares, incidents of police harassment, and the like, that they experienced may be quite enough to pervade the lives of interracial couples with concern, caution, and defensive efforts unnecessary for same-race couples.

9

IDENTITY

For centuries, Americans in interracial relationships have struggled with identity issues (Johnston, 1970, chap. 8). In the past, identity had much to do with legal standing, rights, and life chances. Nowadays, identity is more a matter of self-concept—what one thinks of oneself. A person's major commitments, including choice of a partner, affect and are affected by the person's self-concept. How others react to one also stems from self-concept (see the discussion in the previous chapter on how one carries oneself) and has a major influence on it. For some people, being in an interracial partnership is not necessarily consistent with their self-concept as a member of a racial group member or as loyal to people who oppose such partnerships. Moreover, the reactions of others may threaten a person's self-concept. For example, people's reactions may suggest that one has made a bad choice, has been disloyal to one's people, is a rule violator, or does not belong in a group that one counts as important in personal identity.

THE AFRICAN AMERICAN
PARTNER'S IDENTITY

Historically, there seems to have been less African American than white opposition to interracial marriage. For example, Wilkinson (1975, p. 4) cited a 1972 Gallup poll in which 58% of blacks approved of such unions and 21% disapproved (with the remainder recorded as "no opinion"). By contrast, only 25% of whites said they approved and 65% disapproved. If approval from one's own racial group is part of personal identity and if what held in the 1970s were true today, we would expect fewer interracially partnered African Americans to report identity concerns as a result of their interracial relationship. But quite a few African Americans talked about identity concerns related to their interracial relationship.

Challenges to Black Identity

Some African Americans felt that their identity was challenged by other African Americans during discussions of white racism or when hostility toward whites was expressed. An African American partnered with a white may be automatically discredited in such discussions and, particularly if refusing to be drawn into opposition to all whites, may have his or her identity questioned.

> If I'm at meetings, [where] the rhetoric is antiwhite . . . , people sometimes associate whites and oppression. So if they're talking about political stuff and talking about racism, I have no problems with people discussing racism, [because] I feel it is a racist society. But that doesn't mean to me that because I feel it's a racist society I'm antiwhite. And I think that's where there's always a real shaky kind of thing, when I'm in these discussions, because they can end up sounding antiwhite, and so then it's hard for me to kind of bridge that gap because I'm married to someone who's white. . . . I think specifically about the situation where I was with a group of women who were part of the community I was working in . . . ; it was someone's birthday . . . and I was just dropping something off. And they were getting into this white people smell thing, which I thought was just the same thing white folks said about black people. . . . When people get into that stuff, then that's when I

. . . start to say . . . what I'm feeling. But you always feel people will discount because you are with someone white. It's like, "Well, we know where you stand!" . . . In some ways, that has been the most difficult piece of it, because I think people will assume a lot about your political beliefs, about how you grew up. . . . When people start robbing my identity from me and kind of making statements . . . or discount me because I'm with someone white, that I have no concern about the black community, I'm not black identified . . . that's been the hardest thing to deal with for me. (Gloria)

Partnership with a white can threaten an African American's credibility in the black community and, as a consequence, threaten personal identity. For example, a teacher discussing black history with black students could find himself challenged because of his marriage to a white woman, and that challenge could lead him to question his identity.

GREGORY I was teachin' a history class . . . and . . . one of my students [said], ". . . How can you say that? Your wife is white." . . . That threw the whole class into chaos. . . . It was like, "How can you teach this class if you're married to a white woman?" . . . If I was married to someone of my own race, . . . and this is just my projection and my imagining, I think I have more access in the black community. I mean, there's a certain thing in the black community. It's called legitimacy, that you attain with who you are and what type of outward appearance you have. . . . If you're an African American man and you're in a relationship with an African American woman, the African American community sees you in high esteem. If you're an African American man and you're married to a non-African American woman, then there's segments of the community who say, "This guy's gotta be viewed with suspicion. He (laughs) broke the code." The code is that if you are going to marry, marry in the race. And it's very strong! I think a lot of people think the African American community is very liberal about that, [but] that's one of the few things that a person can do to really kinda chop yourself off at the knees! If you're plannin' on goin' anywhere in the community, they're gonna look and say, "You talk a good game, brother, but who'd you marry? If you married her, how can we trust you on other issues?" . . .

INTERVIEWER Do you experience that as a loss?

GREGORY In some ways I do. In some ways I do. I think that if I were an ambitious person . . . I would feel a loss a lot greater. I'm not overly ambitious. I don't see myself bein' sort of a community leader . . . and in that respect I don't think the black community's any different than any other community. . . . I certainly don't think a white politician would stand a ghost of a chance of gettin' elected if he married someone who's non-Caucasian.

INTERVIEWER Have you in your community had to prove yourself as an African American? I mean, has that identity been questioned, that you're sort of less African American because you're married to a white woman?

LORENZO Yeah, all the time. Yeah, it's a frequent occurrence. . . . I was in a position some years ago where I had to yank some support, federal dollars, from a program that I was administering from a [service agency] that was owned by a black proprietor. She was just livid over what was happening to her, and she was sure that she was being messed around with only because she was black. So she comes into the office to try to see if she can get it reversed, and who does she deal with but me. So at first, she tried to beg for clemency because she figured, "OK, well, I'll get it from a brother." The truth was she was running a shitty program, and I had to tell her that. And so she got very nasty and said . . . it's pretty much what she'd expect from somebody who was married to some honky bitch. . . . That was an extreme example, but . . . I don't think a single month has gone by of our life as a couple . . . when I haven't gotten some bit of negativity from somebody about being married to a white partner.

I've been reading people who talk about how consorting with white people compromises one (laughs), or can, and can constrain you in various ways. And I can see that it does kind of weaken your position (laughs), depending on what you have to say. . . . I'm writing a history of Africans in America; I'm doing research now, so I've been thinking about this a lot (laughs). . . . It's an interesting position to be in. . . . As far as I know it doesn't matter between Laura and me. But when I'm reading certain authors, for instance, . . . Third World press out of Chi-

cago or . . . militant black nationalists people, it makes me think
(laughs) . . . about how, for instance, I would make much more sweep-
ing generalizations if I weren't married to Laura. . . . I have thought
more about what other people might think because when I write about
. . . black things . . . I wonder how [my marriage] would be received. I
wonder how people will read me differently because of that. . . . I'm
not doing anything differently, but I do think about it. (William)

As the three men just quoted suggest, marriage to a white person
can close doors in the black community, can restrict access to leadership roles, and can restrict how seriously one's words, writings, or
actions are taken. As the following two statements suggest, the door
can also be closed to membership in certain groups in the black
community.

INTERVIEWER Have you felt in your career that there have been times
          where being married to a white man has been a disadvantage
          or has limited what you're doing?
GARY . . . In [that sorority for black women], did you ever think that
          there was any influence on how high you could rise in that
          organization?
PATRICIA Oh, I think so. . . . Although they have white women
          members who are married to black men, it's a traditionally
          black woman's organization. And I know that I'll never be
          invited to be in that group.

EMMETT There are definitely moments of self-doubt. I run into
          people constantly who are of the attitude of, "Well, are you
          abandoning your background?" . . .
INTERVIEWER . . . Have you had people accuse you of being less black
          because you're involved with a white woman?
EMMETT Pretty constantly. . . . There's the whole thing with [a black
          organization]. . . . We constantly get word back from [them]
          as saying that no one who [is in an interracial relationship]
          . . . [is] black enough to [work with them].

When others raise questions, one has to look inside to see who
one is.

I'm sometimes challenged about my black identity. . . . When I challenge myself . . . about it, I come to my own defense by saying that I have what's inside of me because of who I am. . . . [But] people will question whether you know who you are, because of your [wife being white]. . . . To me it's *absurd* that they would think that, because they don't know what I'm doing to make it better for other people of my . . . race. . . . I know what I'm doing. (Ed)

For an African American partnered with a white, the challenge to black identity may also come from whites. A particularly painful form of challenge is when whites assume that, because one is in a relationship with a white, one must be antiblack.

BARB I . . . frequently have experiences where people who know me very well and know my family make racist remarks about black people, particularly black men, that somehow it's OK for them to say those things to [me], or know that they wouldn't say them to another black person. And I find that personally offensive, and when I've had to remind people of that they seem kind of startled, as if they thought, "Oh, shit, we thought you were on our side with this issue." (laughs) . . .

INTERVIEWER So you're saying people who are white . . .

BARB Yeah.

INTERVIEWER assuming that because you are in a relationship with a white man that maybe you've crossed a certain line.

BARB I'm assuming that that's what they are saying.

Continuing to Have a Black Identity

No African American talked about giving up African American identity. One man talked about the enormous diversity among African Americans and about the core of black identity that involved caring about certain things.

As a black person I can't buy everything another black person says. You really can't. Even though it's nice to want to come together with other black people because we know we need to unify ourselves so we can be strong, but you just can't, man. Everyone . . . doesn't think the same way that I think. Everyone's not spiritual; everyone doesn't believe in the same thing that I believe in. . . . They all care about some of the things I care about, and . . . I don't want to split myself up from being a black person. I am always going to be a black person. The way you identify me is my skin color, but . . . I don't want [people] to think that all black men are spiritual or we all believe in God, 'cause in fact a lot of us don't. So them are the things I'm working on as a black person, and trying to educate other black people about, especially black women. I didn't marry my wife because she is white. Sometimes, they think that. It's sickening. We went to see [*Jungle Fever*]. . . . And that hurts; people are already saying, "Oh, he has jungle fever." It's stupid. (Houston)

Another man who talked about continuing to have a black identity said that the challenge to his identity began before marriage, as he realized he was entering a serious relationship with a white woman. He also talked about how the unhappiness of some black women with his choice of partner was a source of discomfort for him. Implied in that discomfort was a sense that a man who is identified as black should not cause black women he cares about to feel unhappy.

I grew up in a very political family, although both of my parents give some due to sort of the Afrocentric worldview, and neither of them really, in their heart of hearts, thinks that that's particularly important. I mean, it's never been a driving force for them, but it's been something of a force anyway, and it was a very interracial environment in which I was raised. . . . As I was growing up, Africa, things relating to Africa, that side of my heritage, was always very important to me, and so I asked myself some questions about what am I doing when Virginia and I got together and geez, you know, am I really going to get married and have kids who, yes, we will identify as black, but we also know are in fact biracial. And what is it going to mean for me personally, like on a level somewhere between the social and spiritual 10 years from now, 20 years from now, to be married to this white woman? . . . I . . . wrestled with that stuff but decided at the time that it probably wasn't really all that important and that the love and my hopes for the relationship were really the more important thing, and that I would just deal with it. And I have, and I can't think, honestly, of any moments when I've had to . . . seriously wrestle with it as an issue. But I still think about it sometimes. I think about it especially in connection with the distance emotionally that there is between me and several black female friends who I have just accepted that there is kind of always going to be this little bit of a gulf between me and them because of my marriage. . . . They have such strongly, overwhelmingly negative feelings, and because they care about me they sit on it, and we don't talk about it, but I know they're there. (Lorenzo)

He went on to talk about the value to him of being firmly rooted in his heritage, saying that without those firm roots he would have great difficulty in an interracial marriage and his children would have serious identity problems. He believed that being married to a white person and parenting biracial children required a strong black identity.

I would . . . say that when the black partner in a couple has a really weak or undeveloped sense of . . . self as a black person, as a member of the African American community, I think that's a real setup for all kinds of problems. It's a setup for problems with them as a couple, and it's a setup for kind of everybody's spoken or unspoken fears about what about the kids, which the in-laws always bring up. Because if the African American parent can't carry the ball in terms of helping those kids mold their self-identity. See, choices don't get made in the family then that support the children's need to build a strong self-identity, because, ostensibly, it doesn't matter to either parent. Families like that tend to build and strengthen this very insular and false notion that it's OK to shut out the rest of the world and forget that people are going to see their children as black children and forget that race does matter very, very much in the United States and instead cling to this kind of creative little bubble world within the family that because we say . . . we love each other that race doesn't matter. Just go out there and tell people . . . that you're an American. And on one level there's nothing wrong with that thinking. . . . But people have to understand that there's a worldview that you keep for yourself and your family and friends in much the same way that if you are Orthodox Jewish or Fundamentalist Christian that there are certain things you would say within your family that you say because you're all of the same faith, that you'd be stupid and disrespectful to say at public school. . . . People don't want to hear that mess. They don't want to hear that there's only one way to salvation, that you happen to know it and they don't. And it's not the same thing, but it's similar. . . . There is a thing that we say within our family that everybody should accept everybody for who and what they are. . . . But if the kids are brought up expecting, because this is what they've heard at home, that this is what they should also demand and respect outside, it's a recipe for disaster. And I've seen so much unhappiness on the part of both the broader families involved, and specifically the kids, that I would very, very passionately and specifically counsel families who think this way to . . . reexamine where they are now. . . .

There are 28 million black people in the United States and . . . 28 million different ways of . . . being black in America, so you can't tell somebody who just doesn't feel culturally black and doesn't feel that they have much of a connection with the African American community that . . . they better go out and get that for themselves, but . . . you certainly have to be aware of it and take responsibility for the fact that, however you are going to try to do it, it's your job as the only black parent to help your kids get ready to deal with the world that you find offensive and didn't create . . . but you've got to deal with it and [so do] your children. So all this stuff about . . . perpetuating this cultural and racial ambivalence in another generation of kids is, I think, a real problem with a fair percentage of interracial families. Not anywhere near the majority but with a sizable minority, about whom I do kind of worry, and you know, some of your kids I wind up interacting with on one level or another [as] a sort of unofficial uncle out in the community. I try to give them something. But it's very hard if they don't get some good strong bicultural home training at an early age. That's a problem for anybody, no matter what your background is. But if you're going to have to be in a position to . . . defend yourself, . . . you damn well better get some help learning how to do that. And I see too many families in which it's just this lala land version of reality that's given to the kids. (Lorenzo)

Another black man, who felt that at one time he had come to minimize aspects of black culture, said that one needed a strongly rooted black identity to get along well in an interracial relationship.

I have been raised and educated in my family as a more traditional integrationist, which I have always believed and still do believe is a good thing. I believe in the concept of the melting pot. And the moment you do that to synthesize into something that is truly American, there is going to be a blending of cultures and races. I have since come to realize that an aspect of that was my, if not giving up something of a black culture, at least minimizing it. . . . I'm beginning to realize that there is a real possibility of keeping a separateness while building some kind of melded unit. . . . The fact that we are of different races does make a difference in our relationship, and I think we are continually . . . aware of what it is to be of a particular race, and it means that you do identify, keep with, study more about what makes you you. (Emmett)

He also discussed identity and loyalty doubts stemming from his interracial relationship.

There have been times for me where I have seriously questioned am I being too selfish in my relationship with her? I have done work in race relations; I am a chairman of a EEO [equal employment opportunity] committee in my union; I am on the national committee; I've gone to Washington to lobby for the Civil Rights Act. . . . It has at times engendered a kind of self-doubt in the sense that, "Am I being selfish in a relationship with the woman that I love as opposed to finding a relationship with a black woman, specifically with the idea of raising a child and perhaps somehow advancing the race?" I mean, that's in quotation marks and tongue-in-cheek, but yet that is not tongue-in-cheek. Those doubts do exist, but relationships are tough anyway. . . . I think there's going to be all kinds of doubts, and I don't think that you can avoid that kind of doubt.

Being Too Much in the White World

Another aspect of identity that some African Americans mentioned was that a partnership with a white person put them more often in an all-white environment. Visiting, partying, praying, shopping, and so on in an all-white world can be an identity challenge. For many people, identity is sustained by being among others who are like themselves and in places where they are not the only person of their group.

GREGORY There've been some . . . events that Joyce has wanted to do, and I just said . . . I can't do it; I'm not gonna do it. I've just had too much of a European focus this week; I'm not gonna do it. . . . Joyce [has] been understanding and [said], "Oh yeah, OK. Say you've got your basic European overload, right. . . . You don't want to do it; I want to do it; I'll do it; fine."

INTERVIEWER What are those events?

JOYCE Well, like going to the country, for example. Or like being totally away from black people, going and spending a week away from the city, or going to [a town where everyone is white] (laughs). Going someplace that he knows is going to not feel comfortable.

GREGORY . . . I don't want to look around at an event and see I'm the only African American there. . . . It's . . . sort of like a psychological type of oppression when you're the only person from your race somewhere. And so it's not that people are saying that . . . "We don't want you here" or "You're not wanted" or any of that stuff.

Talk about needing a respite from mostly white social situations is presumably talk about both a desire to be free of being "the other," the person who is different, and also a desire to be free of having to be vigilant—the awareness of being onstage that some blacks talked about (see especially Chapter 8).

THE WHITE PARTNER'S IDENTITY

More African Americans than whites talked about challenges to identity. One reason for the difference may be that in Minnesota it is easy for a white to spend most or all of the day in an all-white setting, whereas there are few all-black settings available for African Americans. The difference may also arise from the ways in which white privilege and racism operate. White privilege enables whites to go through daily life with an ease that is denied African Americans (McIntosh, 1988). Whites can expect to see newscasters of their group, can expect to walk through a store without extensive surveillance, can expect to return merchandise without having to present three forms of identity, and so on. Their privilege may make white identity of no particular significance to many whites; their identity is not an issue because white privilege is so automatic. But for African Americans, the denial of privilege and the potential of white racism to appear in encounters with whites may make it important to have a respite from being too often in all-white or mostly white social situations. It also may make joining with other African Americans important in terms of comfort, if not safety, and as part of developing a personal identity strong enough to withstand white racism. Whites may feel much less need to band together and much less need to bolster their identity by joining together with other whites.

Whites Coming to New Identity Awareness

Some whites said that their identity was affected by their marriage. One part of it is that many whites, at least in the upper Midwest, do not think of race as a part of identity. Particularly in a mostly white or entirely white community, racial membership is not a part of white identity. Once they became linked to a black person, however, the way society defines them, as part of an interracial couple, pushes them to include race as part of their identity.

DOT As little as white people think about their race . . . I never thought of, I never defined myself as a white person growing up. Unlike black people who have to think of their race every day. . . . It isn't something I think about daily. When outside forces come into play, then I do think about it. . . . As far as society's concerned, I need to be ever mindful that I am in an interracial marriage. Society views me differently because of my interracial marriage.

WILSON . . . Just growing up in the United States as a black child, I was aware that I was different (little laugh). . . . I understood that I had to be conscious of what's going on about me. . . . Over a period of time, it becomes a burden, which I think affects most black people as far as hypertension, stress. It becomes a heavy burden to carry from day to day. When you get up . . . in the morning and look in mirror, the first thing that comes in my mind, "I'm still black. I'm still beautiful, but I've got to [go] out there and deal with these ignorant people."

DOT That's what I mean by the white people don't think about their race. Never a day in my life that I look in the mirror and think, "You're white," because I was surrounded by white people.

Being in an interracial couple can lead some whites to assume (or to have imposed on them) expertise about African American life and issues. One white man talked about how he needed to work at not presuming to make an expertise he did not have part of his identity.

There are times when I don't feel it's even appropriate for me in . . . a particular situation to try to speak to an issue that has to do with being an African American. . . . I have to be careful about that. . . . Because I'm a member of an interracial family, . . . it doesn't make me African American. (Adam)

Not Becoming a Marginal Member of One's Own Biracial Family

Typically, the children of an interracial couple were defined as black. As their children developed a black identity, some whites who were interviewed felt marginalized. They might feel that aspects of their identity were not being transmitted to their children, even though those aspects of identity may not, in the past, have been very salient for them. For some white parents, like the one quoted next, feelings of being marginalized led to a digging in, an effort to count as a person if not as the dominant identity source.

ADAM I have to watch out and make sure that my kids recognize that I'm not the odd man out. . . . [Our daughter] and you have had these discussions. "[Child's name], you're an African American."

WANDA Yeah, they feel sorry for him.

ADAM . . . "We're African American"; you know, what it means to be African American, all of that. . . . "Dad, what are you?" "Ah, ah, white. I'm different," and you don't want that either, I mean, entirely, but . . . you want your kids both to recognize . . . the social reality and . . . how you're viewed.

In another family, having the children identified as black made the white parent feel that part of her identity was being slighted. But she was also amused that the matter made a difference to her.

JOHN You just feel kind of slighted, don't you, that the kids *were* black? . . .

LIZ Why do I have to call *them* black? . . . Then I don't get my ethn-, they don't carry my identity. They don't, and then all of a sudden I realized I was labeling myself white, and it was, like (laughs), well, I didn't know I really labeled myself white, and there I did it.

SUMMARY AND CONCLUSIONS

Interracial partnership can lead to questions about one's identity. To the extent that identity is linked to group connections, questions about belongingness arise when one is strongly committed to someone from another group and associates frequently with people from that group. Interracial partnership does not obliterate one's ethnic, racial, or other identities (Spickard, 1989, p. 17). It may, however, lead to questions from others and oneself about one's identity. Despite the relatively great acceptance of interracial partnerships in black families, quite a few African Americans talked about the ways their credibility was challenged in their community. Other people questioned their expertise on matters relating to African American life, questioned their standing to speak up against racism, closed out certain jobs and organizational memberships to them, and questioned whether they had the right to lead in the black community. White people might also assume that a black person in an interracial relationship does not have a strong African American identity and might even feel that they can safely say antiblack things in front of such a person.

Despite the ways others might question their identity, the black partners who spoke about matters of identity all felt identified as black. None spoke of wanting to drop that aspect of identity. If anything, they saw a strong black identity as important in maintaining an interracial relationship and in properly bringing up biracial children.

White partners spoke less often about identity. All live in a part of America where a white person can spend all or nearly all of every waking moment entirely surrounded by white people, so it is easy to understand why whiteness might not be central to the identity of whites. Nonetheless, entering an interracial partnership could make race a salient aspect of identity for a white person, partly because others have reactions to a white who is joined with someone of color. Racial matters can also become more central to identity as others define one as an expert on black America and, for couples who have children, as race becomes important in the identity and socialization of children. Included in this, for some whites, was discomfort over their biracial children being labeled as black and identifying that way. A white partner for whom race was never part of identity might feel pushed to make it part of his or her identity as a child moved toward black identity.

10

CHILDREN

Sixteen couples in the study had at least one child together, and the woman in another couple was pregnant with a first child. As far as could be determined from what parents said, the children were living normal, healthy lives. Nonetheless, racism can pose challenges for an interracial couple raising a child.

For centuries, the racial identity of a child had enormous implications for the legal standing, rights, and life chances of that child (Johnston, 1970, chap. 8). Parents had to struggle to help a biracial child deal with a legal system that created hazards for biracial people. To the best of our knowledge, there are no longer laws on the books that single out biracial individuals. But raising a biracial child can still be challenging. Parents are still challenged to help a child to cope with racism. Some of the racism a child must learn to deal with is identical to the racism directed at any black child, but there are also racist words and actions directed specifically at black-white biracial children. The existence of biracial children is a challenge to racist thinking, in part because those who need to fit everyone into a clearly defined set of categories can be resentful when a child straddles the boundaries between categories. Biracial children may also threaten white racism because of the claim biracial children have to property, power, and privileges that in the past were reserved for whites (Kitchen, 1993, pp. 65-66).

BIRACIAL CHILDREN
AND WHITE GRANDPARENTS

In understanding the special challenges of parenting a biracial child, it is revealing to look at the child's relationship with her or his white grandparents. As discussed in Chapter 5, white family members who objected to a couple's getting together often raised concerns about children the couple might have.

> The reason Dad was telling me that black and white people shouldn't get together is 'cause of the kids. The kids wouldn't know what they were. And I was saying, "That's a bunch of bull. . . . Kids are kids, and you treat them as such." (Liz)

One might assume from the concerns raised about children that the parents of a white partner would distance the interracial couple's children. That rarely happened, however. Typically, a white partner's parents who were bitterly opposed to the interracial relationship became very attached to the children of that relationship. As indicated in Chapter 5, children could be the key to the white partner's parents becoming reconciled to the interracial relationship.

> We had it out that one time about he wasn't gonna talk to me anymore if I came home with a black man, rethought it and said, "No matter what," and they've just kind of stuck with that. They really love the kids. . . . He had a heart attack in, was it in January? Yeah, and I think he thought he was going to die, and he kept calling and asking for [our son] to come stay with him. So the kids are really important to my parents. (Liz)

> My mother, once we got married and it was apparent that she couldn't do anything about it, then she kind of switched sides, and she will now get very intense with relatives (laughs), I mean, racial problems and

stuff, and she'll confront people about stuff. She's very protective of
the kids, particularly when they were little. Somebody would be sitting
next to her on the bus, would say something and she'd . . . say, "Well,
you're talking about my grandchildren." (Virginia)

There were also families in which even though a white grandparent
felt very attached to the children, he or she still kept a distance. In
one case, the couple suspected that the woman's father feared the
stigma of being seen with a biracial grandchild.

ROSEMARY [Our son] is almost 7. He's probably been out to my dad's
    and stayed with him twice, which is just absolutely pathetic.
ED . . . I'm driving . . . out on [the highway], and I see her father and
    his wife driving another one of their [grandchildren]. . . . But
    that never happens with [our son].
ROSEMARY That right there, that's racism. . . . Oh, but my dad just
    loves [our son]. I mean, . . . he just pours him on. But . . .
    does not take any of the action. . . .
ED And [our son] is starting to question his grandfather. . . . Like,
    "Why didn't we get to go to Grandpa's this Easter?"

ADVANTAGES
TO A CHILD'S BEING BIRACIAL

In America, racism can be a burden for a biracial child. But some
people also saw real advantages to a child's being biracial. It would
be a mistake to accept a simple notion that biracial children have
more troubled lives than other children. They may have some trouble
because of racism, but they also have major advantages over children
who are not biracial (see Kouri, 1994).

I think biracial children are luckier. . . . People . . . always want to talk
about the negative things, but our kids are going to grow up in a world
with all different kinds of colors. I think that's neat. (Eve)

ADAM The kids that succeed . . . often develop skills so that they can
    sort of live in both worlds. . . . It's . . . a strength. It's like
    learning another language. . . .

WANDA . . . There are . . . things that you give to your child that
[couples who are in the same culture] may not be able to do.
There's some parents out there who will give . . . the cultural
lessons to their children regardless of what race they are, but
that's pretty rare.

In addition to the advantages that come with knowing two worlds
and having dual perspectives, a biracial child can gain from educational benefits available to children of color. These benefits have
been established to achieve educational goals for the whole population and to attempt to reduce the damage caused by racism. As part
of their efforts to integrate their schools and to provide the highest
quality education for all children, Minneapolis and St. Paul both
developed magnet schools. Educational resources have been concen-
trated in those schools, so white families throughout the metropolitan
area compete intensely to enroll a child in one of those schools. For
a child of color, admission to a magnet school is easier than for a
white child.

There are times when you recognize that you may even have an advantage, as in the case of school systems. [Our daughter], light
skinned, we wanted to get her into a magnet school. Check off on
the form, African American. All the white places fill up quicker. . . .
[She] gets in. Are you going to feel guilty? . . . No. She is African
American. (Adam)

BRINGING UP A BIRACIAL
CHILD IN A RACIST SOCIETY

The Reality of Racial Categories and Racism

Parents of biracial children have to face the reality of racial
categorization and racism (Kerwin et al., 1993; Tizard & Phoenix,
1993, pp. 140-145). The children will be racially labeled, even
though that may seem irrelevant to the children and their parents.
One mother told about a labeling event that occurred while she was
visiting her mother.

These kids kept coming to my mother's house saying to [our son], "Are you black or white?" . . . They weren't tormenting him with it. They felt like that they really need to put him in a category, and finally, he says, "I'm neither" or "I'm both" or something like that, and they went away. They never bothered him again or said "hello" to him again or wanted to play with him again. They had their answer. (Patricia)

Biracial children may draw inordinate amounts of attention in situations in which the usual racial category system has no clear place for somebody who seems not to fit in one category or another.

Goin' down to see his family. . . . Boy, what an experience. I've never had 200 people get out on the lawn; they want to see what a biracial kid looks like. . . . Everybody in the neighborhood came through to meet me and to see our daughter. They wanted to see her. I mean, actually get up close and kind of study her. (Kate)

Biracial children risk encounters with racism on a daily basis. Being categorized as "half white" or "mixed" or something else biracial will not erase the problems caused by racism. In fact, being categorized as biracial brings an additional load of stereotypes. For example, the children may also be labeled as dysfunctional.

[People] always bring up [biracial] children, saying that they will be mixed-up. (Eve)

Parents of biracial children face the challenge of how to protect a child and the even more difficult challenge of accepting that they cannot always protect a child (Brown, 1987). A white father thought that he might be physically dangerous to anyone who directed racism at his children.

I'm very antiracist. I think that if the opportunity (laughs) arised, I would be militarily so. . . . I hope that I don't ever see anybody hurt my children because of their . . . race, or the fact that it's interracial. Because I don't know what I might do. I think it would *really* make me mad. . . . That's how strongly I feel about protecting my children, and their *right* to be protected; I think that they should never have to feel that. . . . I might be dangerous (laughs) in a situation like that. (Tim)

Yet the reality is almost certainly that he will not know some of what happens to his children and that they will at times be on their own in dealing with racism (cf. Kerwin et al., 1993; Tizard & Phoenix, 1993, p. 147).

Partner Differences in Knowledge About Dealing With Bias

In an interracial couple, a black parent, much more than a white parent, will have life experience on which to draw in helping a child to cope with racism. A white parent may well have entered an interracial partnership not only not paying much attention to matters of race but feeling that the moral thing to do is to ignore racial matters. Once that parent has a biracial child, it may be crucial in parenting the child to be constantly aware of the possibility that race matters to someone with whom the child is dealing.

[Color] is not . . . in the forefront of my mind unless somebody else brings it there. It's not an issue. I think more so now that we have a child, it's come more into play of how is he going to be viewed. (Jill)

LIZ I hadn't really even thought about the racial issue very much until John brought up he would like the kids to be in a day care situation with other black kids. . . . I started thinking about it, like, are they really black, and do they really have to go to this black day care, or is it important that they be with other black kids? And so that's when it became more of an issue that there was a race difference.

INTERVIEWER And what did you decide when you asked yourself that question?

LIZ I don't know if I decided anything. I got the picture that the kids need to be prepared for society to see them or label them as black. . . . Other people see the race more than I do. And that they [need] to be prepared for that; I don't have to, in my

house, like, tell them, "You're black." I don't need to get into
that at home with them.

We had a [racial] incident with our daughter last summer, with a little
white girl. And this little girl's dad about had a fit. And I was at work
and the dad of this little girl ended up coming over and having a long
conversation with Robert. And what did he say about 200 times during
that conversation? "But I'm not a racist! But I'm not a racist!" (laughs).
And Robert just said, "Look, you're entitled to teach your children
what you want to teach them. You're entitled to believe what you want
to believe and . . . think what you want to think; however, when it in-
fringes on my family . . . then it becomes my business. If your child
ever bites my daughter again because she doesn't like black people,
we're going to have a serious problem." (Kate)

The pressure on the white parent to pay attention to matters of
race comes not only from society and from her or his spouse but also
from the child.

ANN [Our older daughter] is starting to talk about race. . . . I think
about what toys we have in the home. I think a lot about what
friends she has and if she has enough friends of color. . . .
She knows what color she is; she thinks [her sister] is white;
she says [her sister] is white like Mom and she is brown like
Dad. . . . Her teacher says one time she said she wishes she
was white, so that made me feel real bad. . . .

BAYARD [Our older daughter] talks about it more, so we have got to
deal with it. . . . I knew it would come.

In raising a child to deal with bias and to develop a healthy identity,
the African American partner has all sorts of life experiences, learning, social connections, and perspectives that the white partner does
not have. A white woman who had a biracial child from an earlier
relationship talked about how much she thought her child gained
from her having married an African American man.

INTERVIEWER Did your son have any bearing on how you decided to
date after he was born, in that . . . your son is [biracial]?

LAURA . . . Yes, it did; it had some bearing. And . . . I think for a while
that was my thought, "Well, . . . I don't feel it would be fair,
somehow, for him to have a white stepfather; I don't feel he
would get what he needs." . . . I think that would be a real
point of tension that I would have to live with if I had married
a white man. Within me, I'm very comfortable with [him]
having William for his stepdad.

Some black parents expressed concerns about their spouse's ignorance of how to socialize a child to live in a racist society.

Having a child, I'm probably more on Kent to be aware of black history and to convey to [our daughter] his interest in my culture along
with his culture. [Before], if he didn't sit down and watch a program
with me that was on TV, I wouldn't give him a hard time. . . . But now
I kind of feel I don't want to give mixed messages to our child
(laughs), and so I want him to also watch things or attend things so
that she feels as proud of both sides of her heritage. . . . If Kent is not
aware of when things are going on, . . . who's going to pick up on it
for [our daughter]? So I feel the need to, that he's as conscious of it all
as I am, so that he can help her as she's growing up. . . . I don't know
if I should relate this story, but I think it reminded me of the difference
between being black and white in this society. . . . He doesn't have that
kind of paranoia that I think black folks in this country (chuckles) just
have to have because you *don't know* sometimes what people, the moti-
vations for saying or doing the things are; you don't know whether it's
based on your color or based on something you actually did to them.
. . . Ya know, something simple like I tell him, like, if he walks into a
store without a receipt, he doesn't bother carrying a bag in (laughs)
with the merchandise, and I just would be afraid to do that. I would
feel like a, in fact, I've felt people following me in stores. And it's a
constant reminder to me as a black person that no matter how I dress
or how I look or what I accomplish that there are gonna be people
who're gonna be looking out for me because I'm black. And I don't
think he has to experience that as a white male. (Gloria)

We have different modes of child rearing we were raised with. And . . .
it's related to the privilege and not having to be afraid of what your
child does if they're white. And be very afraid and protective of what
your child does if they're black. (Patricia)

Later, Patricia gave an example of an issue that she felt required different child rearing in black than in white families—rearing a child to deal with the police.

> I am very afraid to have a minority child at this point. I mean, all I can think of is, "OK, in another year he's going to college, and he will be in sort of the safety of a college campus. I want to be very careful about where that is," because, I mean, he's been stopped twice by the police. You say to yourself, "Well, what is that related to? Was he doing something?" And I've tried to say to him, ". . . Cops make their living off of minority teenage boys. You can't be out at night. Your freedoms have to be curtailed, because they wonder why you are on the streets. When you're stopped, be polite. Don't give them any reason to hurt you." No [white] parent has to worry about that kind of stuff.

One black man was even concerned that his white partner might teach their child to think in racist ways. The following came at the conclusion of a discussion about the white partner's assumptions about black teenagers entering a store where she clerked.

> When I'll get upset and get angry is that [if] it ever has any affect on the kids. You know, if our kids start looking at people and getting these preconceived notions, then that'll make me upset. So don't teach our kids that stuff. (Bayard)

White Parent Struggles
Over a Biracial Child's Identity

White parents, particularly mothers, worked at finding play and learning resources that would enable a child to build a strong, positive, resilient identity. Parents might hope to find resources tailored specifically for biracial children, but they might settle for and be glad they found materials for African American children. They might also struggle to teach the child about their white or ethnic heritage in a way that makes it seem to be more than just the heritage of an oppressor.

> DOT In terms of my daughter, she's just my daughter. But sometimes when you're out you [are] forced to think about [racism]. Then it becomes a factor. . . .

WILSON My daughter makes me think about my interracial marriage
because she has to know from where she came. She has to be
aware of what's going on in society, what to expect in
different occasions. . . .

DOT Society has made up nothing for the biracial child. I would buy
these Golden Books by the stackful. . . . There were none
with biracial children in them at that time, but I found myself
looking for ones that were illustrated with black children.
. . . When you look into a book and you're a little child, it
would be nice sometimes to see a brown daddy and a pink
mom. . . . When it came time to buy the Barbie dolls, I was
real conscious of having both, and I used to say, "Well, what
a shame they don't make biracial Barbie. . . ." I found it to
be very important that she be proud of her African heritage,
and I also found, there have been times when I am ashamed
of my German heritage. You all know the German history is
not a pretty one. It became more important to me to find
things in that to be proud of. . . . One time, she said to me,
"Mom, are we, are you a Jew or a Nazi?" It was like whatever
she had heard on TV there were only two choices. . . . I found
myself quickly beginning to look up things on Pennsylvania
Dutch, which is what I am, and I would point out the art of
the Pennsylvania Dutch and things like that. . . . It became
suddenly important that she be proud.

As others have observed (Gibbs & Hines, 1992), there are social
pressures on biracial children as they grow older to identify black.
Some whites grieved and resented the need for a child to be socialized
as black and identified as black. It felt like a violation of marital equity
and a loss of a connection of personal identity with the child.

Why do I have to call *them* black . . . ? Then I don't get my ethn-, they
don't carry my identity. (Liz)

Liz also grieved that her children would have to face racism.

I think that's gonna be something I have to deal with for the next 18
years, or forever. . . . I started uncovering different levels of, I didn't
want to admit that my kids were going to have problems with racism.

Or that that could be a problem for them, and I think it is. . . . Realistically . . . they are going to encounter problems with it.

The Child's Sense of Identity

Many parents talked about its being absolutely essential that a
biracial child have a clear, positive, resilient sense of identity (cf.
Tizard & Phoenix, 1993, p. 139). Like parents interviewed by Kerwin
et al. (1993), they talked about biracial children needing to be
prepared to face racism. They also talked about the identity confu-
sions that biracial children might experience because they embody
two racial groups that are defined very differently in the category
system of American racism. Many parents spoke of supporting a child
in facing the challenges by helping the child to know and to accept
who she or he is.

It's very important that we're sort of politically and socially kind of
conscious of who we are, sort of identity-wise, especially in terms of the
kids. . . . What we've done for [our children is] talking about their identity
and providing materials and books, and I think the biggest piece, providing family and play family and extended family that's both cultures. It
seems to me . . . those are the important connections. (Joyce)

I think that it's important that we teach our children, all interracial
couples, when they say, "What are you?" I teach my children, I got this
from reading, "We are—I am biracial." And then you can go into the
fact, biracial, two races, what; we're more than that, but we're just
gonna break it down—"We're biracial." And then what does that
mean? "Well, we're black, and white." Then you can go from that,
'cause if you say "biracial," nobody's gonna, "What you talkin'
about?" They're probably gonna leave it at that. So we try to teach our
children what to say when people, especially now they're going to . . .
school, and it is predominantly white. And I know that they're gonna
come across that, OK? So I really, especially last year, started working
on, what do you want to call yourselves? We're black and white, and I
want to make sure that you know that that's what you are. You're not
just black because somebody on the Census says that you are. And
you're not just white; you are both. . . . It's important to me that they
know that they are both. (Flora)

A black father talked about a biracial woman, interviewed on television, who had not been brought up with a clear, affirming identity.

> What she explained was that her racial identity . . . wasn't clearly defined to her. So she was kind of like this floater, this person without a race. And then her mom took her to live in a predominantly white neighborhood where the kids . . . teased her about racial difference. And her not having any . . . foundation as to what she belonged to, she kind of went into a fantasy, wishing she was white. [But] wishes don't come true. . . . She didn't really have any exposure to positive blackness, and the exposure that she had to the Caucasian race was negative. She was this lost person. (John)

Some parents said that an important part of socializing a biracial child was to expose the child to appropriate films, books, television programs, and adult models.

> Now they're in school I have material in my house on African Americans. He goes to the library and he gets things about black people, and both of them are interested in things they see on TV, 'cause I want them to be involved. They're gonna get both sides; they're gonna get the side in school; they're gonna get what their dad gives them. My husband's family is real close-knit. They see their family a lot on his side more than they do on mine. So I'm gonna get them involved with the positive things; they see enough negative from both sides on TV. . . . So now I see that they're interested in the black American and the African roots, and I'm very happy about it. (Flora)

Exposing children to appropriate films, books, television programs, and adult models is more challenging when the white partner has a great deal of responsibility for child socialization and is rather ignorant about how to go about guiding a child of color.

> I worry more about teaching her by lack of exposure than anything else. Like, I really knock myself out for books. But what movie do I pick for her, and who does she want to be? She wants to be Maria in *Sound of Music,* and I used to think it was enough that Bayard is black. I wasn't going to have to worry about it. My kids were going to be

fine, and I thought, well, "He's biracial. I'm not going to have to worry about it. Oh, he can help me through everything. He's biracial. He's done it all. He can help them." And then I realize that it's not that way, because she identifies so strongly with me. I mean, I'm her mother. She's with me all the time, and I'm really glad that _____ is my only black woman friend, and I'm really glad she's my friend, and I'm glad my kids can be around her because [our younger daughter] does not really know any black women, and that's why all of a sudden I'm hot on finding her a school with black teachers. I realize that it's not . . . enough that Bayard is there, that there need to be women of color in her life as role models too. . . . So I'm real hot on that now, and shopping for schools, and finding out how many people of color do you have teaching. If you don't have any, what's your plan on getting them in there? (Ann)

Consistent with findings in a study carried out in and around New York City (Kerwin et al., 1993), a number of parents spoke of choice of community as an issue in raising biracial children. For example, one couple talked about the value of bringing up biracial children in a neighborhood where there were many African American children.

VIRGINIA   It's an interracial neighborhood, highly interracial neighborhood.

LORENZO   Right, which I think will stand in good stead later. It would have been nicer to have been more affluent for [our children], as they were growing up, but actually really horrible . . . if for the last 10 years or so we've been in a predominately white suburban community, because they wouldn't 've had a chance to literally every day of their lives interact with a reasonably healthy, sane now, and for recent years, predominately black community, although it is continued to be racially mixed, where they've had a broad range of experiences. Because . . . the more middle-class environment creates this whole other level of alienation. . . . I've got a couple of adult friends who really struggle with this now, feeling like they're very thoroughly acculturated black folks with only the most tentative and tenuous ties to what they see as the vast majority of the African American community. And so it's possible to be very dark and come from two black parents and be a great deal more alienated and less connected to the

African American community as a whole than many children
of mixed heritage wind up becoming as adults, purely by
virtue of their environment and the atmosphere in which
they grew up.

In facing issues of child identity, parents had to deal with the way
their parenting reflected their own identity. For example, a black
parent could feel uncomfortable around black friends if she were not
using enough of what she considered "black" parenting standards.

Sometimes when I'm with friends who are ethnically very African
American, whatever that means, and have raised their kids that way,
I feel like . . . I should try and be more black in my parenting. And
I fight that feeling. . . . [A friend] was over the other night, and when
. . . my younger daughter, I wanted her to be sure that she said,
"Hello," and, just kind of that down-home kind of home training,
like (laughs) you speak and you act decent and you're not flippant.
But . . . our older daughter can be very flippant and is very comfortable with strangers and will say absolutely what she thinks, whether
you're an adult or not. . . . I never worry about that, except when
we're in the company of other black women. I think, she's probably
. . . showing that she hasn't been raised right. (Barb)

Some parents worked at bringing up a biracial child to have a black
identity. They did so because they believed the child would be defined
as black by the larger society and because they believed that a child
defined as black would benefit from being connected to the black
community and acquiring the strengths and survival skills that can be
learned in that community. But some parents talked about wanting a
child to be raised with a white identity as well as a black one.

When we got married we were looking for a culturally diverse environment in a church setting and that would not only focus on black [but]
focus on white, European, other cultures. . . . We have a multiracial
church. . . . What attracted me to that church, the congregation is very
warm, they are multiracial. We feel like we want to bring our kids up
in an environment that don't speak to one or the other but an environment that speak to the whole. That my daughter know she is both
black and white, our son know that he is both black and white and that

he is judged by who he is rather than what he appears to be on the outside. (Robert, who is black)

One man who defined himself as black but had a white parent talked about his identity struggles while growing up. What he had to say helps to make clear what many parents said, that proper socialization of a biracial child can help the child come to terms with matters of identity.

BAYARD For a while . . . I considered myself and used the term *mulatto*. I stopped using that after I became a little more aware of what it meant. . . . It's derived from the word mule or the word mule is derived from the word mulatto. So I stopped using the term. . . . For a while, I was real adamant about when I had to check race on some sort of form, . . . I checked "other" and put "mulatto" in there. But after I decided to stop doing that, I just would check "African American" or whatever. . . . I never considered myself to be white. I [don't think I] ever asked my mom or told my mom I wanted to be white. I can't remember anything like that. . . . But my mom from the very beginning told us that we were black kids. My father was black and we had black relatives. Although I didn't see my father much, I saw my father's brothers and aunts and cousins, . . . so I had contact with my black side of my family when I was young. . . . When I was real young, my mother's mother is from Germany, . . . so I went through a phase when I wanted to be a black German. I took . . . years of German in junior high and high school and . . . college. . . . When I was real young, about 6, 7 years old . . . that was something me and my grandma would joke a lot about, being a black German. . . .

INTERVIEWER Have you ever wished that the culture had more of a way of identifying you as biracial?

BAYARD I guess my desire would be that . . . nobody would have to identify themselves as far as race is concerned, being black or white or biracial or what have you. . . .

ANN It bothers me about our children. I mean, what box do I check for [our daughter]? Our kids are a quarter black. Does that make them black? They're not white; they're not black. . . .

I guess I say she's a biracial child or we're a multicultural family. . . . She's going to be a biracial child, and I'm not going to tell her she's black. How can you tell this kid she's black? I mean, she doesn't look black, and she can think whatever she wants. She can grow up and think she's white as long as she understands her dad is black. . . . She can identify whatever she feels is most comfortable as long as she accepts what her heritage is.

Some parents had strong reservations about the identities "biracial" and "mixed," identities that do not provide a person with a large, identifiable, culturally defined group with which to affiliate. For the child, however, there can be concerns about identifying with only one side of the family.

VIRGINIA [Our daughter] is calling herself mixed these days.

LORENZO Yeah, we have to have another talk. Kids speak to each other obviously, and their own peer group has a huge effect on what they say and how they see themselves, and for her, certainly, knowing a fair number of offspring from other interracial homes, it's an issue that they talk about amongst themselves. And so whatever she winds up ultimately feeling comfortable with, from her point of view, is what she's going to go with, but I think that "mixed" is a mistake too and kind of we're . . .

VIRGINIA (laughs) This is a fairly recent development. . . . I think she used to identify herself as black, and she's going through a phase where she's identifying herself as mixed. . . .

LORENZO Yeah, well part of it I know has to do with feeling personally . . . and culturally different from . . .

VIRGINIA Black kids.

LORENZO Yeah right. And she feels it's sort of odd and uncomfortable that she gets to participate in programs that are specifically designed for minority youth, where she gets an advantage that she thinks may be . . . a little unfair, and she's just not sure how she really feels about it.

VIRGINIA She's at this point being very hotly recruited for colleges and being sent all sorts of information on scholarships. . . .

She's had privileges that other people don't, and therefore, why should she be getting this stuff?

LORENZO . . . She feels kind of like she's double dipping.

The couple went on to say that in their opinion there is no value to identifying [as] mixed.

VIRGINIA There is no mixed community . . .

LORENZO where it was deemed a desirable thing to have an interme-
diate group of people with whom one could deal, who could
kind of consciously be there to straddle the worlds. And since
the legacy of colonialism in the Caribbean didn't hold here,
there has never been any social or cultural meaning to being
a so-called mixed person. There is a little bit in . . . like an
isolated pocket like parts of New Orleans or other parts of
Louisiana and a little bit in South Carolina, but that's outside
of the experiences of a vast majority of Americans for whom
you are either, it didn't matter a bit; I mean, that's why we
have this whole series of ridiculous words like *octoroon*. It
didn't matter what percentage of black blood you had by
state law in state after state. If you had one drop of black
blood you were black. Period. And so there was no sociopolitical meaning to the word *mixed*. . . . Since that is still very
much where we are, it doesn't really make sense to encourage
a group of people, just because they have mixed racial
heritage, to . . . carve out [a] niche for themselves that makes
them different from the rest of the community of color to
which they ultimately, because of how things are, . . . belong.
Now that's why I'm saying that family mythology and the
family trip about who we are is different, and you are going
to know because you've encouraged your kids to develop
radar too, and they just kind of have, just by you modeling
that to them, they will know, increasingly who it's OK to talk
about these things with, and who it's not. And you just know
those things and go on with your life. . . .

VIRGINIA I see it in terms of survival skills where I think that part of
our responsibility as parents is to teach our children to
survive in the world, and that's on all levels. And with racially
mixed children, that includes dealing with the broader world

on racial issues and that they get from identifying with those who are black and not by playing games or expecting the white community not to see them different. The white community will see them as different, and . . . they just need to get that stuff straight early on. They know who their mother is. They know what their family history is, . . . and so I never felt like I've heard other white women say they felt like they were left out or something. I never felt that. I just see that the survival skill that they need to understand how to function in the world, and I can't teach them that. And if they tell me that something's happening and that they think it has something to do with race, I'm sure it does. They would know that more than I do, but in terms of who they are as an identity, I think it is a saner and more useful thing in terms of how they see themselves to identify themselves as black. . . . There's too many other things in life to worry about, and the black community has had a history forever of accepting people of all shades, and that's a much easier thing to deal with than to be thinking that somehow they're different. I think that any ambivalence the kids have has more to do with not feeling like they really came out of a hard-core black community. They go to private schools, that kind of stuff.

WHEN SIBLINGS DIFFER IN SKIN COLOR

An important issue in bringing up biracial children is to deal with what skin color and other physical features mean to others. For biracial children who look white, there are potential benefits and challenges that are not present for those who do not look white. They may avoid racism if they can pass (Daniel, 1992) for white, and passing can be tempting. An African American parent with a child whose skin was white and hair was straight talked about the advantages of the child passing as white and his own difficulties growing up African American.

Yesterday I was looking at . . . our son, and I was thinking about how straight his hair is, and how light it is, and how light his skin tone is, and I was remembering the first 2 years in high school, 9th and 10th grade. I went to a private Catholic school, 96% white. At this time, *Roots* had just come on TV, so of course the ignorant white children didn't quite understand what that story was all about. To them it was just a joke. There was no common ground for them to relate to it, except me. So I would get the jokes and the nicknames, Kizzy or "You're my nigger." Crap like that. And I was thinking that [our son], being so fair skinned and his hair being so straight and fair, that perhaps he'd be spared that, which I don't know, maybe it's avoidance of the actual problem, but I don't see that I'm going to change the world. I have no fantasies of that. But I don't want him to have to go through the same feelings that I did. . . . I'm sure my . . . mother thought it was best for me when she put me in that school. It's a very good school. Now it's almost 30% black, but unfortunately, sometimes being a trendsetter puts a lot of stress on an individual, especially an adolescent male with an ego that outweighs common sense. So a lot of times, I would confront those situations with violence. I just don't want [our son] to have to deal with those things. . . . I would rather him be on an equal footing with everyone else, even though I realize it's pie in the sky, at this time anyway. I want him to be judged like I would want myself to be judged, on my merits, my intellect, rather than the color of my skin or how curly my hair is. (James)

As James said, passing can be tempting. Perhaps part of the temptation is the possibility of covertly subverting the racist category system (Daniel, 1992). Passing, however, can bring with it a lifetime of identity struggles, the unpleasantness of secret keeping, and personal and family pain arising from efforts to hide the existence of relatives of color from certain people.

Another kind of problem related to the physical aspect of racial categorizing arises when one sibling in a family can pass for white and another cannot. The one who looks black may be the target of racism outside the home, whereas the one who looks white may receive privileges society denies to the darker-skinned sibling. Those differences can create resentments in a family and barriers to sibling closeness.

BAYARD I think it's . . . real important that we . . . tell [our older daughter] that the people she deals with at school, society,

whatever, when they see she has a black father, they are going
to consider her black, regardless of what she thinks she is.

ANN Yeah, I worry a lot about our kids having completely different
experiences [because one looks white and one does not] and
that there being some resentment . . .

INTERVIEWER Between the two of them, you mean?

ANN Umm-hm. I think that's going to happen. In fact it already does.
. . . They're going to have a different life experience.

In one family, the differences in appearance between the children
led to differences in treatment by the extended family and to
parental concern that certain feelings of a black grandmother might
need explaining to the children, particularly to the child who looked
white.

> The first time that my younger daughter, who is white appearing to a
> lot of people, was with my mom alone . . . my mother was uncomfort-
> able with people staring, and she thought, "They probably think I'm
> some servant." (Barb)

In that family, the skin color issue even showed up during family
play.

> Race is a really interesting thing to [our older daughter]. And we used
> to [have] wrestling meets, and [she], especially when [her sister] came,
> we had the whites against the blacks. But that was always [our older
> daughter's] idea.

A white parent said that strangers questioned his relationship to
his darker-skinned child but not to his lighter-skinned child.

> [Our son] is recognizably a minority. . . . When I'm with [him]
> you'll get different reactions than when I'm with [our daughter].
> When I'm with [our daughter] we could be white. When I'm with
> [our son], . . . "Well now, is the kid adopted or is he" mine?
> (Adam)

CHILDREN FORCED TO DECIDE
WHETHER THEY ARE BLACK OR WHITE

Some parents worked at socializing a child to have a biracial identity, but biracial children seem pressured by peers to fit into a category system that excludes biracial as a possibility and that is guided by simple physical notions about racial categorization. Adam, who was just quoted, talked about how, even in the lower grades, there are such pressures.

> In the . . . Minneapolis Public Schools, . . . differences are brought out. . . . Kids . . . see [our daughter], they'll make a judgment on [her]. . . . She'll say, "Well no, I'm African American." "Well, no you're not," or then even if they get through that, then they'll see us together. . . . Kids, of course, at that age are [very open]; nothing's hidden, and like, "How can this be?" They would ask questions like, "My mommy told me . . . this doesn't happen" (laugh). Or as [our daughter] said, one kid . . . thought that she had to be adopted.

It seems that when children reached junior high or high school, they could no longer have a biracial identity. They were pushed by peers, and perhaps by themselves, to be either white or black. In the Twin Cities at the time of the interviews, there seemed to be no interracial peer group.

> While [our children] are in grade school it seems like . . . things are fine; things are fine. So they walk into high school. Things aren't fine! Things change when you go to high school! Whoa! They change, and then kids are made to choose. OK, so one parent's black and one parent's white. What are you? Which group you gonna be with? Can't have both! You can't be with white people one day and black people the next. . . . Here's the line drawn down the middle; choose up. (Gregory)

SUMMARY AND CONCLUSIONS

By all accounts, the children of these couples were consistently doing well. Nonetheless, parenting biracial children can pose challenges. Although biracial children sometimes had a special power to bring white grandparents to reconcile with the child's interracial parents, there were white grandparents who kept their distance, possibly out of not wanting to be seen in public with the child.

Although there was talk of the problems of grandparents who distanced and of painful incidents of racism, there was also talk of the advantages to a child in being biracial, particularly the value of knowing multiple perspectives and of being able to relate to people in more than one group.

For a biracial child to reach adulthood without being hurt by racial categorization and racism, parents worked at socializing the child to have a strong, positive, confident sense of identity. Parents talked with a child about identity; provided strong support from the extended family, play family, and friends; provided identity-bolstering books, toys, and films; instructed the child about what to say in various situations; found the child strong adult role models; and built good connections to a strong black community. African American parents often were seen as in a better place to accomplish some of this than white parents, and some white parents clearly struggled to learn what they needed to learn, whereas some black parents both supported the child and worried about whether the white parent was up to the job.

The personal identity issues of some parents seemed entangled in how the parent dealt with the issue of child identity. Some parents learned things about their own sense of identity as they worked at bringing up their child. In particular, some white parents learned how race or membership in a racial community was part of their own identity. For some, this was a source of frustration, as a child developed an identity that seemed to exclude the parent's own identity community (Cauce et al., 1992). Many parents seemed to want a child to identify as biracial or with both black and white heritages and communities. But some parents also felt that there was no biracial community with which to identify and that the larger society (including schoolmates of the child) were pushing the child toward identifying as exclusively black or exclusively white. At the same time, a biracial child who identified as only black or only white could be concerned about cutting off part of her or his background and family.

11

LEARNING FROM EACH OTHER

In any couple, partners will learn from one another. They will learn each other's expectations, needs, preferences, preferred coping strategies, dislikes, experiences, habits, and so on. That learning occurs as their observations of one another, their conversations, their disputes, their joint decision making, their hearing of each other's stories, and their other shared experiences accumulate. One way to think about the importance of such learning is to think of every relationship as intercultural.

> We have cultural differences, and that can be very enriching. . . . We all come together with different backgrounds; . . . we all grow up in differ-ent families. . . . You can just kind of come together and . . . learn from each other. (Rosemary)

Partners in black-white interracial couples inevitably bring differ-ent backgrounds to the relationship. The black partner's experiences with racism and the partners' differing experiences in white and black communities mean that there is much for them to learn from one another. It seems unlikely that an interracial couple could stay together long without learning about some of their differences in background and experience.

> It would be a real burden if you tried to somehow not address racial ... or cultural differences in a relationship, if you somehow said a way of dealing with it is to not deal with it. Then you're going to have a real sense of friction and tension. But that would happen if I was from a very strong Italian American background and she was from a strong German American background. This, it's (pause) all the problems with the relationship aren't necessarily, you can't put your finger on what the cause is. Generally, the cause is people don't know how to work through the relationship. I tend to keep coming back to that. (Emmett)

Every black partner has had innumerable experiences of racism and continues to live in a world where each day can bring new dangers, frustrations, deprivations, and humiliations.

> The feeling that you're a suspect all the time. You're always suspect. And I guess you have to carry yourself accordingly, and that's a stressful way to live. . . . I like to get up sometime at 4 o'clock in the morning, 4:30, take a walk maybe a mile or so. And . . . that can be pretty danger- ous. . . . Living here for 17 years in my own neighborhood . . . and you still feel uncomfortable out there getting up early in the morning to take my walk. . . . Just painful, it is really painful to see that . . . just to feel the tension which you carry around from day to day. (Wilson)

> I was . . . raised by my mother to understand that as a black person [racism] is part of the experience in this country. And it doesn't matter. My mother used to say to us, "I don't care how much money you have, how many fur coats you own. You can drive up to the biggest hotel in town, and the man who parks your car will find some way to remind you that you're black." And I used to think, "God, that's really silly." But I think it prepared me so much for life. (Patricia)

Although they may not be aware of it, race also shapes the lives of white people (Frankenberg, 1993). Frankenberg (1993) argued that any system of differentiation shapes the lives of all who are in it. She asserted that in America everyone is a victim of racism. Because the daily risks of victimization are far more palpable for African Americans, they are under much more pressure than whites to be knowledgeable about the racist system. A white partner, therefore, is in a position to learn quite a bit from an African American partner about the system in which they have both lived. An important part of that learning may be about the ways the system is unfair and injurious to African Americans, but another part of the learning may be about the harm the system causes to white people (e.g., keeping them ignorant of the unearned advantages to being white, enabling them to support an oppressive system without their even intending to do so, and depriving them of the richness, warmth, and joy of close friendships with African Americans).

WHITE PARTNERS LEARN ABOUT
RACISM THROUGH THEIR PARTNERSHIP

Most, if not all, white partners seemed to enter the relationship with a lot to learn. Although having had previous interracial relationships made a difference for some whites, even some who had dated interracially before the current relationship reported considerable learning about racism from their current partner. It seems that growing up white leaves one with substantial limitations in perceiving and understanding racism in America and with an enormous amount of learning still necessary to understand even the basics of what any African American knows.

Henry has said on several occasions that it's real important, that he wants me to understand certain things about his background, his culture, what's happening in society, 'cause I do walk around not knowing, sometimes. I don't see those things, and sometimes he'll sit me down and tell me these things are going on, and that's fine. So I feel that I have grown as a person, because of that, because of becoming more aware of things that I was not aware of before, not out of, didn't want to know, but I just wasn't knowing. (Donna)

You a product of your upbringing, a product what you live in, like, people like to say, I may say something to Kate which I know she see'n' it from a different eye. She see'n' it from an eye that she never experienced before. So I expect her to be less conscious about that particular issue. So sometimes when we discuss some issue together, as a couple . . . she'll say, "I never thought about that. I see why you approach this situation the way that you did now." And all because of her white upbringing, she never had to look at it any other way. (Robert)

SHIRLEY Shane has taught me how to recognize false behavior.

INTERVIEWER Can you say what it is that you have learned?

SHIRLEY Body language, I guess a little bit, and don't trust everybody right away, like I was brought up to be; get to know them first.

SHANE Oh, I think that's the whole thing. You gotta know people before you can trust them. It just doesn't work if you jump right into something.

I think part of the education for me was if the discrimination was not absolutely blatant and in my face, I would often not notice it. And Patricia would point something out. "Did you see that this happened?" "Let's see, yeah, I remember that." And she'd say, "You know what that means." And then I, "Oh, I suppose." (Gary)

We did get into an argument (small laugh). We were watching that race program on TV. What was it? *Racism in the 90s* or something. But I think it was for my ignorance because I really didn't . . . understand the difference between racism and . . . prejudice. I wasn't using it right because I really didn't understand, and I remember us getting into a big argument. (Jill)

Not only does a white partner need that learning to travel comfortably and safely with a black partner where interracial couples might be targets of racism, but she or he needs that learning to be an understanding partner.

One thing I think that has . . . been a great help in our relationship is Dot understanding of man and his inhumanity to man, all the things that are going around which surrounds me as a black person. I think

without that insight . . . I probably might have not been attracted to
her. But I think that understanding . . . and the awareness (pause)
makes a great deal of difference. . . . Somebody's in lala land somewhere, I don't think we could make it. It would be very difficult.
(Wilson)

Put another way, black partners must know the white world to be
comfortable, do well, and survive. White partners are much less likely
to have had reasons, or even opportunity, to learn about the black
world. So in a sense, the black partner speaks two languages, whereas
the white only speaks one. But the language the white partner speaks
that deals with the white world is not the language of the white world
that the black partner needs to know. One white man spoke about
learning the language an African American learns while navigating
the white world.

Wanda has in a sense had to learn another language. I think it's important for me to learn that language as much as I can but remember that
there are times when I am . . . a foreigner still. (Adam)

It was not merely that many white partners were unaware of what
was happening to African Americans but also that they were unaware
of the ways in which they unknowingly supported a racist system and
the ways that system affected them.

I've seen like a different side of the world being married to him, and
I've been exposed to some things that I wouldn't have been exposed to
had I married a white male. So I think my views are evolving, and
every day I learn something new, and I'm hoping that I'm changing for
the better. (Eve)

The "changing for the better" that Eve referred to seemed to be
the realization of how she, as a European American woman in a racist
system, had benefited from the racist system and contributed to it.
Her comment may represent a desire to stop supporting the racist
system and to fight it and in the process to change the ways she has
been defined in that system. As the following comment indicates,
some African Americans could also see, and feel positive about,

changes in a white partner's awareness of place in the system and orientation toward that system.

> I see her become very racially aware of things, in terms of racial injustices. I see what, I know it might be arrogant to sound that way, but a certain growth in her that has really helped me. I mean, in some ways I think she's made me more aware of some things. (Emmett)

Learning About Racism and How to Deal With It

What might a white partner learn from a black partner? An important element of it is learning to hear, see, and understand the verbal and nonverbal vocabulary of racism.

> I am more aware of the struggles that he as a black male faces. And I realize that my life if I were married to a white male would be very different. And I am thankful that I am married to him because I can see that. I am more aware of it because I see every day the things that he has to go through, and nobody else understands. And I try to share with people that it's important, that issues that affect him really affect all of us, and I try to share with my friends . . . things like that, but they don't understand me because they are not living with it every day like I am. . . . Just subtle things. The way that I've been treated differently. Just like, for example, going to the grocery store and getting the third degree when I'm trying to write a check, you know, with him. You always wonder, "Is this racism? . . . Am I feeling what it's like . . . ?" Because I don't know, and he always says, "It is, it is." But I really don't know what racism is, so I'm learning. . . . At first, I didn't realize what it was, and . . . I wouldn't know if someone was being racist to me. . . . I'm beginning to learn what it is, but it's still really new to me, and like I said, sometimes I'll ask him, "Do you think that they said that or did that to us because of race," and he always says, "Yes." He always thinks it's a racial thing, and now being with him longer, I'm beginning to think everything's racial too (she laughs). (Eve)

As Eve implied, part of the learning that a white partner acquires from traveling with the African American partner is how to detect racism. Other whites also talked about acquiring racism-detecting radar.

INTERVIEWER Do you both carry [the same sixth] sense about what's going on around you?

JOYCE . . . I think I'm developing it more.

INTERVIEWER Uh-huh. So that's not always been part of your way of doing it, but you picked up on how to do it, either from Gregory or just your own experience.

JOYCE I think, yeah, especially, I mean, just his awareness, like I'm tuned into that.

INTERVIEWER Did that take a while to develop?

JOYCE Yeah, it did. I think I definitely had kind of a naïveté about that.

Even though a white partner may be learning, there still may be a well-grounded belief that the African American partner is a better detector of racism.

> I can't imagine being in a relationship different than this, because it's very good for us. And I think it's made me a much better person, and I think that we learn a lot . . . about people and about ourselves, and we learn a lot about, unfortunately, some of the bad things in life. But he's sensitive to certain kinds of bigotry or racism that is harder for me to pick up. Whereas I'm sensitive to other things. (Christine)

In learning about white racism a white partner may also learn verbal and nonverbal ways of communicating about self (including the carrying of self that was discussed in Chapter 8). One couple talked about their experiences learning how to "speak" well in a potentially racist environment.

HOUSTON One thing I was telling my wife is when you're around other people, I notice she kind of hangs her head down. Well, "Don't do that, 'cause we're from the old 'You keep your head up high!' " My dad was like, "Keep your head up!" But she . . . put her head down. I said, "Don't do that around me. I don't like that." When you're around people that you know are racists and that are going to be prejudiced toward you, you got to be strong. You just can't let them see that you're weak. . . .

EVE I've been trying to think about what he said that maybe I do it because people are looking at us, so I've been trying not to do it. But it's a hard habit to break. And maybe I do do it because when people, especially white men, stare at us, I don't, he looks them right in the eye. But I just, I just would rather look the other way. But he looks them right in the eye, and he always tells me I should too.

Another kind of learning centers on being statistically in the minority. What is learned in that case may be the feeling of being outnumbered, a feeling of anxiety, of situational insignificance, of being relatively alone, or of being dominated by people who see one as different from themselves.

> We went to . . . this party . . . that was real scary. Not just because there was a lot of people. . . . This place . . . was just wall to wall, just packed. And I would say 90, . . . 95% of them were black. You could see the whites, the other whites, you could see that they felt pretty uncomfortable. And that was not out of fear. It was out of just like, "Whoa! This is a new experience!" (Rosemary)

> This past winter, my husband was accused of doing something that he didn't do, and we had to go through court, . . . and it was really hard on us. And the one thing that I noticed that when we got into the court was that, well, first of all, everyone, the judge, everybody else was white; everyone on the other side of the system was a minority, Native American, black. . . . And I realized when I saw him in there charged with something that he didn't do that those other people just saw him as a black man, not as a person. He was just another black man who committed a crime, they sort of thought, which he didn't do. But it didn't matter if he did it or not. He was just another black man. (Eve)

Disputing a Black Partner's Perceptions

A white partner does not necessarily accept all the education offered by an African American partner. There were couples in which it seemed as though the white partner did not want to see white racism as the black partner saw it. There were also white partners who seemed to understand white racism as the black partner did and granted that the black partner had much more experience and knowledge of it but who felt that the black partner was wrong in seeing racism in certain instances. One couple discussed their differing perceptions in general and a specific incident that was mentioned in Chapter 7.

HENRY I think that there are other facets in the community, that . . . we don't look at it the same way. I am constantly on guard; I hear and see things that are around us. . . .

DONNA That I don't hear and see.

HENRY That she doesn't hear and see (both laugh). An example is that we were in Sausalito a couple of years ago. . . . We were walking down the street, just sight-seeing, and doing what tourists do. And this guy's coming up the street, and . . . as he approached us, he kind of said under his breath, "White girl, wake up." And what she heard was, "Wake up." I heard the entire statement. . . .

DONNA That's the only comment that has been generated at the two of us. Nobody's ever said anything to . . . our faces.

HENRY That was audible anyway.

DONNA Yeah, behind our backs I don't know what people are saying.

HENRY But they're expressions that you read, of course (laughs).

DONNA He reads 'em.

HENRY . . . I do read them, and I've learned. At first, she told me that I was overly sensitive. But I didn't let that bother me because I've known myself long enough to be able to trust my reactions to what's going on.

In another couple for which there were differences about what the black partner labeled as racist, it seemed as though the white partner was growing into being her own person on many issues, including race. Her comments that follow seem to reflect that increasing self-confidence, with her feeling that she had valid things to say, even in areas in which he had much more life experience than she.

GREGORY Yeah, I [talk about white racist acts]. . . . (everyone laughs). It's mainly cause I'm ragin'! "Why couldn't they get their act together!? Oh! Joyce! No offense!"

INTERVIEWER . . . And . . . does that offend you? I mean, have you ever gotten mad about that?

JOYCE Yeah, sometimes I have. . . . It's good to talk about that because it's like I can take it personally, but he doesn't mean it personally. . . . I think . . . it's easier for me to express my feelings . . . if I'm feeling hurt by something, or if I feel personally hurt, to say that. Just sort of clear the air. . . . I can understand how he feels . . . a little bit. But sometimes it's more that I might have a different opinion about it. . . .

INTERVIEWER In other words, he's made it a racial issue.

JOYCE Right. When sometimes I'm feeling it might not be. And I think in the past I would tend to not state my opinion, 'cause it feels like, well, if it's about race, then of course he's gonna be right . . . because he's black . . . and he knows. . . . But I don't feel that way anymore, and it feels like I can express my opinion even if I contradict him on race. And that's felt like a really big step, to be able to do that and feel comfortable about that.

INTERVIEWER Is that because you've gained information or experience, or is it because you've claimed your own authority?

JOYCE . . . I think it's authority; claiming my own authority and feeling that my opinions and feelings count too, even on those things. . . . It feels . . . like . . . personal growth; . . . I don't feel like I have any more authority about it. . . . I'm not a very political kind of person; I don't keep up on the news, which is kind of an issue between us because Gregory is very tuned into what is going on, with the whole Baby D, the adoption case, for instance. . . . Sometimes, I would feel guilty that I'm not as aware of what's going on. Or that I should feel like definitely, definitely this child should go to a black family, whereas like I feel more now I can say, the child is attached. I mean, it's like, I feel like I can debate it. I don't feel like there's just one right answer here.

INTERVIEWER Was there any help from Gregory for you to have that growth? Did he stay in a combative position and you just sort of had to work that out, or did he hear that struggle?

JOYCE . . . I think it's more, I mean, we're in a couples group together, and I think just being able to be more honest with each other; I mean, that's kind of grown out of that.

One African American seemed glad that his wife challenged some of his interpretations of events.

> I learned a sense of identity with [my] culture without getting a total comfort of being with that culture. I think being with Nora keeps me exploring that but makes, I don't know how to explain it, somehow I feel much more identified with it. I'm not defending it as something I'm born to. It's a part of what I carry with me in the world, and she helps me stay aware of it and at the same time not use it as something to hide behind or something to be defensive about. Nora can cut through a lot of the bullshit. I can say that *XYZ* happened, because I'm black or because so and so was black, and she will confront it as, "No, probably not, because they're loud obnoxious people." (Emmett)

Although some white partners seemed to feel that at times the black partner labeled as racism things that might be something else, there were also white partners who felt the black partner failed at times to recognize racism.

> He'll give, I think, sometimes white people more benefit of the doubt than I will, because I will be with him, and I hear them say what they really feel, whether it's polite to say things in front of him. (Christine)

For the most part, however, it was the black partner who saw racism more often and who encouraged the white partner to see things the same way. One of the arenas for learning was the socialization of a child. As mentioned in the previous chapter, it can be challenging and difficult for a white partner to face the realities and complexities of socializing a biracial child to cope with racism. Although many white parents worked at learning what was needed, at least one white parent at first balked at doing the learning.

JOHN I was talkin' a reference to the children and at least feeling proud or having a healthy self-esteem about themselves, havin' black blood in them or whatever. And not have it to be an issue that later on in life they have to adjust to. I'm thinkin' that if they grew up with acceptance and love for themselves, just who they are as a person, it would be much better for them all the way through their lives. And I also

thought that with the kind of people that we are, I know that
they're gonna have a lot of love and support, so for the other
people who had an issue with race, whenever they ran across
one of these children, they would have to rethink their
position on what they thought black people were. . . . So
when I brought this up to Liz, she went through the roof.

LIZ . . . I just didn't feel able to talk about it, and I asked him not to
talk to me about it, because it's just overwhelming; and I
didn't really know why or what, I couldn't even figure out
what all was involved with it, and I knew I wasn't able to talk
to him about it.

Some things may be too hard to learn. Lacking a lifetime of
experience dealing with racism directed at oneself, one's family,
friends and community, white partners are probably never going to
understand fully what it is like to be black.

It's very hard for a white or Caucasian person to understand how it is
to be black. (John)

As a white person, it's your first experience really with prejudice, with
how that feels. And so it's been a learning experience. And I'll never
get to know what Gregory's experience is like or what our kids' experience will be like, [but] it's like kind of an opening. (Joyce)

WHAT WHITE PARTNERS
TEACH AFRICAN AMERICAN PARTNERS

Given the emphasis in the interviews on racism, talk about learning
in the relationship seemed to center on white partners learning from
African American partners about racism. Even in the rare instance
when an African American partner might seem to say that nothing
was learned from the white partner, however, the African American
partner still seemed to talk about learning some things. For example,
in the following comments, an African American talked about what
one could label the learning that comes with confirming what one
previously believed.

I don't know that I've learned anything actually. She has, rather, confirmed some notions that I used to have. When I went from thinking
that . . . essentially we were all the same and the other stuff is really
kind of superficial. Going from there to, "There are major (laughs)
differences that are important; they're learned, but they're important
just the same, . . . so might could just as well be a gene as far as most
of us are concerned." Now I'm back to (laughs), "We're all essentially
the same" (laughs). Could make ya dizzy (laughs), so I don't know if
I've really learned anything new. I've just kind of come back to what I
was several years ago. (William)

Some African American partners talked about the value in learning
the white partner's perspective on events.

[When you are married interracially], you tend to know more. You are
exposed to her experience that you don't know exists. Because you
marry somebody different, you make your life not to be boring, so it's
just excitement. (Isaac)

SUMMARY AND CONCLUSIONS

One of the tasks of any committed relationship is to learn from
one's partner—expectations, preferences, dislikes, needs, experiences, habits, and so on. Partners in interracial couples will also have
to learn from each other things that do not often cross the gap created
by racism. The white partner may have to learn about white privilege,
about the many forms that racism takes, about the pain and injustice
that arise from racism, about black defenses against racism, and about
the ways a person who does not intend to be racist may support and
benefit from racism. Although some of the white partners had previous interracial relationships, many white partners talked about how
much they learned in their current relationship about detecting and
dealing with racism. Similarly, Frankenberg (1993, p. 110) found that
white women in interracial relationships were much more fluent at
naming racism and identifying its impact than were white women in
same-race relationships. White partners who were interviewed for
the present study also might learn what it is like to be a statistical

minority, and those with biracial children talked about learning to bring up a biracial child in a racist world.

A white partner might dispute a black partner's perceptions. The dispute might represent genuine differences in perceptions or differences in willingness to read racism in various events. The dispute might also stem from processes of personal growth that lead the partners to speak with different voices about things important to both of them.

There was much less talk in the interviews about what the white partners taught black partners than about what the black partners taught white partners. That may be an artifact of the interview focus on racism, a topic about which African Americans have much more life experience and cultural grounding than whites. It is also possible that, as a result of being in a statistical minority and in a system in which whites oppress blacks, black partners might have entered the relationship much more expert about the white world than white partners were about the black world.

12

RACE IN THE
COUPLE RELATIONSHIP

WORDS SAID IN ANGER,
CONFLICT, TEASING, OR SARCASM

Because they live in a society in which racism is so significant, it would not be surprising to find racism, accusations of it, or suspicions of it in interracial couples. The couples in the present study were asked if race had ever been a part of their conflicts with each other. In contrast to an interracial couple described by Frankenberg (1993, p. 117), there was no couple in the present study in which conflict was always made, in part, a racial issue. In a few couples, however, racial epithets or racial attitudes were expressed in words said by one partner to the other. Sometimes, such words were said in anger. At other times, they were said teasingly, humorously, or sarcastically when the couple was dealing with a difference of opinion or of cultural background.

JOHN One time, I think I called her a name, didn't I?

LIZ Yup.

INTERVIEWER A racist name?

JOHN Yeah, . . . in an argument, yeah. In fact, I wasn't even aware that I said it.

INTERVIEWER And did that generate concern about whether you could work at having a relationship together?

LIZ I was really alarmed when you called me that. . . . I still wonder about that. . . . You kind of said, "You're like all those other white people." . . . That was my problem, that I was this white person, and I thought, "Well, that's insurmountable. . . . If he's thinking that white people are fucked up and I'm a white person, and he has this underlying hatred of white people, if that's really there, then how could he ever really love me if . . . this thing's buried in him that's like, antiwhite?"

INTERVIEWER Do you believe that's there?

LIZ In him? I think it's probably there. If he said it, . . . but . . . I think it's not a big part of him.

INTERVIEWER Have there been times where race has been a part of your conflict?

GREGORY You mean when we get into a conflict with one another and it takes racial overtones?

INTERVIEWER Yeah. Or that you have operated from some stereotypical posture. . . .

GREGORY . . . Being sarcastic, it might have come out like that. I bet that has happened; it's been in a sarcastic vein. But has it been like in a heated conflict?

JOYCE . . . I think we deal with it more in kind of a joking way.

GREGORY Yeah. Yeah. . . . [For example], Joyce will ask me sometimes about "Why aren't you on time?" and I'll say, "Well, you've been married to me for so many years, don't you understand the concept of CPT? When you gonna learn CPT?" [They went on to say that CPT stands for "colored people's time."] . . . Or if Joyce makes a meal that I find to be rather "flat" in taste, I [might] get sarcastic and say things like, "This is white people's cooking; why don't you learn how to cook colored?" It comes out that way, sort of sarcastically. . . . I haven't experienced it where it's been there when we've been really hostile and angry at each other, and we start [a] big, big thing, or the hostility comes out because of racial differences. I can't say that that happens.

INTERVIEWER And so if Gregory would make a comment like that about your cooking, is that something that's hurtful, or is that a joke to you at the time? How do you respond to that?

JOYCE I think now it's a joke. I think initially when we were first together, it was more hurtful.

In a few other couples, words about race showed up in ways that the partners defined as teasing or playful.

SHIRLEY Sometimes we tease each other, . . . something like (laughs) his friend's father used to call us, he and his friend, "Wooly-headed . . ."

SHANE "Afros," yeah.

SHIRLEY "Wooly-headed" something, so I'll throw that out at him sometimes, but it's certainly not insulting. They're endearing, if anything.

SHANE Yeah.

GARY We've made a lot of racial jokes . . . and continue to do [so], . . . crude racial jokes, . . . the kind of things that if they're made by other people you'd [be] immediately offended. . . . I think I used to say when you'd come in the room at night, . . . "Got to turn on the light. I can't see you."

PATRICIA Yeah, something like that. Or sometimes, when I get mad, I'll say, "Well, we black people, we got lower impulse control" (all laugh). And so we sort of laugh about it like that, . . . but when I look at Gary, I don't think, "You white m-f." I just think, "You m-f; I'm really pissed at you right now." It doesn't have anything to do with the fact that he's white.

GARY But I've seen certainly you did that to other white people, as last week when that man pulled out in front of you, and you called him a "pea-eyed pecker head" (all laugh). . . .

PATRICIA Those are old terms that I heard my parents and my grandparents use in the South. I mean, despite what most white people think, we talk about them too.

GARY . . . [When] some white person would do something in a car, . . .
I remember hearing expressions I never heard before in my life,
"tallow-faced" this or that.

> There are times that racial attitudes can be a source of irritation. I
> mean, I will say things that are absolutely absurd and racist just be-
> cause that's my style of humor that I know annoys her, but the issue is
> the type of humor I will use. It's not the fact, the nature of our rela-
> tionship. . . . "White women are horrible drivers when they get older."
> You know, that kind of comment. (Emmett)

One couple noted that although racial matters were not part of the
expression of anger in their own relationship, they had seen how race
could surface during angry exchanges in another couple.

> We [know] one couple that whenever they would argue in front of us
> and, unfortunately, the words *black* and *white* would always come up,
> and I would say there that then interraciality is a real factor within
> their home. . . . It would be, not necessarily name-calling, but he
> would talk about her white brother when he was angry. . . . I guess I
> never heard her use "black" and that with him. But we do not do that,
> so . . . within this household [race] isn't a factor. (Dot)

Differences of Opinion as Matters of Culture

In some couples, interpersonal differences of various sorts were
defined as cultural differences. Defining differences as cultural is an
acknowledgment that the two partners came from cultures different
in many ways (linguistic expressions, religion, preferred foods, money
management practices, etiquette, preferred musical forms, etc.). One
could speculate that a consequence of defining differences as cultural
is that it makes it easier to be understanding of disagreement, to frame
differences as matters requiring cultural understanding rather than
angry accusation.

> We recognize that we have some cultural differences. . . . We like the
> same music, but the artists were very different. . . . I think there's just
> some things like that. I mean, there are things that you're brought up
> with culturally. But I don't think we see it as particularity mattering as

much as sort of learning more about each other in terms of depth. Because . . . there are layers of knowledge, and it takes a while before you get to those kinds of things, and it's like any relationship. You're obviously dealing with a lot of other things. It takes a while before you get to know . . . each other in a sort of a detailed sense of the word. Certainly in terms of cultural things, a lot of it has to do with what . . . kinds of things were a part of your family. And some of them are African American for me; some of them are very southern. Some of them have to do with that sort of Cajun side, or I call it the "hot pepper side." . . . I don't necessarily point to those as sort of racial. . . . It has something to do with skin color because of place of origin. . . . But more to do with . . . the kind of culture you embrace and bring into your lives and that your families have. I mean, I think that's the real difference. We still have this thing about catsup, either cooking with it (laughs) or where it's put. (Wanda)

I think that sometimes Lorenzo assumes that (laugh) I don't under-stand or don't give . . . value to certain things that have to do, that ultimately probably go back to race. . . . He thinks that I don't take certain things seriously. . . . Our kids are in private schools, and I have always, well, this is important to both of us, but I've always been real insistent on that. And oh, we look at schools, and we've done this several times, and we're looking at changing schools. We've always looked at race as one of the things, and I would suspect that race is more important to Lorenzo in a school than it is to me, that is, balance of race, and so we come out fighting about it. . . . But I don't think it's serious, and it really is a matter of priorities rather than a disagreement. (Virginia is white)

RESPONSES TO RACISM AROUND THEM

A white partner in an interracial couple may have grown up aware of racism in an abstract sense but indifferent to or unaware of racism in many specific instances. But having been in a relationship with an African American, one might expect that the white partner would be much more advanced in recognizing, being concerned about, and opposing racism. Some white partners talked about their encounters with racism.

I think there was only one incident where I kind of had to come back at somebody because of something they said to me . . . about the relationship in terms of our racial differences. . . . [A coworker] just said something about, "Well, is it true what they say about black men?" . . . Implying their virility, their sexuality, and things like that, and I just said, "Well, if you mean that they're kind and wonderful and sensitive kinds of people, yes, it is true." . . . There have been times when it's been kind of awkward because I didn't know whether, I mean, it's not the kind of thing you just want to blurt out [that I'm in an interracial marriage]. And I don't want to sound defensive about it, but yet, if somebody is saying something that verges on being biased or racist or something, I want to make people aware that they can't talk like that in front of me. I don't care; they can have that attitude. I'll do everything I can to educate them a little bit, but I don't want to hear that crap around me. (Nora)

In some couples, perhaps particularly those in which the woman was African American and the man was white, the white partner seemed, at least some of the time, disinclined to challenge racist remarks. Several white partners talked about times when they had not said or done anything in response to racist words.

INTERVIEWER Have you been in that situation where you're in an all-white group and someone makes a racial joke?

KENT Yeah.

INTERVIEWER And then how have you handled that?

KENT Generally, pretty delicately. . . . There are certain times when you can speak up and say, "Well, that's not appropriate," and other times where you just don't. You just leave it at that. And so it all depends on the situation.

I work in a [mall], and there was a white man who came in. We had these little black [baby dolls]. And he was a real nice customer, him and his wife, and he picked up a little black boy and showed his wife, and he said, "Oh, we should put this on a little noose." And I just sat there, and I was really, I was stunned. I should have said something, and I didn't, I mean, I let him just walk out of my store, and I felt really bad that I didn't say something to him like, "Wait a minute. You're talking about my family. You can't assume because I'm white that you're not going to offend me." (Ann)

We have a neighbor who will often talk to me about "the niggers." He knows who I'm married to. . . . He sees us every day. But he'll talk to me about that, and I've had a number of people tell me what I should say, and I'm mulling it over. I don't know. I'm pretty much nonplussed when it happens. I'll be out back knocking off branches on a tree, and he'll say, "Did you see that nigger walking down the alley?" Now, he knows. It's not just like he forgot. (Roger)

What might a white partner be thinking who lets racist remarks go by? Presumably, there is something about the situation that makes challenging the remarks difficult or inappropriate—for example, the white partner's attention is divided; the presence of others would make it harder to get by the defenses of the person who made the remarks; or a confrontation might risk the white partner's job, risk ending a valued relationship, or risk making the person who made the remarks even more racist. Sometimes, the person making the racist remarks may seem so closed to changing that there seems to be no point to challenging the remarks. Also, at times, a person might be so stunned by racist remarks that no reply comes to mind; it is only in afterthought that the person realizes what one might have said.

JOYCE When . . . our oldest daughter [was a baby] . . . I was at the pediatrician, and I think it was, she was fairly newly born; it was maybe her first exam. And he looked at her, and he said, "Now check under the fingernails. She'll be a little bit darker, but not too bad." . . . I've wished I would have reacted. It was kind of like I didn't know what to say to him. . . .

INTERVIEWER What might you say now if you were in that situation, knowing what you know now?

JOYCE "I don't see it as probably being bad; I mean, I really feel like you made a negative comment, and I don't appreciate it. Not very sensitive."

For some white partners, there might be a process of learning how to confront racism. Earlier experiences with racism might have thrown them, but they might feel, after more experience, that they know how to confront it.

It depends on the person, . . . and . . . the older I get, the more likely I am to try to educate . . . or to scream and holler . . . or something like that. Years ago, I had a really horrible period at work, racially speaking. And my reaction was to go to the bathroom and cry. I was so hurt, you know. . . . I worked the midnight shift, and . . . it never entered my head that any of these people had ill feelings towards me because of my interracial marriage. It just never entered my head. And there was one good ol' boy. . . . He worked . . . the afternoon shift, so as I was coming in at midnight, he was getting ready to go home. . . . There's an employee's club close by there. One day . . . they were having a party over there. The afternoon shift had left work early to go, and the midnight shift had come in early. . . . I had parked my car in the parking lot and walked over to the club. Well, this [man] came up to me in the club and says, "I was wondering if I can give you a ride back to the building when we leave, because there's some matter I need to talk over with you." Now the office scuttlebutt had it that [he] and his wife were having trouble, and I was enough of a, I guess, a egomaniac thinking that he was going to come for help; he was going to ask me what . . . can I do? I'm older than he is by a few years, and a lot of people tell me their troubles. I just thought that that's what it was. OK, so I said, "Yeah, that's fine." So we left the club, and it's only two blocks, and all the way back . . . he didn't say anything. So we got to the parking lot . . . so I thought to myself, "Well, this guy didn't re- ally want to tell anything personal." . . . And he said, "Well, just a min- ute, I haven't said what I needed to say. . . . Have you ever noticed that you come in at night and some days I'm friendly and nice to you and some days I don't speak at all?" And I said, "You know, I have noticed that." And he said, "Well, now why do you think that is?" And I said, "Well, I always assumed that you're moody. And I certainly know that by the time your shift is over you're so beat so that you don't want to talk anyway." And he said, "No, no you're wrong about that." He said, "Some days, you come walking through there, and you've always been nice to me." And he said, "And I say to myself, well, she" (pause), you know, friendly and smarter (pause), and some days you come in there, and I look at your face and all I can think is "married to a goddamn nigger!" And I was so, it was like somebody had hit me physically. I, I went back against the car seat, I, and the only thing that I could say (voice shaking) was, "Oh, [Butch]!" And I got out, and I went in and I punched in, and I went to the bathroom and I sat there and cried. In fact, I was so, it isn't that [he] personally meant anything to me, but I was so taken aback and I was so hurt, and the sad part of it is, the worst part is that that all took place in 1976.

I still work in the same building, not the same area, and he still works [there] too. And I see him, three, four times a week. "Hi, . . . how ya doin'?" He's just as friendly as can be. That affected him not at all, and it's 15 years later, and I'm sitting here telling you about it because it still hurts me. And he truly does not know what he did. He does not know that he hurt me. Now if that happens today, I would do more than say, "Oh, [Butch]," and get out of the car. I had some more instances, . . . and I went to the boss and asked him to transfer me back to where I had been before, where I worked with all women. And I thought that it was because these were all white men that they were, some of them were like that. But now, I would raise more of a ruckus. I would contact the EEO committee. (Dot)

In the beginning of our relationship, [I didn't take] a strong stand on making ignorant people knowledgeable. I think I . . . didn't feel like I was on solid ground, because I didn't know how far to push it, how to take control of the situation to combat the comments these people were making. And I think I went from that extreme to not even wanting to deal with ignorant people. If it's a personal attack, definitely, but the interracial attacks or the biased opinions for me are few and far between. . . . I worked with some girls that are just, I'd swear that they lived in a closet all their life! I mean, just the view of how they are, like one of them saying that that's OK for you, but my parents would never accept that in my life. And I know a lot of them censor things as far as . . . their comments, and it's just how they were raised. Their parents raised them that our relationship wouldn't be acceptable and to say things in slang or derogatory as if it's not a big deal. But to me, I find it offensive, but to other people it's not a big deal. So I think a lot of people knowing that I am in an interracial relationship and that I am very overopinionated, . . . I think they buffer things that they say around me. I really do. (Jill)

For African Americans, too, sometimes the decision was to let racist remarks go by, perhaps as a way of putting themselves above such things, perhaps as a way to head off additional remarks, or perhaps because they did not want to take on the responsibility of educating someone who was ignorant.

Sometimes, I do not react to racist remarks. . . . And [then the person making the remarks might say], "Oh, well, I guess . . . that doesn't phase him." (Ed)

With me it would depend on the situation, and I guess how I felt that day, as to how I was going to respond. I would hope I respond without causing an altercation. And on other days, that would be all right too. (Wilson)

The fact that [our friends] approve of us doesn't mean they're not racists in that racist comments continue to be made in my presence about black people and about Hispanics and others. And not realizing that I have a very strong feeling about racist comments. . . . And I don't always correct them. (Patricia)

Sometimes, people felt that racist remarks were made by someone who did not matter enough to deserve a reply. For example, a black woman whose white husband is quoted earlier as saying that he doesn't respond to the racist remarks of a white neighbor said,

[That neighbor] is such a nonentity in my life. I mean, if it were a family with kids or something, and our kids were playing, it would be really difficult. But I think because he's just somebody, I mean, he's like a piece of lint. . . . It's not . . . [an] issue. (Barb)

It is difficult to say whether a white partnered with an African American was more likely than the African American to let racist remarks go by unchallenged. For anybody, issues of timing, of the apparent educability of the other, of the press of other matters, and much else might have an influence on what they do about racist remarks. Some of the white partners, however, seemed to have entered the relationship without much experience at recognizing and dealing with racism. With time and experience, however, some had changed their ways of responding to racist remarks.

White Partner Indifference or Lack of Awareness

Sometimes, a white partner—and all the examples we heard of involved a white man—seemed indifferent to racism experienced by his partner or child. It sometimes seemed as though the white partner lacked the background or even the motivation to be aware of racist words or actions.

> I think Gary was less concerned than I was, initially, and I think part of that had to do with . . . being a white male and not having to be concerned about, because I remember . . . in early years, people would do things, like, they'd get in the elevator and assume we weren't together and stand between us. And Gary didn't notice those things, and I would notice those things, one, as a female, that as a black female, where you were always, you sort of have that, always that sense about somebody is doing something different to me because of the color of my skin. So I was really, I think, I took strength from the fact that he wasn't, he didn't seem as concerned. . . . We would go places, and people would look at us, and I don't think he would notice that they were looking. And part of that's his personality, but part of that I think, if you grow up in a smaller town and you grow up as a white male, you don't have to be concerned about those types of things. (Patricia)

The indifference, at least in retrospect, was not necessarily a problem for the African American partner.

> There wasn't a difficulty. I mean, we would talk about it, and sometimes we would laugh about it. And I would joke about the fact that he hadn't noticed it, and I actually kind of enjoyed that. But no, I didn't see it as a difficulty. (Patricia)

However, there might be an occasion when the indifference could seem to the African American partner to be dangerous.

> I can remember one time when I really felt that we were in danger. . . . I was pregnant. We lived in [a midwestern city]. . . . We were having an ice cream after a movie, and some guys came by and made this comment. And Gary was sort of just standing there, 'cause I don't think he heard them, and I said, "I think we need to leave right now," because I've had some pretty bad experiences in [that city]. . . . So I had that sort of sense of danger about me all the time when I was out. And it may not have been a dangerous situation. But that in particular sticks out in my mind. . . . I was frightened at the time. (Patricia)

Sometimes, a white male partner's indifference to or ignorance of racism could in a sense diminish the black partner and support racist views of the world. For example, a white partner might seem to be so ignorant of racism as to blame a spouse and child for racist actions directed at them.

> I told him someone yelled, "nigger." I was on the corner down there; I was with the baby, just driving by. And his first reaction is, "Well, what did you do to provoke that?" (laughs). And I thought, "That's the difference between being black and white. Why would I have to do anything to provoke it?" (Gloria)

One could interpret the husband's question about provocation (a) as a result of his choice to be ignorant about racism (and to make other things more important), (b) as a result of some sort of block (in the man or in the couple relationship) to his learning about racism, (c) as an expression of his theory about racist acts (they are caused, even if they are unjustified), or (d) as a product of his theory about strangers yelling epithets (they only yell when irritated by something). He may not have been innocent, but one could get, from the next quotation, a sense that white male privilege can allow a white male partner to take a kind of guiltless, insulated stance about racist words and actions.

> It was an emotional choice [to marry her]. And . . . one of the things that I increasingly believe is that the more typical American you can be, or the approach, and I hate to say this, but I think it's true, is that white males are what America's all about, is that the more you can afford to not think about stuff. Like, I think you can do things that other people can't do without thinking very much about it if you're a white male. . . . I think it's easier to do certain things if you're a white male, just simply easier to do them without thinking about them. . . . I think I can walk through a situation where other people might feel very, very frightened, or very, very intimidated. . . . There's lots of situations where other people feel this kind of pressure and intimidation and all that, and you . . . can go into it and wonder why everyone else was so tense about it, and just, "Why did that bother you?" And so among the things I think of is, I don't think I notice racism very much. . . . I've fallen back to that very comfortable white male situation where there

are times when I just don't know. . . . So when we got married, what, how old was I? I was 25, something like that. I don't think it struck me as anything unusual at all. I mean, just moderately maybe. We were an unusual couple to begin with. I mean, we were a strange couple beside being interracial. And I think that I just thought of it all as, to me it was not a dramatic thing. It was as strange as having long hair, and it was as strange as having different kinds of clothes. That was it. (Roger)

His wife both agreed and disagreed with his analysis, saying that at times, she thought she had seen white privilege leading him to tune out racism directed at them, but at other times she thought he was more attuned to it than she.

Early in our relationship, when people staring was a concern, it would irk me that it never seemed to bother Roger. And I always thought that that had to do with being white. You know, they just don't, it doesn't bother you (laughs). But other than that kind of thing, I can't think of that ever being something that I notice. . . . I mean, Roger lots of time is more aware of things or questions things that have to do with racism or potential expressions of racism than I am. (Barb)

ONE'S OWN BIASES OF
THOUGHT AND FEELING

Part of being an adult who cares about ending racism is to search out and neutralize one's own racist thoughts and feelings. Being in an interracial relationship is no guarantee that one is free from such thoughts or feelings. In fact, several white partners and one African American partner talked about their awareness of their own prejudice and stereotyping (of people of other races, of people in interracial couples) and of their efforts to eliminate those patterns of thinking.

I am pretty aware of people's stereotypes about these kind of relationships. I have them myself; I mean, I do the same kind of projecting on other people. . . . I sort of catch myself, and I'll go, "But you're just making a judgment. You don't really know what their lives are about." (Joyce)

Sometimes I catch myself when I see an interracial couple with the man is black. And I think, "That really, I'm really affronted by that." And I think (laughs), "Wait a minute. Wait a minute. You know, they have enough problems without you dealing." . . . I have ownership of some [prejudiced garbage] too. My first thought . . . when I go on Lake Street and I see these women who are probably fairly poor and uneducated and they have biracial kids, I get real mad at them. I think, "Why would they bring these kids in the world who have a big problem to begin with, and then they don't have anything going for themselves?" And I think, "Well, you know what? The men that they are interested in, no black woman would want 'em anyway. Nobody wants those people." . . . We are all socialized by this stuff, and at the same time, I say, "I don't care what the community thinks, 'cause I don't want them intruding at me." I am putting my opinion on those people. How do I know what they have, or whether they're good mothers or whether they're capable? The most important thing is, "Do they love their kids?" (Patricia is black)

Where I come from, coming from a small . . . town, I see it as being extremely racist mainly because . . . there isn't anybody else there but people who are just like them. There were two little Korean girls in town, and there was one Jewish family who had one little girl, and she was tormented all the time. And the N word was used fairly freely to describe anything derogatory, and teachers used it in the Lutheran parochial school that I went to. I had a sixth-grade teacher who . . . I'm sure he was a purebred Nazi who whipped children, literally whipped children, and if somebody was misbehaving he would call them the N word. So I had a lot of that stuff that is really programming that I had to kind of clean out, and I really had to face a lot of how I was raised and question so much of that that was real basic to me. . . . It's just a new awareness where I don't just fall back on old prejudicial ideas in a lot of different ways. Once you start questioning one aspect of your beliefs, you start questioning a lot of them. (Nora is white)

In some cases, an African American partner was helpful in a white partner's recognizing personal prejudice and dealing with it, although that help might not have been without discomfort for the white partner.

The more black women I know, the better it is for me. I mean, joining our church has been good for me because I've gotten to know black women that are really warm toward me and accepting. . . . It helps me get rid of *my* stereotyping. . . . I've become a lot more aware of my prejudices, and it's coming out more and I think he's hearing it, and he'll respond and I don't like his response. I mean, we get more into discussions about race than we ever had before. . . . I work in a store, and I'm realizing I told him I thought I'd get more sympathy from him, and I didn't get any. I'll explain to him how nervous [I am] when these kids came into my store . . . black kids. . . . Bayard is always on me, "Well, how do you judge who's a good . . . shopper at your store? . . . What makes you think they're not there to buy toys?" . . . It's always like a real mind stretch when we talk about it. . . . I feel really bad that I'm feeling these things because I'm afraid he's seeing a side of me he's never seen, and he's always thought I was this totally unprejudiced person, and then all of a sudden he's seen these prejudices I have, and I'm really afraid he's going to be real disappointed to know that I carry a side of this, and so that's been hard for me to tell him how I feel, and, like, I thought he was going to support me this one time, and, like, no way, he was not going to back me up. (Ann)

Although I've heard a lot of people go through a lot more than we have, . . . it also takes being open to your own racism. It's all well and good to be sensitive to others in how they react to you, but you ought to be a little bit sensitive when you can and recognize your mistakes, try to learn why what you've just said or done offended . . . your partner or somebody you know, or maybe . . . there's an experience where Wanda would say, "Yeah, I understand that," and I, "I don't understand it. What was happening? Help me here." (Adam)

So some white partners worried that their own racism could alienate their partner. At the same time, they realized that efforts to end societal racism had to begin with what was inside themselves. For white partners, it was not only a matter of learning to navigate in a racist world but also learning how to know themselves. This is not to say that anybody who was interviewed said that personal racism or partner racism was a serious problem in the relationship. As Liz said, "I think it's not a big part of him." The racism that was of primary concern to people was the racism of the larger society. Statements of concern were overwhelmingly statements like the following:

I am proud to be in a marriage where we've . . . overlooked some of
the things that society might say or the differences, not let those
differences part us, and that we have grown with those differences
and enjoyed those differences in each other. It doesn't matter to me
what society's standards may say as to whether or not interracial couples are OK or not OK because society—I don't trust their, or its,
opinions. I believe more what God says, or some of my close
friends or people that I will let be close to me say, more than what
society says. And I believe that things like institutional racism . . .
permeate . . . the government. . . . And among white people, OK,
you've got . . . "I don't want you to marry her because she's not Meth-
odist," or whatever. So the government, I think, and society always
kind of keep us all screwed up, in a way that we're not gonna identify
the precious things in us. (Kate)

INTERPRETATIVE CHALLENGES
FOR INTERRACIAL COUPLES

Things that might be taken as matters of racism could also be
framed in other ways. There is always room for interpretation when
difficulty arises in a relationship. Partners in an interracial couple can
wonder whether their conflict about a certain matter is a result of
genuine differences of opinion, personality differences, background
differences, or the bias of one of the partners. Some people talked
about the ways that cultural, gender, rural-urban, or other differences
made problems for them. Quite a few talked about differences with
the partner in a way that made it clear that they struggled to decide
whether the differences were matters of culture, gender, class, personality, life experiences, racism, or something else.

When we've felt sort of a distance, it felt like our worlds are so different. . . . Like in our couples' group, a couple times when we've felt . . .
distant, it felt because our worlds are so different, but . . . part of it is
because he's black, I'm white, and part of it is I have my women
friends, he has, ya know, we have different groups of people. It's like
we do some things together, but we do a lot of things separate, too. So
it's just sort of part of the dynamic of that whole thing with how to
have our worlds be together and still have our separate lives and sepa-

rate identities. . . . My women's group is very important to me, and things that Gregory goes to if he's with [his black friends] are very separate. (Joyce)

ROSEMARY I think sometimes he thinks that I'm just that naive white girl, and I just don't really [know] what it's all about. He . . . doesn't give me any credit for having any . . . street smarts.

ED And she has.

ROSEMARY Probably more than (laughing) he has ever had. . . . I just know that I've got 'em. And that's why I feel very angry when he insinuates that I don't. He sometimes will give me the impression that, and I think this is kinda of a male-female thing too, that I can't make it up to the store and back. . . .

ED Sometimes Rosemary will *sound* real white to me, like real pritzy little white girl. Sometimes she talks like that.

ROSEMARY Well, I am white (laughing). What . . . do you want me to be?

ED But sometimes it takes me by surprise, 'cause it'll come out of nowhere. Just like how I will talk black . . . with certain people. . . .

ROSEMARY I can tell if he's talking to a white person or a black person by how he talks on the phone, immediately. The other thing is, Ed used to have some problems with escalating with his temper, which he has since confronted. But when he escalates and starts getting real angry, he starts talking real, I don't know what the word is.

ED Real black.

ROSEMARY Real Chicago, street, jive, black. It was like the exorcist. . . . It was like going into this cold, I didn't know, this person. . . .

ED It was like, it's not, it's not my normal persona. . . . It was like, son-of-a-bitch, mother-fucker coming out very eloquently.

ROSEMARY No, it wasn't just that. It was . . .

ED A rage of anger. . . . My dad was that way, and that's me being my father also, 'cause that's . . . one of the snapshots that I kept of him was his anger and his rage.

INTERVIEWER So how have you worked that through in your relationship with each other?

ED . . . I've gone through domestic abuse programs and men's support groups. . . . But it never was black and white, because . . . my ex-wife [who is black] . . . said, "Remember . . . you are a hitter, and you better remember that." . . . I struck her once. And so . . . it's not . . . white and black. It's just that that's a problem that I've had.

HOUSTON How I was raised is totally different from how she was raised.

EVE Yeah, so I don't know if it is necessarily a race or cultural thing.

HOUSTON It's culture. . . . We know that race, that's man-made.

EVE And also . . . he was raised in a big family; I was raised in a small family. And my friends that have been raised in big families are a little more like his family in that he always told me, "Don't feel offended if my parents don't send us a birthday card" or, you know what I mean? Well, with 15 brothers and sisters I don't really expect them to keep track of all of us. So I look at it that way too. But it's our family size that makes a difference.

HOUSTON Just like you said, there's . . . things that we think differently on, even . . . how we want children to be raised. . . . I took care of kids when I was young, so I know . . . what it's all about, and Eve didn't, but she is a really good mother and I am still learning too.

I think that there have been . . . difficulties that have been related to, like cultural things on a broader sense . . . and class . . . because of the whole bunch of understandings, misunderstandings, and myths and just sort of baggage that goes from having been raised in one class or another with a certain set of expectations and experiences and then having sort of a gap that you have to work around. And so because that kind of stuff is more fundamental, communication's kind of a problem. Those don't wind up being real serious either because you wind up kind of figuring that stuff out after a while and you say, "Oh, well, OK." (Lorenzo)

Whether partners interpret differences as matters of race or something else, to sustain a relationship, they have to assume that there is a basis for trust and mutual support.

When we have our differences, whether culturally or racially, in expressing ourselves with each other, it's hell. . . . It's really hard, because I like to feel that the issues are never more important than the
relationship and the two people. And hopefully, we'll both come to
that communicative awareness to do it that way; we have something
that we have to discuss, but it's not more important than you, and it's
not more important than me, and let's keepin' that way. . . . I don't think
that so much of our differences have to do with her race or my race. . . .
It has to do with me and my struggles to become a person. (John)

Racist thoughts and feelings, perhaps even the awareness that
differences of opinion can be matters of race, could undermine a
couple's trust in each other. Because of this, some couples may try to
keep racism and race out of their interpretations of their own or their
partner's thoughts, feelings, and actions (see Brown, 1987). So when
couples said, as many of them did, that racism was not a problem (or
not much of a problem) in their relationship with each other, we can
wonder whether in other situations they (or somebody else) might
give a different interpretation to some of what goes on in their
relationship. Similarly, some couples may work at keeping race a
small part of their relationship (or their interpretation of their
relationship) as a counter to people who stereotype interracial relationships as being focused on race.

We talk about money; we talk about the other things that couples [talk
about]. . . . People assume that when you have arguments or discussions it has to be about race and race is so *central* all the time to what's
going on. I'm not saying race isn't there, but it's not like we spend
more time talking about, or arguing about, things related to race. I
mean, we've never called each other any racial terms the whole time
we've known each other. But I think people assume that that goes on a
lot. And so I think to normalize these relationships—there's all kinds. I
mean, there really is a continuum. Maybe you would get that with
some couples, but I just think interracial couples go the gamut the
same way as same-race couples in terms of issues. (Gloria)

On the other hand, there is certainly a danger that what is a matter
of culture or class or gender could be taken to mean something about
race. In that sense, it might be very healthy for a partner to be able

to say of something disagreeable in the words or actions of the other, "That's not race; that's just how women (men) are (or how people of my partner's class or people of my partner's culture are)." The following, for example, seems to be a statement about matters that were initially interpreted in terms of race but are now mostly or entirely interpreted as matters of class, culture, and gender.

INTERVIEWER You said that sometimes Rosemary would talk or act like "a pritzy white girl." . . . Could you say more about what that is? Or how you see that?

ED . . . When she does that, it's OK. I've accepted it. But . . . I didn't know she had that character in her . . . the little Bambi reindeer, passing through the forest, like that particular little white, suburban, middle-class protected Ozzie and Harriet. . . . When I see Rosemary, I see a liberal, advanced woman of her time, and then when I see her go into this . . . what's the word, *debutante,* beauty queen person, that's not what I saw or imagined. . . . I thought she was fucking with me at first when she did. I thought she was pretending.

SUMMARY AND CONCLUSIONS

In a few couples, there had been remarks or epithets that could be labeled racist or at least be labeled matters of race. Those remarks and epithets would most commonly be uttered in anger or in playful or not-so-playful teasing. The racism might, in these cases, be a matter of habits leftover from the past, a matter of preferred epithets when angry, a matter of residual discomfort, or something else. In some couples, words or differences of opinion that could conceivably be interpreted by someone as prejudiced or as matters of race were defined as something else, perhaps matters of playfulness or cultural differences.

Given that white racism is a presence in society, white partners might have occasion to deal with white racism in the words and actions of others. Although some white partners worked hard at opposing racism, in some couples, perhaps particularly couples in which the woman was African American and the man was white, the white partner seemed to be disinclined to challenge racist remarks or actions. In not confronting, a white partner (or for that matter, an African American partner) might feel that it was pointless or that there were some risks in confrontation (e.g., the possible loss of a job, a possible physical attack). Sometimes, the racism, or at least the way it was expressed or the situation in which it was expressed, was so new that a person had trouble coming up with a reaction. There were times, however, when a white male partner might seem indifferent to racism experienced by his partner or their children. Sometimes, the indifference was not a problem for the African American partner, but sometimes it was. In situations in which a white partner did not react to racism or did not offer support to the African American partner, it seemed as though some white partners were in a process of learning how to perceive and react to racism. It is also possible that there were some whose experience or well-learned ways of thinking made it unlikely that they would come to perceive racism or understand it as an African American would.

Being in an interracial relationship is no guarantee that one is free of racism. Some people talked about freeing themselves of racism as a lifetime project, and some white partners found their African American partner helpful in that project, although the help might at times involve some discomfort. It is important to note, however, that in no couple was partner racism said to be a big problem.

One can wonder whether matters of race are more significant in some of these couples than the partners think. Admitting that matters of race are quite significant could threaten some relationships, make for intense relationship conflict, and support stereotypes of interracial couples. On the other hand, most people who were interviewed spoke about how they were just trying to live a good life with each other (see particularly Chapter 3). With attention focused on love, grocery shopping, raising children, making out tax returns, doing the laundry, planning vacations, washing the dishes, and all the other details of a shared life, it is easy to imagine how matters of race become insignificant.

13

THE SPECIAL BLESSINGS

Facing hassles from their own families and with an awareness of how societal racism and even personal prejudice could play out in their relationship, it is easy to imagine that some of the people interviewed were reluctant at first to go forward with an interracial relationship.

> A lot had been going on in my mind, same time that I was dating Kate, about . . . the races back home and the trust issue. . . . But as I got more involved in the relationship with Kate, those issues . . . slowly and gradually disappeared from me. . . . Ya know what I'm sayin'? . . . The race issue, the fear, . . . those potential issues that are gonna come up in this relationship. Why don't we just drop it now, and go out and find me a black woman? (Robert)

But everyone who was interviewed did go forward, and everyone seemed to have good feelings about the relationship. So it seemed appropriate to ask whether there were special blessings in the relationship. Many people lit up when asked about the special blessings. The question resonated with what they thought and felt. Moreover, some people commented on the need to make clear how much good there can be in an interracial relationship.

> I'm glad you asked that question, because my pet peeve for years and years . . . has been studies that focused on problems and I think because of that give an extremely distorted view of what's going on. I would say that not only the interracial marriage but children . . . has probably broadened and enriched my life in ways that no other single experience could do. And I think that for the kids too, that they would say and see themselves as being wealthier culturally rather than having any problems. And that's absolutely across the board, and it far exceeds any of the minor inconveniences and hassles. (Virginia)

BLESSINGS THAT MIGHT
BE PRESENT IN ANY RELATIONSHIP

Consistent with what people had said about the ordinariness of their relationship (see Chapter 3), quite a few people talked about the blessings of their relationship in ways one might imagine hearing from anybody in a satisfying relationship. Some people may have gone through considerable difficulty in other relationships or in the current one to get to where they were. But it was striking how positive most people were in talking about their relationship. In most, if not all, relationships, the blessings seemed to far outweigh the difficulties.

Children

In almost every couple with children, one or both partners said that their children were a blessing.

> The most important thing that happened from that, in terms of biracial relationship, are those beautiful offspring. (Robert)

INTERVIEWER What have been the special blessings of your interracial relationship?

JOHN . . . These two last kids right here. . . . They came at 7 months, and they went through quite a struggle to stay on this planet with us. We spent a lot of time in the hospital, watching them puttin' needles to try to feed 'em intravenously. . . . And that kind of gave me a reevaluation of life, in a real outrageous way. Make me rethink my love for my other kids. . . . And I think that I grew so much as a person, just havin' these two kids. (John)

Connections With Each Other

Some people said that the partner, the relationship, or the family was a blessing. Again, some of what people said might be what anybody in an ordinary, satisfying partnership might say.

When me and Liz have fun, when we're gettin' along, and the planets are all aligned, the gods are pleased, it's real good fun. (John)

HOUSTON Our relationship, the strength we have, it's grown. And the thing that I'm working on now is us becoming one, because it takes a long time to become one with your spouse. . . .

EVE To me, like he said, getting to know another person. I mean getting to know him as my husband. . . . Just sharing our lives together.

HOUSTON I have learned a lot just from her . . . a different way of living, because, personally, financially I never could manage myself properly. She's good about that. I always told myself, "Hey, look, when I get married I am never giving my check to my wife. . . . Those mens that do that are crazy. . . . Never going to do that." But I do that. . . . It benefits me, as opposed to, you know, I was getting my check, it was like, "OK, you charge here, go over to the car company and buy a new car, go out and buy some clothing." Now it's different. That was really hard for me to break. I mean, . . . it's just like a addiction. It's just like a person on drugs. It's hard to break those habits. And people don't look at those habits like that, but yet I had to give up; I used to smoke cigarettes, too. She was really helpful with that, really, because you know if a person is not hounding you all the time, of course it makes you sick. . . . I really wanted to stop. And just like, someone helped me. A *lot* of different things like that. And I been off cigarettes for more than 3 years now, 3 in July.

DOT I have more love in my life than a lot of people ever will. . . . I feel lucky in the love department. . . .

WILSON I've had a lot, a lot of down experiences, and without Dot it would have been some very, very bleak days. Her kindness and (pause) and just to know that there's somebody that care about you more than anything else in the world. . . . Just to feel that somebody's there close to you who cares more about you than anything else in this world, and has helped me come through so many bad moments. And I don't think I could have gotten, it has enabled me, you have enabled me to carry on because there have been times in my life here, in the past few years that I have gotten to the point where I could just (makes a sound like cutting his throat), as far as Dot has given me a reason to live. And then when [our daughter] was born (long pause) I had no choice but to say, "I'm going to make it." (He is crying now.) So they have given, they have sustained my life. To the bone (still sniffling). . . .

DOT No one has ever loved me unconditionally in my life, until Wilson, not my folks or, no one. I've always depended on how I acted and how smart I am. . . . One time, I don't know if I was seeking to find if this was truly unconditional love or whatever, but . . . I told him the worst thing I'd ever done in my life (laugh), something that I never told anybody else. And I told him, and you know, he just accepted me in that.

GARY I think that the benefits have so surpassed any possible problems that there's no question now that our relationship has been very strong and has sustained both of us and sustained us where we went, and that happens so rarely in marriages. . . .

PATRICIA We had a wonderful kid. I think we blew our wad on that one (all laugh). I think [another blessing has been] a real closeness and a real honesty in this relationship. I mean, I can come home and rant and rave and say everything I think, without feeling that it's not going to be OK when it's done. . . .

GARY Our relationship has been so much better than any that I'd ever experienced, and so most of my friends . . .

PATRICIA And that's white-white and black-black. It's true.

GARY . . . It so strengthened us. It so enabled each of us to do things
we couldn't have done otherwise. . . . That's the big blessing.
. . . It seems to me that the relationship continues changing
and continues growing.

> I've got the best wife in the world. Flora is a hardworking, dedicated
> mother and wife . . . and my best friend. . . . I have a hard time trying
> to understand why anybody would be against an interracial relation-
> ship, because ours has gone so smoothly. (Tim)

> I think for me . . . the blessing has been that our relationship and . . .
> the connections that our relationship allows us to make has kept me
> thinking and kept me . . . on my toes, . . . kept me aware and alive
> about things, issues and topics. One of the things that I always feared
> in adulthood was that adults weren't paying attention to what was go-
> ing on, and I'm still frustrated with the fact that people don't want to
> do something about things, . . . just becoming less aware that things
> are going on. . . . My family is in some ways very, I think we have a cer-
> tain warmth about us. But we're not very physical, and . . . we're still
> very . . . formal (laughs) in some ways. . . . I think . . . our relationship
> . . . allows me to continue to develop those things that I thought were
> missing. . . . We do talk a lot and share emotions and feelings and
> things like that, which is something that I really didn't grow up with.
> (Wanda)

Some people talked about the blessing of having been joined with
members of their partner's family. Much of what they had to say
could be said by anybody in an ordinary relationship who felt good
about in-laws or stepchildren.

> My family is in Ohio, and I've been here since 1973, going to college
> and working. I actually got a new family out of this. Her family is
> great. (Shane)

> Another special blessing of the marriage for me is [my stepsons]. There
> are a lot of stepmothers who don't enjoy the relationship with their
> stepchildren. When I met him, I was prepared to love them because I
> loved him when I met him. And now I love them in their own right.
> (Dot)

BLESSINGS PRESENT BECAUSE
THE RELATIONSHIP IS INTERRACIAL

People also talked about blessings that perhaps can only exist in a relationship between people of different races. That suggests that some who felt that they were in an ordinary relationship could see extraordinary features to the relationship. One woman, for example, talked about how the interracial nature of the relationship helped to make it special by pushing the couple toward more openness than might exist in a same-race relationship.

> I think when you have something that is as obvious as race that you have to get over or not—not to get over, but you have to deal with early on in your relationship—I think we naturally have maybe a more open relationship than a lot of other people do. We can talk about anything with each other. I don't think that we both have secrets or things that we won't reveal or don't want to reveal. . . . But I think we probably have a more open and communicative relationship than a lot of people. It baffles me sometimes when I hear about people saying, "Oh, I can't talk to my husband or wife about that. They wouldn't understand," or something like that. I think we do have certain things that we do have problems with, but I think we just got to be pretty open and honest with each other. (Nora)

Healing

Quite a few people talked about the blessing of "healing" (healing the "paranoia" of being an African American in a racist society, healing the prejudice and ignorance that comes with being white in American society).

> I'm not as paranoid as I used to be. I used to be really sick, as far as my paranoia. . . . Being in this relationship has helped me get over that. (Ed)

> I feel more relaxed and confident with my ideas and my feelings because, I think being raised in a prejudicial and biased way there's that little voice in you that says you shouldn't be telling those kind of jokes; you shouldn't be saying those kind of things. And finally, when

you're out into the real world and you can definitely say, "No, those jokes are bad; they're wrong. I'm not going to do that anymore," you feel a sense of peace and a kind of acceptance. (Nora)

Consistent with the idea that an interracial relationship can heal, one woman talked about being able to bridge the historical, cultural, attitudinal, and experiential gulf between black and white people. She saw the bridge as necessary to an interracial relationship and as a contribution to healing the wounds of racism.

When I was watching this [television program], *Diary of Black Minnesotans,* the discussion in this program turned into a very black separatist discussion. And I felt like that I'm beyond that, that I *have* to be beyond that. And I think that is a blessing. It's like a bridge, a bridge between races, and I've felt this way too; another real positive feeling for me was when I went to an event at Holy Rosary Church this summer . . . and they had all these cultures there. It was an event with music in the evening, and they had music from South America, and they had Native American music, and they had black drumming. . . . I brought the kids, and just the diversity of people that attended, and I felt like I'm a part of people who are bridging the hatred. (Liz)

One man who talked about the thrill he got from his own interracial family and from seeing other interracial families seemed to be talking in part about the thrill that came from knowing that healing was going on, that black and white could be united.

When I was growing up, there were certain experiences . . . that would give me that real tingling sensation, that real thrill. However bad the day had gone, however bad whatever was going on in your life, there was just the special kind of feeling like, "God, life is good!" It just hits you. It's not there for very long necessarily, but it's enough to sustain you. When I was younger, it might come when I hit a 20-foot jumper at the buzzer, or when I kissed the girlfriend. . . . I think I find that every time I make a . . . connection with people like you, with other people involved in interracial relationships or when I see us or when I feel that people are responding to us in a way that genuinely opens up their eyes or maybe opens up our own. We see our kids, . . . we see all these interracial kids running around, I get that kind of feeling. I guess that's certainly something that is blessed for me. (Adam)

Another man had a similar view, that the children of an interracial relationship represented a healing.

> Part of being interracially married is a spiritual peace about the children being sort of the blending of the races. (Ed)

Enrichment

Another blessing that was mentioned, more often and with more detail by white partners than by African American partners, was how enriching it was to be partnered with somebody from a different cultural-racial group. The white partners might speak of learning about a world they had not known, learning different ways of looking at the world, or learning about racism. The African American partners might speak more generally about learning more about the white world. This blessing was often mentioned in conjunction with some version of the blessing of healing the wounds of racism. Here are comments by a number of white partners about the blessing of enrichment:

> I just feel my life is so enriched. I mean, that whole process I described when I was a child, trying to break down color barriers, trying to get to know . . . the black race. I'm still trying to get to know black people completely in this racist society. . . . But Charles has afforded me the ability to go into all-black churches. . . . The opportunities are unique. (Janet)

> Just the insight and awareness, the richness of living in more than one culture at the same time. It's like, wow, ya know! It's great—that's a special blessing. It's real invigorating, adds new insights that I know help me a great deal in just my day-to-day living. (Kate)

> The [neatest] thing for me has been . . . the cultural difference and learning something about Ed's [world]. We're like soul mates, and yet . . . we've come into the relationship with a lot of experiences that the other hasn't had. . . . One of my favorites, that I would never have experienced, is going up to the barbershop on Fourth Avenue and 38th. . . . You have to come first come, first served. And people just wait, and so you can go in there, and you're like maybe 20th in line. So you

sit there all day . . . not minding it one bit, because I'm learning something . . . and you're listening to these people talk. . . . They're not that different than me. And yet there *is* a cultural, there's just something. And they're yelling back and forth, and so part of it's . . . their cultural stuff . . . and then watching them get their hair cut. I *love* watching them cut the hair. . . . I can remember one time when a woman . . . had fallen asleep while she was getting her hair cut, and it was a woman cutting her hair, a woman barber. The woman woke up, and looked at her hair, and she was just like, "Oh, girlfriend! Girlfriend!" . . . Experiences like that are enriching. Or if you haven't gone to Chicago with Ed and meeting . . . musician friends of his. . . . There's this one guy that, I mean, he's just the coolest guy in the world, a trumpet player. . . . Meeting his mother. I would sit and listen to her until 3 in the morning telling me stories. (Rosemary)

GLORIA   I don't think this is so much for myself, because . . . I was really exposed, particularly in my high school, to lots of different cultures, and so it didn't seem that unusual, I mean, I don't feel like I've learned that much more about his culture, his European culture, by necessarily being married.

KENT   But I've learned a lot more about your culture, by far.

I feel that as far as just the interraciality that there are *so* many people out there who never get to know anyone of a race other than themselves. . . . The other day . . . my boss was . . . trying to get some cultural diversity stuff going at work. And they sent a thing around saying if you have any articles or whatever to bring them, . . . having to do with cultural diversity. . . . He's a white man who is not an evil person, but he's one of those who keeps the old institutionalized racism going. . . . So he said, "Well, now, you bring these articles in, but then don't bring anything that's going to upset people. . . ." And I said, "Well, I'm bringing in all my stuff on Malcolm X and Mr. Louis Farrakhan tomorrow. We're going to read that first thing in the morning." And he said, "Na na na na. I'm a nice guy. I don't want anything controversial." So then I turned from being totally joking with him to kind of serious. And I said, ". . . You're a lucky fellow. You don't have to have any controversy in your life. You're lucky." I said, ". . . My life has controversy." Then I sat down at my desk and I started thinking I was dead wrong. I am more lucky. [He] is not lucky living a life where there is no controversy. I'm lucky, and I wouldn't trade . . . what I have for *any*thing in the world. The parts I consider controversial have helped me to learn; they keep me seeking to learn. I will never stop being amazed at racism. I hope I never get to the point where it no longer shocks me. I will never stop fighting in my own little way. (Dot)

Black people have to know their own culture, and they also have to know white culture. They have to speak two languages. And the advantage for me is that I also get to learn a second language. . . . Given the direction that I was headed . . . when I was headed off to college, the chances of me being in a place that was intellectually stimulating 20 years later . . . I mean, I'd probably be sitting around the officers' club talking about our Desert Storm victories . . . and no more aware of the variety of culture available in this country . . . than I was in 1968. I mean, it just seems to me that I benefited greatly. (Roger)

I think that for me a special blessing [has been the] personal knowledge. I have learned so much. . . . I've learned that people are people. . . . I've learned so much from being with him and the knowledge from his culture that he's taught to me that we can share . . . that I think a lot of same-race relationships don't get. . . . There was just so much that I've learned about African American history that I never was taught . . . in a school or read in a book, that he's taught me. (Jill)

We celebrate Kwanzaa connected with [the] . . . families from that workshop that we've been going to for years. It feels like that's been really rich in friendship. . . . We've made more of an effort to be more diverse and to include more people as family than I think I would have been. (Joyce)

Here are comments by several African Americans about the enrichment that comes from being partnered with someone of a different culture or race:

Some of the things that you get from a multicultural relationship is that perhaps you have access to opinions . . . that are more diverse than, say, two individuals who come from the same region and the same culture who were perhaps raised more closely in relation to similarities than she and I. (James)

You learning more from the cultural diversity you're in. You learning more about, and I think especially for myself, given the uniqueness of how I grew up . . . , I had to take and learn that indeed what my father was saying to me was correct, that they aren't all alike. . . . It made me become more aware of myself. It really brought out the things in me that I needed to deal with . . . as an individual with a lot of hang-ups. . . . It's very challenging all the time. I know all relationships may be challenging but this one even more so because of all the negative that society put upon it. So it bring out the best in you . . . because we know that there [is] a lot of anger against us out here. So we have to . . . withstand all of those angers . . . , people callin' you names. . . . Why did she marry that nigger? Why he marry this poor white trash? . . . So all them negatives out there, it really make you feel more strong. It make you feel more stalwart, so unique, and so special. (Robert)

I think one of the special blessings has to do with our kids. I mean, they have a unique look and will have a chance to grow up and get advantaged from different cultures and have a claim to different cultures, not that people who don't have that claim are any less, but I think it's nice that they will have that. (Bayard)

Possibly, some of the enrichment that can come to an African American who joins with a white partner are the benefits that come from white privilege. If whites, on the average, have more access to the material and social benefits of being in a privileged group, an African American may gain access to some of those benefits through partnership with a white. There was not even a hint that any African American entered a relationship to gain access to white privilege, but a few talked about increased access to specific privileges that came with their partnership with a white. One African American woman, for example, talked about career advantages from her marriage.

In terms of my career, . . . it may have been an advantage in some respects [to be married to a white man]. Because of his career, I was in places that I wouldn't have necessarily been, I don't think. So sometimes I think it's an advantage. But . . . I'm my own person. And I'm well qualified, so I certainly don't think I've gotten anything because of him. But I think I've heard of opportunities because of him. (Patricia)

As Patricia said, being in an interracial relationship affects who one meets. Others also talked about how being in an interracial relationship influenced who they met.

You meet a more, *enlightened* is the word that comes to mind, . . . strata of our society that's going to be more educated, more liberal. (Emmett)

Withstanding Racist Opposition

Some of the blessings people said they experienced were the blessings of having stayed together, withstood, and overcome racist opposition to their relationship.

After getting so much negative feedback and absolutely no support from anybody, it's just such a wonderful relief to see that we made it and that we're happy and we get along. So it's just kind of all just self-affirming for me. (Christine)

If one has challenged one's family by being in a relationship that some family members intensely opposed, one can feel that one's relationship with the family has passed a crucial test if family members are still loving.

Ya know I think the other blessing I've got to is that I know my parents love me (laughs). (Liz)

In the process, one blessing may have been that one learned patience.

Patience, maybe patience with other people too, 'cause, like I said, my dad did come around. He did that all by himself. I didn't have to try to show him what the world is all about. . . . Patience worked for him. (Shirley)

Although most people answered the question about blessings by emphasizing what they had experienced as individuals, as a couple, or as a family, in talking about weathering racist opposition, one white woman described the contribution her relationship made to her family of origin.

> I think it's been very good for [my parents], very, very good for them because they don't really know what, like the only contact that people in a town like [theirs] have with people of different races are when the county fair comes through. And there are carnies and things like that in that, so they think that all black people are carnival barkers or something. And I think it's been very good for my parents. (Nora)

SUMMARY AND CONCLUSIONS

Although this book deals at length with difficulties that may arise from racism, the couples also had plenty to say about what was positive in their partnerships. In fact, it was important to some of them that there be more of a balance in what was said about interracial couples, partly as a rejoinder to racist stereotypes about interracial couples. Some of the blessings people described for their relationship were blessings that might be found in any ordinary, satisfying relationship—the blessings of delightful children and of love.

Many of the blessings people talked about were blessings that could only be obtained in an interracial relationship. Three blessings were mentioned often: (a) healing—healing individual wounds from racism and healing the wounds in society that have been caused by racism; (b) enrichment—the enrichment of self, partner, and children that comes from the joining of groups, of perspectives, of cultures; (c) weathering racist opposition—as individual and couple, getting past racist opposition and getting to better places with family members who had opposed the relationship.

14

FINDING SUPPORT

A ny couple without supportive family, friends, neighbors, and organizations is likely to have a more difficult life. Couples have to sort out who is supportive and who is not. They need to find people who are relatively accepting of who they are as individuals and as a couple and who can provide some of what they need individually and as a couple. Interracial couples need support just as any couple does. Most of the support they need might be support that is not directly linked to their being an interracial couple. That their relationship is interracial means, however, that they have some special needs. They will need to find people who are not so racist as to undermine them as individuals and as a couple. They may need to find people who can support them in dealing with family and community opposition and in dealing with any expressions of racism they experience. They may also need to find people who, like they, wrestle with issues of personal identity, child rearing, and coming together across racial and cultural differences.

SEPARATING SUPPORTIVE
PEOPLE FROM THOSE WHO ARE NOT

Most individuals and couples probably engage in some kind of ongoing sorting to find reasonable amounts of support. They have to get to know people, work out their relationships with people, and recognize when their own needs change or when the support someone else provides changes. Many of the couples we interviewed had achieved levels of support that they felt good about, and some talked about the sorting process that enabled them to achieve that support.

> I think we've received tremendous support. I mean, of the people who don't support us, we don't associate with them anymore. I remember being very hurt by a woman who I, in college, and I'm her daughter's god[mother], and I haven't seen the child since probably 2, 'cause she wouldn't have anything to do with [me] after that. I remember some friends in Texas . . . making some comments; . . . I got a letter from this friend sort of ranting and raving about it. . . . I probably was initially hurt, but I'm not friends with them anymore. At our wedding, it was an incredible amount of support. I mean, people came, and Gary's mother's friends came, and, in some ways, we laughed about that, it was like attempting to show how liberal they could be, because we got *fabulous* wedding presents. (Patricia)

She went on to add something that many respondents could have said, that they often felt supported (or at least not undermined) because they avoided people who were not supportive and because people who were inclined not to be supportive often kept quiet about their feelings.

> We've tended to be around people who are very supportive, and the people who aren't have tended not to say anything. . . . I remember [a preacher] saying, "When you have an education, you can . . . be around people who . . . will either be supportive or have sense enough not to say anything." And I think we've experienced a lot of that.

The process of sorting may always be interactive, with potential supporters announcing their support and the individuals to be supported evaluating the degree to which those others can provide support.

LIZ [My friend's] mother wrote me a letter, kinda saying how hard she knew it was for me. . . .

INTERVIEWER Was it a supportive letter?

LIZ Yeah, she was trying to be supportive.

One couple, in talking about finding support from an old friend of the husband, revealed how high the stakes can be in determining who will be supportive. Sorting out supportive people from those who are not supportive is not necessarily a dispassionate process, especially when it risks face-to-face rejection and the possible weakening or destruction of long-term, important friendships.

PATRICIA We were surrounded with a lot of friends who were very supportive. . . . [So], if we chose to expose ourselves to the other parts of the community, that was fine. But within our niche, . . . people were real supportive.

GARY And it was actively discussed in our community and with each other. I remember my black male friends, bringing it up with them. Just [asking], "How do you feel about this? Is this gonna be an issue?" And one friend . . . I remember telling me that he really didn't believe in interracial relationships and would never choose it for himself, but it looked like it was going to work for us. And my best friend in college, a black man . . . , I wrote him and asked him what he thought. And he didn't reply. And I was so worried that this was going to hurt our relationship. So we went to [Pittsburgh] to visit. He just had gotten married.

PATRICIA And *I* am getting physically ill . . . because I'm really frightened.

GARY He said, "Come ahead," but he hadn't said anything.

INTERVIEWER And you were physically ill and frightened because?

PATRICIA Because . . . Gary got no response from [his friend]. We didn't know what his response was going to be. Maybe this was going to hurt their friendship. And so I have built up to this monumental headache, and I'm sick, and . . .

GARY Well, we went to the house, and he didn't arrive right away. And this woman was there, this white woman who seemed to expect us.

PATRICIA And I thought she was there cleaning the house . . . ; I didn't know. And then, but as it turned out, she thought we knew they were married! Oh, they were going to get married. That's right. They were going to get married, because they got married almost at the same time as we did. But it was like I had to leave. I said to Gary, "You have to take me back to the hotel, because I'm feeling really sick." She, not knowing that we didn't know who she was, thinking this woman is strange, I'm sure. So we go back to the hotel, and then we get back together again, and find out that this. And you know, the reason [the friend] didn't respond is because it wasn't an issue.

GARY Well, but he was seeing it as a great joke that I'd be worried about it. . . . Rather than tell me, let us *see* that that was not going to be an issue in our friendship.

Gary and Patricia went on to say that when support is found, typically, it is based on a broad base of friendship, with the interracial nature of the relationship being a minor matter.

GARY We've gotten a lot of support of all kinds, emotional support, financial support, and we've been [in] difficulties.

PATRICIA Yeah, and I don't think it's so much with our friends' support because we're an interracial couple. I think it's because they liked us, and so they support us. The fact that we are an interracial couple is kind of secondary. So it's a friendship, not based on the fact that people feel there's a deficit in us and some dysfunction and that they need to try to help us do it, because we're just another couple of people that they like. . . .

GARY I'm not at all sure that all of our friends as a result of knowing us approve of interracial relationships. They approve us.

PATRICIA Yeah, that's probably true.

Virginia talked about how the sorting process, at least as regards matters of race, seemed to be more significant early in a couple's relationship. After an initial sorting on matters of racism and acceptance, a couple will have identified family and acquaintances to distance and those who are good candidates for continuing closeness.

By the time you're married or shortly after, the family and friends have sorted themselves out. [Race] is no longer an issue.

In a couple for which the white partner's family had initially opposed the relationship and then moved to be accepting and supportive, the early sorting process included struggles with and among the white partner's family. But by the time of the interview, years after the couple relationship began, the early struggles were no longer in evidence. There was only support, although as the woman in the couple said in the following comment, the support may be a kind of generalized couple support, not support directed at concerns and issues that an interracial couple might uniquely have to deal with.

[Our families] are just supportive, and not everybody has that in their relationship, for lots of different reasons. But they're just supportive. . . . , and . . . you're firmly in the extended family, even though Adam's family is not that extended (laughs). So there's always a sense that they can be counted on. . . . But that's just barely a basic kind of need for any relationship. I don't think it really goes beyond, I mean, I don't think they particularly go out of their way to do it for the interracial purpose. That's certainly not the focus. (Wanda)

With some family and friends, a couple may have to work hard to win support, but there are relationships for which support is present from the beginning. In some cases the support was there from the beginning because it involved people who introduced the partners to each other in the first place.

I know that we had the support of our friends, our closest friends, because we met through some friends. (Nora)

SUPPORTIVE FAMILY, FRIENDS, AND INSTITUTIONS

Quite a few people talked about family, friends, and institutions that were supportive. Some emphasized how important it was, perhaps particularly at first, to find people who were supportive of a relationship that was interracial.

> His friends were really accepting of me, but they were musicians, most of them, or students. We socialize more, probably, with his friends right now. My friends in college included a couple of interracial couples, so that, I think, made it easier for me. And then the black male friends I had in grad school . . . were dating all different kinds of people, so what was nice about that was I had a network of black friends . . . who were real open. . . . We didn't have to feel isolated because we were making a choice that, say, a fair amount of people didn't accept. (Gloria)

For most of the couples who were married, the relationship had gone on long enough by the time of the wedding for there to have been quite a lot of sorting of people in terms of supportiveness. Emmett talked about looking out over the people in attendance at his wedding and seeing the support there, both in terms of the attitudes of the people who were there and in terms of the racial and ethnic mix of those in attendance.

> It was very nice to look out over the people who were at the wedding with us and see such an incredible mix of people and cultures. It was something that my mother commented on. . . . It was odd to see a white couple or a black couple or an Asian couple.

Sometimes, it seemed that there was no active support among relatives, friends, and acquaintances, although they accepted the relationship. One man had an explanation of that, talking about the way accepting blurs into ignoring.

INTERVIEWER Have you received support from family, friends, or siblings that you know is related to your being an interracial couple? . . . We're in your corner type of support.

JAMES . . . No. See, it's a strange thing about American society; . . . once you accept something, you ignore it. It no longer exists for you. So as a multicultural family, to those who accept it, you're just a family. Therefore, you need no support. Now I suppose if we were down South and we were going through trials and tribulations, having our lawn burned up by fiery crosses or something, it might be a different situation.

Supportive Connections
Between Families of Origin

One way that a couple can be supported is through the connections of their separate families of origin. If, for example, her parents and his parents know each other, get along well, and have regular contact, the couple could feel that their relationship counted with their parents and was supported by them. In fact, in many cultures, including some cultural groups in the United States a committed couple relationship links or strengthens the links between the families of the two partners (Cerroni-Long, 1984). In the present study, however, only two couples mentioned contact between their respective families of origin. Perhaps such lack of contact is also common in same-race couples who are as educated and geographically mobile as the couples who were interviewed. Perhaps it is common in same-race couples when the two families of origin live many miles distant from each other, as was the case for every one of the couples. But it was striking that the black family of origin and the white family of origin almost never had contact. The contacts that were mentioned were positive but rare.

We had a Christmas party here. It must have been like two Christmases ago. My mom was here and my brother, my niece and my nephews, and my brother's ex-wife and her husband . . . [and] Joyce's family. It was probably one of the best parties we ever had. You remember that party? All the singing. . . . It was kind of a flavor for seein' the world through different eyes in a lot of ways. (Gregory)

In one case, the meeting of the partners' mothers had a powerful affect on both mothers and perhaps on the couple, because it established how similar the two families of origin were and that the two mothers could connect with each other.

After our wedding, I think her mother made a big step towards the acceptance of us in that she was able to sit down with my mother and just talk. Because we did most of the stuff ourselves so they had time alone, and in the breakfast afterwards they were just sitting there talking, and they were going through and finding out that their lives had paralleled a lot in terms of the type of work they had done, the types of experiences they had had. And there was a real bonding that happened there that I think was quite a learning experience for both of our mothers. (Emmett)

Community Supports
Specifically for Interracial Couples

As early as the 1890s, there were clubs for interracial couples (Larsson, 1965, pp. 58-61; Lynn, 1953, p. 520, cited in Spickard, 1989, note 19). In the 1940s, there were additional clubs for interracial couples in some northern cities, at least for couples in which the white partner was a European war bride (Simpkins, 1965, Stewart, 1948, and articles in *Ebony,* in 1951 and 1953, all cited in Spickard, 1989). None of the people who were interviewed mentioned attending a club for interracial couples. Quite a few, however, talked about attending workshops, support groups, and other programs for interracial couples and families. Sometimes, these programs made use of input from somebody who was considered an expert on interracial family issues, but the heart of the workshop, support group, or other program was the active participation of those who attended. Some of the people who were interviewed framed their answers to questions about interracial relationships by talking about their relationship-supportive experiences at specific workshops or support groups.

> I think it came up at the workshop Saturday that as a white person, it's your first experience really with prejudice, with how that feels. (Joyce)

SHIRLEY Shane kind of wondered why I had called and said let's participate in this interview. We don't even talk about it or think about it. It's not even like an issue. I said, "Let's just do it, like the workshops that we go to every year." He says, "Why do we have to talk about this? Let's just live our life." But it's, not that it's more important to me, but maybe I'm a little more concerned about [racism]. . . . Shane has grown up with it, lived with it every day of his life, and me, I've only come to deal with it really since I've been with him. . . . And we're not confronted with it very often at all. I'm sometimes very amazed, but nevertheless, it's enough to concern me where I need to find out about other people's experiences. Get support from them.

INTERVIEWER And so when you mentioned going to the workshop, is that something that you have done a number of times?

SHIRLEY Yeah, 4 or 5 years, I think.

Some people felt that their relationship had benefited from their participation in the workshops for interracial families sponsored by a Minneapolis church and Minneapolis Early Childhood Family Education programs.

> I feel like part of an interracial community. We have friends who are interracially married, and then we have a good friend, she and her husband are both white, and they have two children who are adopted who are black. And we—I don't know if you've ever participated in interracial family workshops at _____ Church—we've sort of found people that are supportive of our relationship. (Barb)

> I think that being in this community helps us a lot. . . . Being in . . . interracial family workshops, those kinds of things; . . . it's an injection for us, and that's the value. And being able to expose ourselves to different types of interracial families . . . , I feel very interested and involved and somewhat knowledgeable and interested in the various adoption controversies that are going on. And noticing again in this community . . . the various levels of interracial activity. . . . We've been very steadily active in interracial family workshops at the _____ Church. (Adam)

Some people found valuable support from others who were in interracial couples. One couple talked about support they had both given and received from interracial couples and about the hunger that some people in interracial couples have for contact with others in interracial relationships.

LORENZO [Our] friends . . . were . . . interested in us as people. There was no agenda to take care of us because we were an

interracial family, but there was on the part of other interracial couples. . . . Because for other interracial couples [our
being an interracial couple] *was* an issue. And the fact that
we were early organizers, with a few other people, of the
interracial family workshops and that people found those
valuable and useful and that people really felt that it was a
nice thing to kind of stay in touch with us because they got
something out of those.

VIRGINIA Well, but it even predated that. . . . You guys have probably
felt some of this too, . . . going out of your way to . . . get to
know other interracial couples. And I remember for instance
[that woman] where you used to work coming over when
[our daughter] was a baby and . . . she's got interracial
children. And I remember one day having a conversation
with her that I was certain that she had thought about having
for a long time and just kind of trying to clue me in to a bunch
of different things (laughs), and let me know some things
to look out for. . . . And I felt like that was her decision to
be supportive, and there's been that kind of stuff . . . ,
although I think probably in recent years it's more we've
done that for other people than people have done that for
us. And that's definitely true in interracial marriages. . . . I
was at a picnic this summer with just the kids. . . . There's a
woman that I went to . . . school with that's interracially
married, and we had some bits and pieces of conversation
throughout school. As soon as she figured out that I was
interracially married and she's got, like, really young children, 2 years old, 3 years old, . . . she cornered [our daugh-
ter] and was like (laughs), it was almost a desperate thing of,
like, "Let me know that children can grow up and be OK."
. . . Some of this has to do with the fact that we, although
not recently but for quite a few years, we were involved in
interracial family groups, so I think that we've been together
a *long* time, so I think we basically knew where each of us
stood. . . .

LORENZO Sure, yeah, I'm sure you've interviewed couples for whom
. . . these are new issues, and they're just kind of exploring
them.

VIRGINIA They kind of hear some new things from each other that
are surprising.

LORENZO Yeah, yeah, and we've guided other couples as mentors though this stuff.

It may be a mistake to say that what people necessarily get from interracial workshops or from making contact with others in interracial couples is "support." Sometimes, what they want, at least as they understand it, is companionship or the company of similar others.

> I don't think we'd been going to workshops as much for support as it was for finding common relationships. . . . I guess you can call that support. But I don't think we ever felt we were there [for support]. (Adam)

A few people expressed reservations about formal support programs. The existence of a program for interracial or biracial families, parents, or children seemed to them to exaggerate the magnitude of their potential problems and perhaps to legitimate the racist categories that make terms such as *race, interracial,* and *biracial* mean some of what racists want them to mean.

EVE I know that the Y that we go to, they have a lot of interracial family groups. . . . And my mom asked us, "Don't you guys want to go to that stuff?" Sometimes I think, "Well, yeah, it would be nice," but sometimes I think I don't. I get tired of always dwelling on that aspect of it. . . . Our kids are just kids, and we are just people. And we do have to teach our children to deal with it, but I think that they have a good mother and a good father, and that's the important thing. . . . I haven't felt any need for any support. . . .

HOUSTON We are just human beings. . . . There is that support group over at the Y for white mothers. . . . If you look at it that way, then I guess you probably would need some support. But if you look at it as just a family, you just normal. I mean, this is normal. What would be normal? A male and a female to get together, have children, and be one. . . . If you let the world direct your lives, you would be messed up. And that's what I am trying not to do, to let people direct the way we live. If people want to look at us, "Oh, she's white and he's black," that's the way they look at it. I can't let that affect us. Just like our children, you know, we hear that all the time—"Well, they going to be confused and all." . . . One thing that me and my wife are definitely going to work with them on is teaching them that, "Hey, people are going to say this and that, but you must realize that you are just human beings. You just kids like any other kids. Simple as that."

The interviewers invited a couple in which the man had talked about their being an ordinary couple to talk about what it means for people who consider themselves to be an ordinary couple to seek support groups.

INTERVIEWER There are people who seek out . . . workshops where they're coming together with other people who are in interracial families. . . . If this is no different than any relationship, . . . by attending to the fact that it's interracial, you're acting as if it's different or you're making it different. And I'm wondering if you have some idea about why people seek out those workshops or if you've ever gone to any of them or how you make sense out of that for those people?

JAMES Support. Support groups. It's like Weight Watchers; it's like stopping smoking. Any other thing that you don't think you can handle it yourself.

JILL It's not only that though. . . . It's for just basically getting together and sharing . . .

JAMES Commonality?

JILL Well, it's sharing your experiences, because it's true no matter how much we think that we view our relationship no different than other [relationships], other people view our relationship [differently]. . . .

JAMES Seems to me that's a support group.

JILL Well, OK.

JAMES But I don't really believe in those things. Not in this particular instance. Because, like she said, if you go to those things, let's say you have an experience with your child, and so and so has had the same experience or similar experiences, their response will probably be different than yours. But people do need to talk about their problems. Some people can't analyze a situation without talking out loud. Like some people do with math problems. Sometimes, you have to read them out loud to understand what they are. And they come up with their own solutions.

Although many people who had attended workshops for interracial couples said that the workshops were valuable, the workshops are challenged to deal with the diversity of interracial families. One woman talked about her frustration, at a workshop for parents of interracial children, in trying to find women whose interracial couple experiences were like hers.

> I'd been attending a [support group]. It was a child education type thing that had a special workshop for interracial kids. . . . And I remember going to that, and there was a couple other, there weren't very many people that showed up. That, you know, people keep thinking that we need this kind of bothers me too. . . . I was sitting in there and I was telling my experience. . . . And this one woman just got up and said (imitating angry voice), "Your experience is totally different from mine." . . . It was such an inflammatory attack on me, and she said, "My first boyfriends was black pimps," and . . . she's, like, from the inner city. . . . "You don't know what it's like. You don't know . . . prostituting." She went on and on. . . . I never went back to that. . . . I have nothing in common with these folks. This is not about finding camaraderie because of interracial experiences. (Janet)

SUMMARY AND CONCLUSIONS

All couples can benefit from support. Lots of the support that would benefit an interracial couple is the kind of support that would benefit any couple. But some of the support they may find valuable is support in dealing with issues that can arise specifically in interracial couples and families—for example, support in personal identity struggles stemming from being in an interracial relationship, in parenting biracial children, in dealing with family opposition, or in dealing with partner differences in the experience of racism and privilege.

Some couples talked about a sorting-out process, particularly at the beginning of their relationship, to identify relatives, friends, and acquaintances who were accepting and supportive of the relationship and those who might better be distanced. The sorting process not only involved the couple's making judgments but also other's volunteering their attitudes and family members contending with one another about whether or how to support the couple. The process of arriving at supportive relationships may also involve people who are not supportive keeping quiet about their opinions while interacting with the couple. Although the process may seem dispassionate, feelings can run high for the couple, particularly when first informing good friends and close relatives about the relationship. Early support can be especially welcomed, but as described in earlier chapters of this book, some family support is gained only later on.

What constitutes support is not a simple matter. People may express supportive attitudes; they may support simply by their own racial and cultural diversity. Sometimes, it is difficult to tell the difference between support and ignoring, because positive acceptance shades into a nonsupportive indifference. Perhaps the most supportive relationships are those that provide different positive things on different occasions—playful friendship, help with moving, sympathy at a death, and so on.

The Twin Cities are rich in community supports for interracial couples and families. Some people felt a real hunger for contact with others in interracial couples, and some did not. Some welcomed support; some welcomed something that they would not call support—perhaps companionship with similar others. Some opposed the idea of support for interracial couples, feeling that such support legitimated racist categories and stereotypes. Some who participated in interracial family programs found little support for themselves because of the ways they differed from those in attendance. Others were glad to be involved, both to receive and to give support.

15

NO MORE RACISM!

Everybody who was interviewed spoke of the need to end racism directed at interracial relationships. They advocated seeing people as individuals, not as racial stereotypes, and seeing interracial couples as like other couples.

I really have a hard time with understanding how the choice that someone made can arouse so much passion in other people, to the extent that they want to do harm or they want to harass or they want to ostracize. . . . If people didn't think of differences as being such a negative or such a scary thing, then I think it would be easier for people to make whatever kinds of choices. . . . It's not like I'm *pro* interracial marriage, so I think everyone should get in this situation and assimilate and all become one blend. No, I don't believe that. I just believe that people should have the freedom to do this. And I think in an environment in which people respected differences and didn't get so anxious about them, I think that would happen more readily, that people would just choose, based on what they have in common with the person, how they felt about the person. (Gloria)

I think society sees a black male with a white female in a relationship together, first they say, "Well, he may be a pimp, using her as a whore; she's pushin' drugs for him." Use all these negatives to surround that relationship, right? And because they want to think of all these negative things and make it not work, [we need] to let society know just what type of relationship they have. . . . Only thing different is that we come from different races. . . . I see just like whenever the press reportin' its views in north Minneapolis, always negative, negative, negative, negative. They don't say all the good things, one community trying to do to build themselves over there, do all them other things each day, like work with the children, the youth funds over there, to get 'em away from drugs, and let 'em know whenever a drug dealer come through, "Don't deal with these folks." . . . They don't talk about that. . . . I think we as a couple got to be sure that we don't fall into the stereotype society set for us already. I see this every time I go out with Kate. I see myself settin' examples. . . . Three-piece suit and my briefcase in my hand, right? . . . Every time I go out, I try to put myself in a position to say, "Look, I'm no different than the white couple over there. We're out just having a good time, have dinner, go to a movie, listen to a band, only different because our skin tones look different." (Robert)

I want [people] to know that we are as diverse as they are. Terri and I are no more alike than the two white ladies across the street married to white men. We range from totally ignorant to highly interesting, and we range from dogs to beautiful. . . . We range from thin to fat. Some of us are ex-prostitutes and some of us are not. . . . They can trust some of us and some of us they can't. (Dot)

I want the larger society to know that interracial relationship or not, that people are people. All races of people require the same thing; . . . we all need to breathe and eat, and we all need love and affection. And I think that all mankind should have the right to those things, regardless of what his or her race may be. As far as letting the larger community know anything about interracial relationships, I want them to know that my children don't deserve to be treated any differently than their children. Pity the fool (laughing and making loud sounds—Whack! Whack!) that treats them any differently. . . . I don't disrespect other people's children because of their race, and I should hope that other people wouldn't disrespect mine because of theirs. (Tim)

I think people should . . . simply recognize that people are people and their relationships are complex. If two people can . . . establish a relationship that lasts . . . and bears fruits . . . for the two of them and for the people around them even, then that's good enough. That's a pretty big success these days when you look at divorce rates [and] what people are doing to each other. (Adam)

In talking about their opposition to racism directed at interracial relationships, some people spoke of the richness of black history and of black-white interracial relationships.

We are all God's people, and . . . in this family we have a very, very rich profound union of cultures . . . , and it's perfectly normal, perfectly accept[able]. . . . We are all God's children, and . . . this is unique . . . because of the history of black people in Africa, black people in America. . . . It's special, and if you are fortunate enough to meet and get to know such a . . . family, there is a lot to be shared there. There's a lot of learning and growing that can occur if you choose to partake of that. (Kate)

Ed talked about the beauty of interracial children and the possibility that in the beauty there is a message from God.

We all have to come together eventually, because this separate shit ain't working. . . . I can tell you one more thing. . . . When I went in to look at the proofs for selecting [our son's] pictures, the guy said to me, "Biracial children . . . are the most beautiful children. . . . It's God's way of showing the world that there shouldn't be bigotry."

Some people talked about the burden that racism puts on an interracial couple.

I think that probably the climate has not changed that much in terms of interracial relationships. I think the people are still pretty much opposed to 'em. And certainly, if a kid were to ask me, ". . . Should I marry somebody within my own race or outside of my race?" I'd probably say to them, "You have to do what you think is best for yourself." But then on another level I think, "If you want an easy way out (laughs), marry the person who's in your race, 'cause it's got its own set of struggles." You don't see 'em on the surface when you look at the person. You fall in love. You think this will be a wonderful relationship, and there's a bigger realm outside of that relationship that you have to contend with. . . . I don't know offhand if people . . . give it that much thought. I didn't give it that much thought! (Gregory)

A few people thought that racism would not go away, that racist thinking was too ingrained in society.

I personally don't feel that it would make any difference where you go within the United States. There is always the need within a social structure for the low man on the totem pole. There's always the need to exclude or look down upon individuals or groups and control those individuals or groups, for the sake of ego or economy or any number of factors. I don't think it would make any difference if everyone was pale gray. Then you would find something else to separate out, to strain or weed out individuals who thought one way or felt one way or dressed one way. And I don't see that within this culture that that's going to change. And for all the sanctimonious BS you hear out of Washington on civil rights . . . , I don't see that anyone cares enough or feels that changes could be made. Because it's ingrained. It's a European thought process. And we may be Americans, but we have Western ideals. And they're bred into us, taught to us in school, see them on TV. The changes aren't going to happen. (James)

WHAT WOULD THE
COUPLES LIKE TO SEE HAPPEN?

What would the couples like to see happen in society? Some would like to see complete indifference to interracial couples.

I think that . . . the best message to give if you got to give any message to society at all is just keep on ignoring, 'cause the more that you can work on building family and relationship and the less you have to worry about where you're allowed to live and whether or not people are going to accuse [you] of things or talk to you bizarre ways at work, the longer those family structures can survive. (Roger)

Interracial couples . . . aren't good or bad because of being interracial. . . . It is what that relationship becomes that determines its goodness or badness, but it has nothing to do with the complexion of the people. (Wanda)

Similarly, one man talked about seeing interracial couples as only couples, not as interracial couples.

I don't see people as interracial couples. When I see a few people together, I don't [say] "Oh my God!" My mind don't go, "Interracial couple!" . . . I'm hopin' they are happy, 'cause I know how I'm strugglin' for my happiness in life. And you see two people together you really hope that they're happy. (John)

Some people hoped for more limited objectives, not so much an end to racism as simply more acceptance of interracial couples.

Yes, we are just like everybody else, and that's wonderful, and that's all I need in life. But I am . . . very aware that there is racism in the society and very aware of the hurt it causes individuals and groups, and so I wish that . . . there was some acceptance of interracial relationships. (Christine)

People's ideas of what they would like to see change in the reactions of others to interracial relationships reflect their varying notions of the basis for that opposition. The negative reactions of family, friends, and society that have been discussed in this book represent many different thought patterns, assumptions, intentions, words, behaviors, and origins. There can be so much complexity underlying the opposition that interracial couples experience that sometimes it can be difficult for somebody in an interracial couple to make sense of opposition. One man struggled through a long and complex sentence in getting to his understanding of what seemed to be behind the initial opposition of his parents to his interracial relationship.

Umm, well, yeah, I mean, I, I just think that ah it, part of it was, and part of it just umm, umm, ah, ah, ah, umm, most of it probably would be just the, the lack of knowledge about umm, that, although I don't know what I, how I term it, that type of relationship or the potential for ah, umm, two people who have racial differences to succeed in a relationship, umm, a lack of any information really on umm, ah, what it might or might not take to ah, to support these people—you know, fear. (Adam)

As can be seen in accounts earlier in this book, some people were attached to family and friends who exhibited what could be called racism, and some struggled with their own personal prejudices. Lorenzo spoke with a kind of tolerant understanding about the ignorance that undergirded the opposition of Virginia's parents to the couple's relationship.

A lot of people, but especially the working-class white folks who are involved in interracial relationships, it tends to be with a poor working-class black person. Middle class with middle class, upper class with upper class, and then that's how people generally tend to get together period, so had I fit the expectation that I was also going to be poor and from north Minneapolis, then their experience with poor black folks from Minneapolis was, "Well, sure, this is somebody with, like, no horizons, nothing happening. And, I mean, so she's going to be in a house full of little half-black kids, a house full of little tragic mulattos on the North Side." And they knew that she was this wonderful girl with all kinds of potential, and their view of white women who wind up with black men is that they truly are white trash, the dregs. And so for her to put herself deliberately in that kind of position in life just seemed totally unintelligible to these folks, and I think that's where a whole lot of this comes from. You can be hard on them and then call them total racist pigs. I'm just, you know, that's where people come from on this stuff.

Lorenzo would be glad to see all opposition to interracial couples end, but he also seemed able to be understanding and tolerant of some expressions of opposition to interracial couples.

It is not always easy to decide what is racism. It does not constitute a fixed system of ideas, is not always expressed in a way that is neatly separable from expressions of other sentiments, and is not a property of individuals and institutions that is separate from the words and actions that seem to express them (Wetherell & Potter, 1992, p. 58). Consequently, racism can be thought of as a matter of how one interprets certain words and actions.

Racism can be internalized by somebody who has been a target of it. So freeing individuals and couples from the burden of racism may sometimes involve their changing their self-perceptions and self-limiting dispositions. One man talked about this as he described his struggles to interpret and to decide how to deal with people's reactions to his partner and himself when they were together. As he talked about those struggles, it seemed as though what had to be dealt with was not entirely outside of the couple. Some of it seemed to be inside of him.

> If there is a problem, where does it come from? Is it imposed from the outside? . . . There's no way that we can deny that the relationship and the nature of the relationship is being noticed. . . . How are we who are involved in those relationships . . . dealing with it? Are we creating problems in our mind from the outside, or are people indeed learning to ignore us? And if they are indeed ignoring us, does that make us self-conscious about the fact that we are being ignored? Are we secretly trying to make some kind of statement? And if people start ignoring us, it's like, "Tsk, gee, I've wasted all this time doing this?" (laugh) . . . I think it's more complex than we'll ever know. It's almost on the level of psychoanalysis, the things that you think you're confronting, the problems you're confronting, the benefits you think you're accruing. All of that may be the tip of the iceberg. I don't know how to get down deep in myself in terms of how I'm dealing with it. (Emmett)

HOW TO END RACISM

One can think about there being many different varieties of racism. Efforts to end one variety may not be helpful in ending others. Ending the internalized racism that seemed to be part of what the man just quoted was describing may not help at all in ending the racism of those who seem to need a scapegoat. One kind of racism that John saw in the family of his white partner was a kind of conformist racism.

JOHN I don't think that these people . . . in actuality have a real documented racism mentality or attitude. [It] is something that they just think is expected of them, and they just tryin' to play the role.

INTERVIEWER Almost like a cultural expectation for them?

JOHN Right.

A racism of that sort might best be changed by changing cultural expectations, making it clear in newspapers, schools, church sermons, television programs, and so on that racism is wrong and that the differences that society has defined as racial and important are not a proper or sensible basis for understanding or judging a person.

Racism can be understood as helping a dominant group to maintain privileges at the expense of oppressed groups (Johnson & Warren, 1994). Nonetheless, conformist racism may be the dominant racism among American whites and may not be simple to eradicate, because it may go along with a feeling that "nothing is wrong with this," perhaps even a sense that it is not even racist but only accurate and morally justified. Part of what may be involved in reducing conformist racism is to identify it, to make it clear to people that what they take for granted as appropriate, accurate, or not racism at all is in fact racism and is harmful. One may hark back to other successful public campaigns—for example, persuading people that cholesterol in eggs, meat, and dairy products is harmful to health. It may not be the outspoken racists who do the most damage, but the people who go along with the agenda of racism, perhaps for reasons that have nothing at all to do with racism (cf. Katz, 1993). The staring, the assumptions that an interracial couple could not be traveling together, and the suspicions of a police officer observing an interracial couple may be actions of people who are not racist and who do not even think of what they are doing as racist. There may be a million ways to confront their bias, to educate them, to make their biased thoughts and actions something for them to unlearn.

Family pressures work, which is one reason why so many people who ran into family opposition suffered so much. They felt the pressure. It is also why so many family members came around. For people who recognize that there is racism in their family of origin, opposing that racism may be a most effective way to make a difference. There are quotes in Chapter 5 and elsewhere about confronting bias in families of origin. Here is another example:

> Mom had a family reunion . . . this summer and the kids had had the flu. . . . I was waitin' for them to get well before I came. So I got down there. I think [our older son] still maybe threw up once after I got there, but we were on the mend. This will become significant later. So my mom's sister and her husband are there . . . and then her other sister's there. . . . And what did he say? . . . The reason *our* family is so prosperous or healthy or something was because of the genetic purity. . . . With the exception of these kids here, everybody's blond and Norwegian. . . . He was dealing with me in a really weird way, my uncle was. And then he made that comment, and I thought it was very off . . . like totally disregarding. It was just strange. . . . And then the next day, my mom and dad and her two sisters and a brother-in-law went out to eat. And they came home and several hours later my mom and dad are both sick in the bathroom, and so everybody else got sick too, and *I* didn't get sick, and I figured they got food poisoning, 'cause ya don't get the flu like that where everyone gets the flu at once. . . . And then they kept blaming it on my kids, like they had gotten flu from [my son], and . . . then [my aunts and uncle] wouldn't come back to visit. . . . They never came back to visit my mom, and my mom felt really hurt, and my mom thought it was because of the kids. . . . We talked about it, and she . . . was kind of starting to blame me, and I said, ". . . Either you respect me or you respect your sisters, and I won't come down and visit you anymore." 'Cause it was just like, "This is my *mother.*" She's gotta, like, sit there and pout about her sisters, when they're being racist against my kids. "I'm not going to come visit you," you know. So she kind of sided up with me I guess after all or didn't talk about it. (Liz)

People also can influence coworkers and other acquaintances by acting in contradiction to stereotypes and speaking out against racism. Some white partners offered examples of antibias efforts in the workplace.

ANN If I get a new job, I get a little uncomfortable at first. How am I going to introduce my family to the people I work with so

they can get a chance to know me first? Because I like to look
at it as a way of educating people, and let them come to know
me, and let that blow away all their stereotypes when they
find I'm in an interracial marriage. . . . I don't mind answering [questions about us]. . . . I consider it education. . . .
Maybe 'cause I'm a white person I can get inside white
people's minds. I think society accepts us based on our
socioeconomic status a lot more readily. I mean, if you're a
well-dressed, well-speaking family where everybody is working and educated I think the white community is a lot more
[accepting]. . . . I would tell people everything about Bayard's
color. I'd want them to build their own little picture just so
they could be shocked, so they could realize that, "Wow,
there are these great people who are black, and Ann is this
great person, and she is married and has a neat family, and,
oh, her husband is black, wow!" Kind of open their eyes a
little. . . .

INTERVIEWER How has your educating of the world worked?

ANN I think it's worked really well because people have expressed
how surprised they were. And the fact that they're surprised . . . people will say, "Well, why didn't you tell me
he was black?" I would say, "Well, would you tell me that
your wife has blond hair?" And we would talk about it. It
would open up a dialogue, and if they're people I care
about, we would talk about it a lot, and I would explain to
them.

BAYARD One time, they said, "Why didn't you warn me?"

ANN . . . And I'd say exactly why. "Because I want you to accept me
for me, learn all about me and like me. I mean, if right off
the bat you know I have a black husband, everything I say
you may look at me differently."

Racism can be fought through political activity. One white partner
had fought racism in her community by protesting to government
officials.

There is an activist side to Nora that I didn't see when we first got together. For example, the racist graffiti that you see around on bridge
abutments and stuff like that, I look at it and I ignore it. I think, "Well,

those are sick people. So what?" She goes to the city council people
and says, "I want it erased." And gets it done. (Emmett)

A musician talked about using music to challenge white racism and
insensitivity.

I'm doing it big time now with my album. (Ed)

As discussed in Chapter 8, feeling onstage can be uncomfortable
and can complicate the problems of getting along with one's partner.
But being onstage gives one the opportunity to influence people.

Maybe there are people out there that I can reach and show them
that we are normal humans. You know, "Take a look at how we are,
and maybe you can learn from us." Because, hopefully, there are
some people that are just kind of riding the fence as far as how they
look at race, and they can see that we're OK, we're having fun, we're
decent people, we go to church, pay our taxes and do all those things
that people should do, and maybe you can learn from us. (Shirley)

Similarly, some people seemed to think that ending hostility toward interracial (or multicultural) families was not necessarily difficult if people could be made to see the richness of such families. It
would be almost like pulling up a window shade so people could see
into a rich and rewarding life that was very different from societal
stereotypes or fears.

If people of the larger society could see the richness that comes
into the family when we're, I mean, when I think of how your family
started (he and she laugh) in and how they are now, it's just like,
hey, we have this [Korean-Panamanian daughter-in-law] and all of
her relatives actually. . . . And then our family, and now we have a
niece who is adopted and is from [India], and it's just a great family.
And I think the larger society, I mean, one of my strongest things I
assume is that they think it's really problematic for families to bring
in different races, when it's really been . . . wonderful. (Barb)

I happen to believe that there are good things that come from interracial relationships that can teach and can show people all over about the

value of diversity and the value of people who bring different things to a relationship, sharing those things intimately. (Adam)

In fact, some people talked about changing people's racist attitudes simply by existing in their environment.

If you take the church communities we've been in, as I recall, in every church that we've been members, we've been the only interracial couple. And so people seem to learn about interracial couples by us. And they seem to have changed their attitudes somewhat by connection with us. (Gary)

ADAM We were the first interracial couple on the block. . . . There were a lot of questions. There were certainly a lot of conversations going on, and you could see the level of curiosity. But again, a lot of that is just time and education through exposure. You see, "Oh, they're just normal people" (laughs).

WANDA They had sugar when I came to borrow a cup of sugar.

LORENZO Your whole family has seen a dozen, at least, marriages destroyed and kids run away and freaked out and on dope, and what's happening in this family? Well, nothing but stellar stuff from [our] kids and from you and from me.

VIRGINIA My mother these days calls up Lorenzo all the time and says, "You're the only son-in-law I have" or "the only good son-in-law I have." . . .

LORENZO Because it's been by far the most obviously and visibly successful family anywhere in their universe.

NOT EVERYONE WANTS
THE JOB OF REFORMING OTHERS

Some people, perhaps more African Americans than whites, were clear that they did not want the job of reforming others.

I don't find myself going out of my way to [educate white people]. . . . I guess it's something that needs to be done. I guess . . . I do it more or less by example. Just go about my business and do whatever I would do naturally and not make any preconceived efforts about bringing people one way or another to try to get surprise reactions. . . . I guess when I think of educating somebody, I think of talking about someone who has some real ingrained, preconceived racist notions and that you have to go out of your way to prove that those notions are not true in every case and that there are good black people and there are good interracial things that work out. I know that there are people out there that, because of where they grew up and past experiences—they had maybe an all-white community—may be surprised . . . and I guess that's an education in itself. I guess I assumed when we started talking about educating people, I assumed that we were talking about people that had real ingrained racist notions, and I don't think it's worth the time to try to change those notions, because I don't think you ever can do that. I think [people] pretty much go to the grave with those type of notions. (Bayard)

I think I'm a part of a multiethnic, multicultural family. But nobody else sees me that way. You know, you got to carry something, you gotta have, like a little label on your shirt, because people are willing to say anything at all to you if they think you're part of their particular community. I used to work, I did a lot of labor-type jobs, and I remember people making just incredibly racist comments. . . . And saying these things in front of me. . . . In general, what I do is keep my mouth shut. Unless I feel very, very confident in a situation, I just keep my mouth shut. I don't have a job to do as far as race relations goes. It's not my job to straighten out the world. And so I'll sit and listen very often. It's very interesting. I drove a truck for a while. . . . And the other guy who worked on the truck with me was attending a Bible school. And he made some of the most incredible racist statements I ever heard anybody say. And he enjoyed doing it. He would sit in the cab of the truck with me as we drove down the streets of Minneapolis, and shout out these things. I don't understand how you, how can you square going to a Bible school and being an overt racist, leaning out the window of a truck and saying things to people. I don't, I still don't completely, I mean, I know that there's a great deal of hypocrisy. I'm not naive about that, but it just seems to me that ought to be one of the things you'd screen for in your Bible school. (Roger)

If that's the way you feel, that's the way you feel. I guess I don't go out of my way to try to change what people's opinions are. I'd rather let them see from afar that we're fine. (Tim)

What Tim suggested is that even if people do not want to go out of their way to contend against racism, they may act in opposition to it. Simply enacting antibias actions or simply getting along well with someone of another race may be sufficient to influence many people.

CHANGED ATTITUDES
TOWARD INTERRACIAL COUPLES

Hostility toward interracial couples is declining. In the 1970s, Porterfield (1978, pp. 119-121) talked about white families who sent young white women who were dating interracially to psychiatrists or even to mental hospitals. There were no such reports in the present study. Interracial marriage used to be illegal in many states; now it is not. In contrast to the couples studied by Porterfield (1978, pp. 118-122), very few white partners in the present study were completely cut off from parents or siblings. And the couples in the present study reported few instances of overt discrimination, public name calling, hiring discrimination, and other forms of hostility or opposition based on their being interracial couples. Some white partners even talked about efforts by parents or siblings, who might themselves have been racist at one time, to stop racism in others.

> My mom and lots of my brothers . . . have responded real angrily to people when people have made racist remarks in front of them. And Mom will say, "Hey, wait a minute. You know, you're talking about my son-in-law." And my brother's done the same things. . . . My brother . . . who is a plumber, really blue-collar [will hear racist] jokes, . . . and my brother will say, "Hey, wait a minute. My wife is black." He'll lie; he'll say it just to shock people. And then say, "Hey, you don't know anything about me, and don't assume you can talk." (Ann)

There also may be a crumbling of the rigid, arbitrary category system that underlies racism (Porterfield, 1982). As the boundaries blur in terms of residence, occupation, education, and much else, interracial relationships become harder to recognize as anything remarkable. In that sense, an end to opposition to interracial relationships can be taken as an index of the achievement of social, economic, and political equality (Porterfield, 1982).

The couples who were interviewed may be striving to be unremarkable, yet in their relationships with each other, they have had many experiences of relating and understanding across racial lines that others have not had. Those experiences give them insights into racism and interracial relationships that may be helpful in healing the wounds of racism. Paradoxically, those insights can also make them more tolerant of some forms of racism.

BARB I feel that . . . I'm further developed than people who don't have relationships with cultural [diversity] in them, and I don't think I felt that way, I wouldn't have thought of that earlier. I think we are at a higher point than a lot of people. And I think the kind of work that we've had to do in our relationship is the kind of work that all Americans really need to do. . . .

INTERVIEWER Do you believe that because you are a black and white couple that you had to work more diligently and you have now reaped the benefits of that work?

BARB Yeah, I think so. I haven't always been aware of having to do some kind of work, but I'm aware of growth, and I'm aware that I look at things a lot more broadly than some of my friends who are black and in same-race families and my friends who are white and in same-race families, and [I'm] aware of a lot more stuff than they are. And that just grew out of our life. I don't think that we consciously tried to develop that. . . . I think that I understand a broader segment of the people, and I understand people's reactions, and I can like white people who have ignorant attitudes about race or about black people, and a lot of black people can't do that. And I think it's valuable to be able to understand where people are coming from and all that, where ignorance comes from. I think I'm more open, and I think that comes from probably more than just our relationship, but my relationship with Roger's family. . . . People that I love that are my relatives now I think have really helped me to broaden my perspective and really grow in a multicultural area. . . . I'm able to look at them more as people and that they have a range of everything from wonderful to awful. You can have people in your family with backwards ideas, but you love them anyway because they're your family members. And I think it's a real eye-opener to have that experience cross-racially, to have someone who's a part of your family that you have really grown to love, although they think (laughs) weird things, and some of those things are about race. I think in our society race is such a big, important thing that it's really, I mean, you find out how somebody thinks about you has to do with your race, and then that's all you want to know about them.

SUMMARY AND CONCLUSIONS

It is not necessary for society to change for an interracial couple to have a wonderful life together. Even for couples faced with family opposition, things may well get better whether or not society changes. There are reconciliation processes, and usually, couples learn how to find safer and more rewarding paths as they deal with societal reactions to them and with their differences as a couple. Typically, things also get easier as families come to terms with a relationship.

> The hard part, I think, is dating. And . . . once you get through that and get through the initial responses of people, then it's all easier, and I think it's because the adjustment period with the rest of the community and the rest of the family, and I think that most people aren't really aware of that. That it's the first year or first 18 months or something that's difficult, and once you get through that, it's not a big deal, and I don't think most new interracial couples are aware of that, that it kind of settles down. (Virginia)

Although all the couples who were interviewed had found relatively safe and rewarding paths, everyone spoke about the need to end racism directed at interracial couples. They spoke of the ignorance, meanness, and hurtfulness of opposition to interracial couples and of the blindness of that opposition to the richness and goodness of interracial couple life, the beauty and vitality of biracial children, and the unfairness of the extra burdens that opposition puts on interracial couples. Not everyone thought that racism could be ended, but some of those who did talked about what that end might be like. It could mean that the interracial nature of a couple's relationship would be a matter of complete indifference to others. It could mean accepting interracial couples. It could mean rooting out sources of opposition wherever they are, even in the internalized racism that might be found in oneself or one's partner.

In talking about the end of racism, it should be acknowledged that racism comes in many forms, is represented in a diversity of ways, may be constantly transforming, may in some of its expressions be a matter of interpretation, may or may not be expressed, and, when expressed, may or may not represent deeply entrenched underlying feelings and attitudes. Thus, putting an end to various forms of racism may require enormous diversity of effort. Ending them requires that color no longer mark differences in rights, resources, privileges, opportunities, and the like, but even if that were achieved, the history of racism will be an enormously important reality for generations (Frankenberg, 1993, chap. 6).

The ending of bias may be impossible, but certainly there are resources available to ordinary people to fight it and reduce it. Given the diverse forms of racism, a diversity of resources can be of use. These include the capacity to address the ignorance and conformity processes that underlie what might be called "conformity racism." These include the capacity to point out racism and oppose it in interactions with family, coworkers, friends, politicians, and others. They include our capacity to make music that speaks to people. Given the extent to which interracial couples and families are onstage, their very existence, their diversity, and the ways they are like all other couples are resources for influencing others. Not everyone wants the job of reforming others, but with racism so pervasive, it is probably often the case that a person who does not want to reform others will often act, without intending to make a difference, in ways that contend against racism and other forms of bias.

There seems to be much less opposition to interracial relationships than just a generation ago (Spickard, 1989, p. 7). There has been a partial breakdown in the rigid segregation in housing, employment, politics, and other areas of life that made interracial relationships so remarkable in the past. Perhaps in the long run, the existence of interracial relationships and the acceptance of them as unremarkable will be an indicator of how far society has moved toward equality.

It is not entirely clear what the partners in an interracial couple do with their memories of offenses, stares, family opposition, discrimination, harassment, and the like directed at them and their family and at couples and families like them. Even if there is much more acceptance of interracial couples now than in the past, a person in an interracial relationship lives in a reality that includes the past as well as the present. For example, a person whose bad experience on other jobs has led him to choose to keep information about his interracial relationship from his employer and coworkers may never learn that there is more acceptance of an interracial relationship now than in the past. Similarly, a couple or family whose experiences with racism have led them to circle the wagons may never learn that it is safer now than in the past to join new groups or to travel in unfamiliar places. Perhaps it is in the nature of racism that part of its damage is that it makes it hard for its victims to be open to what life has to offer.

Racism does not have to end for an interracial couple to have a rich and rewarding relationship or for them to learn how to get along comfortably with each other and safely in the larger society. But it is our hope that in the future, this book will be a historical curiosity, describing a time before interracial couples became unremarkable and unopposed. Perhaps for those of us who are alive now, a color-blind end of all opposition to interracial couples is not attainable. Perhaps it makes more sense to work toward the achievement of honest, common understanding across the lines that have been defined by racism. The common understanding would include consensus about the many forms of racism and about the costs of silent or ignorant complicity with them. The common understanding would include awareness of the ways those biases have damaged their victims and, in different ways, their perpetrators and all of society. With that would come a commitment to healing. In this regard, one man suggested that the enormous difference in relationships like his is not race but gender.

What my godmother said when we got married—I call her my aunt, but really she's my godmother—she said, "You shouldn't ever let anybody call you a mixed marriage, and frankly, the only mixed marriage that people ever are worried about is one between a man and a woman." And what she meant was really true, and it is that really and truly there is a bigger empathetic, a bigger more fundamental, more cosmic empathetic gap between men and women than there is between any people of any two wildly disparate cultures that you care to put together in a room. And I think that people shouldn't lose sight of that fact. Different races and cultures enrich the world, and there's so much universality behind what we feel and see and experience that it's an invitation to enrichment, to kind of reach out to different people. . . . Unfortunately, what makes it a loaded issue has everything to do with caste and politics, not really and truly cultural differences. That's nothing. Nothing. It's what we have in a psychological way and a social-political way done to race and culture that's got things all screwed up, and that's where the trouble lies. (Lorenzo)

REFERENCES

Adams, B. N. (1995). *The family: A sociological interpretation* (5th ed.). Fort Worth, TX: Harcourt Brace Jovanovich.

Aldridge, D. P. (1973). The changing nature of interracial marriage in Georgia: A research note. *Journal of Marriage and the Family, 35,* 641-642.

Baptiste, D. A., Jr. (1984). Marital and family therapy with racially/culturally inter-married stepfamilies: Issues and guidelines. *Family Relations, 33,* 373-380.

Barron, M. L. (1972). Intergroup aspects of choosing a mate. In M. L. Barron (Ed.), *The blending American* (pp. 36-48). Chicago: Quadrangle.

Beigel, H. G. (1966). Problems and motives in interracial relationships. *Journal of Sex Research, 2,* 185-205.

Brown, J. A. (1987). Casework contacts with black-white couples. *Social Casework, 68,* 24-29.

Bruce, J. D., & Rodman, H. (1973). Black-white marriages in the United States: A review of the empirical literature. In I. R. Stuart & L. E. Abt (Eds.), *Interracial marriage: Expectations and realities* (pp. 147-159). New York: Grossman.

Cauce, A. M., Hiraga, Y., Mason, C., Aguilar, T., Ordonez, N., & Gonzales, N. (1992). Between a rock and a hard place: Social adjustment of biracial youth. In M. P. P. Root (Ed.), *Racially mixed people in America* (pp. 207-222). Newbury Park, CA: Sage.

Cerroni-Long, E. L. (1984). Marrying out: Socio-cultural and psychological implications of intermarriage. *Journal of Comparative Family Studies, 16,* 25-46.

Collins, P. H. (1990). *Black feminist thought.* New York: Routledge.

Daniel, G. R. (1992). Passers and pluralists: Subverting the racial divide. In M. P. P. Root (Ed.), *Racially mixed people in America* (pp. 91-107). Newbury Park, CA: Sage.

296

Dickson, L. (1993). The future of marriage and family in black America. *Journal of Black Studies, 23,* 472-491.

Edwards, R. (1990). Connecting method and epistemology: A white woman interviewing black women. *Women's Studies International Forum, 13,* 477-490.

Federal government is urged to rethink its system of racial classification. (1994, July 8). *New York Times,* p. A9.

Frankenberg, R. (1993). *White women, race matters: The social construction of whiteness.* Minneapolis: University of Minnesota Press.

Gibbs, J. T., & Hines, A. M. (1992). Negotiating ethnic identity: Issues for black-white biracial adolescents. In M. P. P. Root (Ed.), *Racially mixed people in America* (pp. 223-238). Newbury Park, CA: Sage.

Golden, J. (1954). Patterns of Negro-white intermarriage. *American Sociological Review, 19*(2), 144-147.

Gubrium, J. F., & Holstein, J. A. (1990). *What is family?* Mountain View, CA: Mayfield.

Heer, D. M. (1974). The prevalence of black-white marriage in the United States, 1960 and 1970. *Journal of Marriage and the Family, 36,* 246-258.

Hernton, C. (1965). *Sex and racism in America.* Garden City, NY: Doubleday.

Johnson, W. R., & Warren, D. M. (1994). Introduction. In W. R. Johnson & D. M. Warren (Eds.), *Inside the mixed marriage* (pp. 1-13). Lanham, MD: University Press of America.

Johnston, J. H. (1970). *Race relations in Virginia and miscegenation in the South, 1776-1860.* Amherst: University of Massachusetts Press.

Kalmijn, M. (1993). Trends in black/white intermarriage. *Social Forces, 72,* 119-146.

Katz, F. E. (1993). *Ordinary people and extraordinary evil: A report on the beguilings of evil.* Albany: State University of New York Press.

Kerwin, C., Ponterotto, J. G., Jackson, B. L., & Harris, A. (1993). Racial identity in biracial children: A qualitative investigation. *Journal of Counseling Psychology, 40,* 221-231.

Kirschbaum, M. S. (1994). *Deciding to authorize, forego, or withdraw life support: The meaning for parents.* Unpublished doctoral dissertation, University of Minnesota.

Kitchen, D. L. (1993). *Interracial marriage in the United States, 1900-1980.* Unpublished doctoral dissertation, University of Minnesota.

Kouri, K. M. (1994). *Unifying the races while circumventing prejudice: The parents of black/white multi-racial children.* Unpublished manuscript, University of Southern California, Los Angeles.

Kouri, K. M., & Lasswell, M. (1993). Black-white marriages: Social change and intergenerational mobility. *Marriage & Family Review, 19*(3/4), 241-255.

Loving v. Commonwealth of Virginia, 338, U.S. 1. (1967).

Mathabane, M., & Mathabane, G. (1992). *Love in black and white.* New York: HarperCollins.

McGoldrick, M., & Garcia-Preto, N. (1984). Ethnic intermarriage: Implications for therapy. *Family Process, 23,* 347-364.

McIntosh, P. (1988). *Understanding correspondences between white privilege and male privilege through women's studies work.* Unpublished manuscript, Wellesley College, Wellesley, MA.

Monahan, T. P. (1976). An overview of statistics on interracial marriage in the United States, with data on its extent from 1963-1970. *Journal of Marriage and the Family, 38,* 223-231.

Porterfield, E. (1978). *Black and white mixed marriages.* Chicago: Nelson-Hall.

Porterfield, E. (1982). Black-American intermarriage in the United States. *Marriage and Family Review, 5*(1), 17-34.

Roberts, R. E. T. (1994). Black-white intermarriage in the United States. In W. R. Johnson & D. M. Warren (Eds.), *Inside the mixed marriage* (pp. 25-79). Lanham, MD: University Press of America.

Rosenblatt, P. C., & Karis, T. A. (1993-1994). Family distancing following a fatal farm accident. *Omega, 28,* 183-200.

Schneider, D. M. (1980). *American kinship: A cultural account* (2nd ed.). Chicago: University of Chicago Press.

Schoen, R., & Wooldredge, J. (1989). Marriage choices in North Carolina and Virginia, 1969-71 and 1979-81. *Journal of Marriage and the Family, 51,* 465-481.

Schuman, H., Steeh, C., & Bobo, L. (1985). *Racial attitudes in America: Trends and interpretations.* Cambridge, MA: Harvard University Press.

See, L. A. L. (1989). Tensions between black women and white women: A study. *Affilia, 4*(2), 31-45.

Spickard, P. R. (1989). *Mixed blood: Intermarriage and ethnic identity in twentieth-century America.* Madison: University of Wisconsin Press.

Spickard, P. R. (1992). The illogic of American racial categories. In M. P. P. Root (Ed.), *Racially mixed people in America* (pp. 12-23). Newbury Park, CA: Sage.

Spigner, C. (1990). Black/white interracial marriages: A brief overview of U.S. census data, 1980-1987. *Western Journal of Black Studies, 14,* 214-216.

Stack, C. (1974). *All our kin: Strategies for survival in a black community.* New York: Harper & Row.

Staples, R. (1982). *Black masculinity.* San Francisco: Black Scholar Press.

Staples, R. (1992). Intermarriage. In E. W. Borgatta & M. L. Borgatta (Eds.), *Encyclopedia of sociology* (Vol. 2, pp. 968-974). New York: Macmillan.

Staples, R., & Johnson, L. B. (1993). *Black families at the crossroads: Challenges and prospects.* San Francisco: Jossey-Bass.

Tizard, B., & Phoenix, A. (1993). *Black, white or mixed race? Race and racism in the lives of young people of mixed parentage.* New York: Routledge.

Tucker, M. B., & Mitchell-Kernan, C. (1990). New trends in black American interracial marriage: The social structural context. *Journal of Marriage and the Family, 52,* 209-218.

U.S. Bureau of the Census. (1990). Household and family characteristics, March 1989 and March 1990. *Current Population Reports* (Series P-20, No. 447). Washington, DC: Government Printing Office.

U.S. Bureau of the Census. (1993). *Statistical Abstract of the United States.* Washington, DC: Government Printing Office.

Washington, J. R., Jr. (1970). *Marriage in black and white.* Boston: Beacon.

Welborn, M. (1994). *Black-white couples: Social and psychological factors that influence the initiation, development, and continuance of their relationship.* Unpublished doctoral dissertation, University of Minnesota.

Weston, K. (1991). *Families we choose: Lesbians, gays, kinship.* New York: Columbia University Press.

Wetherell, M., & Potter, J. (1992). *Mapping the language of racism: Discourse and the legitimation of exploitation.* New York: Columbia University Press.

Wilkinson, D. Y. (1975). *Black male/white female: Perspectives on interracial marriage and courtship.* Morristown, NJ: General Learning Press.

INDEX

ABOUT THE AUTHORS

Paul C. Rosenblatt has a PhD in psychology from Northwestern University and is a Professor in the Department of Family Social Science at the University of Minnesota. His most recent books are *The Family in Business, Farming Is in Our Blood,* and *Metaphors of Family Systems Theory.* He has a strong interest in carrying out interview research that can make a difference for good in people's lives. He is currently conducting a study of couples who have had a child die and maintains a continuing interest in farm and migrant farm worker families, families who operate businesses, grieving families, and families affected by human rights abuses.

Terri A. Karis, MA, has taught undergraduate courses in family dynamics and parenthood and has worked as a psychotherapist with individuals and families. Currently, she works as an employee assistance counselor and does diversity training in corporate and non-profit settings with her husband Richard Powell. Terri has a degree in family social science from the University of Minnesota where she is a doctoral student continuing to do research on interracial couples. Terri and Richard have two sons, Kahdeen and Jordan.

Richard D. Powell, MS, has provided direct clinical services to individuals, couples, and families continuously for the past 19 years. He has a degree in counseling psychology and is a Licensed Marriage and Family Therapist. He has worked with the families of seriously emotionally disturbed adolescent children and serious/persistent mentally ill adults, both in residential and outpatient settings. He has provided clinical supervision and consultation to individuals and agencies in many areas, including boundary issues, crisis intervention, suicide prevention, family and organizational systems dynamics, therapy with African Americans, and the solution-oriented therapy model. He has been giving workshops and trainings on solution-oriented therapy for the past 2 years. He is a clinical member of the Association for Marriage and Family Therapy and a professional member of the Association of Black Psychologists. He has a private practice called Discovering Possibilities . . . Solution-Oriented Therapy. He lives in Minneapolis with his wife, Terri Karis, and their two sons, Kahdeen and Jordan.